KV-425-305

JUNIOR ENCYCLOPEDIA

with Fascinating Facts

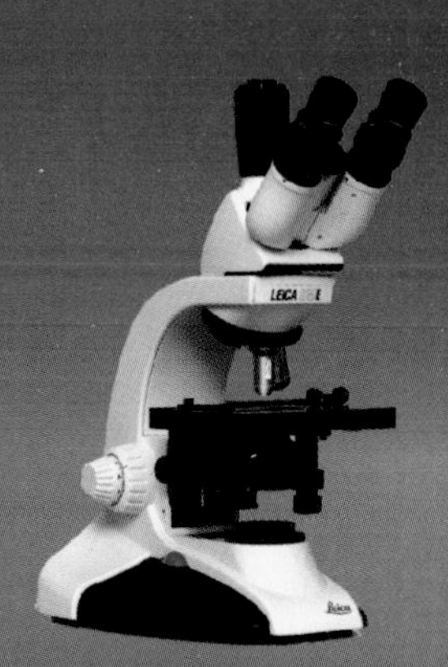

Packed with over 1000 illustrations, photographs including fascinating facts

Information about Earth, Plants, Birds, Inventors & Inventions and History

Junior Encyclopedia with Fascinating Facts

This combined edition produced and co-published in India by
The Book Paradise and Bluebird Books
an imprint of Sachdeva Publications, New Delhi, India
In association with Macbeth Books Ltd, Moscow, Russia.

Original edition published in English as
Junior Encyclopedia Awesome facts about...
Earth, Plants, Birds, Inventors & Inventions, and History

This first combined edition co-published in India 2011 by

13/11, Subhash Nagar, Old Railway Road, Gurgaon, 122001, India
E-mail: bookparadise@hotmail.com

And

An imprint of Sachdeva Publications
4598/12-B, Ansari Road, Daryaganj, New Delhi-110 002
E-mail: Sachdevapublications@yahoo.co.in
Book your copy at -
www.flipkart.com

Printed at Seema Printing Works, New Delhi

ISBN 978-81-7582-133-0

₹ 425.00

Junior Encyclopedia

with Fascinating Facts

Co-published by

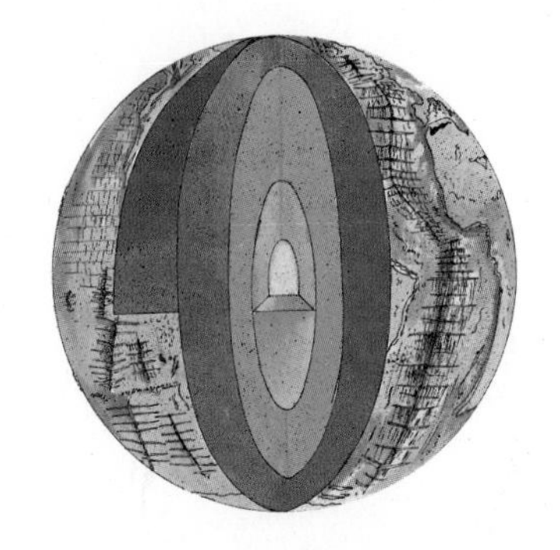

CHAPTER ONE

EARTH

OUR HOME PLANET

NATURAL PHENOMENA

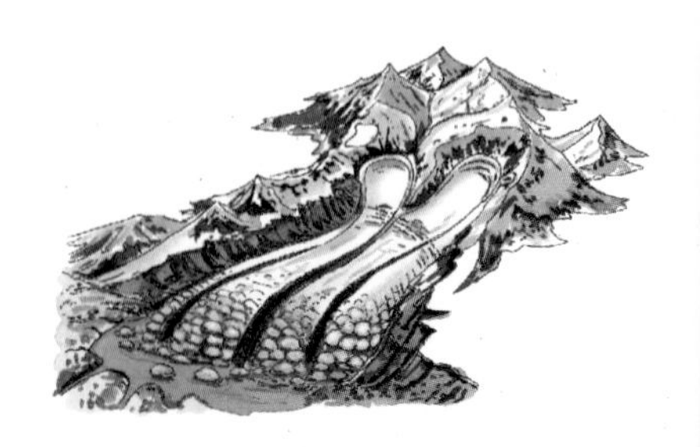

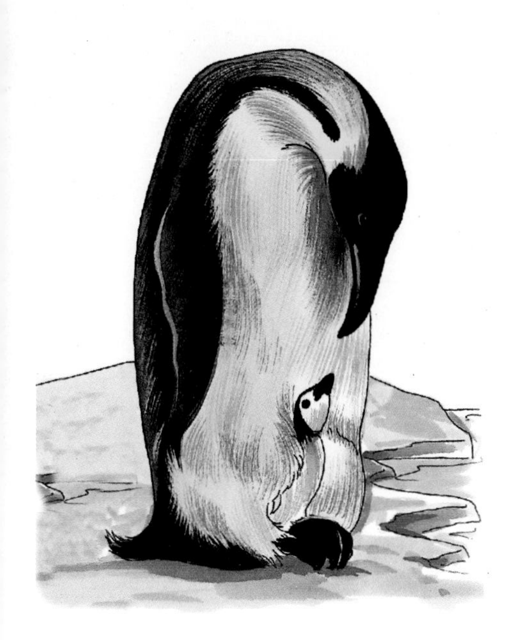

CLIMATIC REGIONS

OUR HOME

PLANET

Planet Earth

Viewed from Space, the Earth appears as a ball of water and land. Our planet is the only planet known to man which supports life. Along with water and land, the atmosphere and the distance from the Sun provide the conditions suitable for the existence of life on the planet. This is what makes the Earth a unique planet.

Earthrise
It was only when Earth was caught on a single photograph frame by Apollo astronauts did we realise that our planet was a unique planet in the entire Solar System.

71 percent of the Earth's surface is covered with water.

Clouds bring rains that ensure that we get a steady supply of water.

A blanket of air, called the atmosphere, envelops Earth and does not let the harmful rays of the Sun reach Earth.

The total surface area covered by land is 152,024,880 sq km.

Living Planet

Earth is one of the nine planets of the Solar System. Do you know that Earth is a unique planet of the Solar System? The reason is that, it is the only planet, which has all the conditions required for the sustenance of life. It is located at just the right distance from the Sun. It is the third nearest planet to the Sun after Mercury and Venus. It is the fifth largest planet after Jupiter, Saturn, Uranus and Neptune. It is at an average distance of 149,598,000 km from the Sun.

Earth is just at the right distance from the Sun for water to exist as a liquid. Because of water, life exists on the planet.

• IT'S FACT •

- Planet Earth is our home. But it is just a speck in the Universe that contains about 100 billion galaxies. Each galaxy contains about 200 billion stars. Other stars in the Universe may also have solar systems.

Formation of Earth

Planet Earth is 4,600 million years old! The Sun and the other planets in the Solar System were also formed round the same time out of a big cloud of gas and dust. At the centre of the cloud, heat and pressure built up and nuclear reactions began to take place. This formed the Sun. Because of its huge size, it exerted a gravitational force on the surrounding fragments. So, some of the fragments collided against each other, while others clubbed together to form the nine planets of the Solar System.

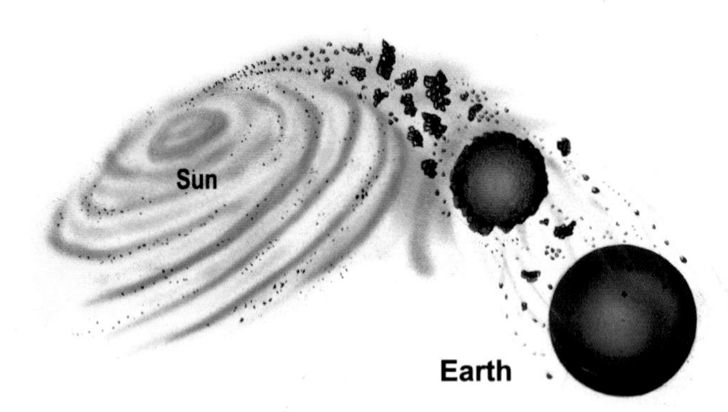

Age of the Earth
Scientists have been able to tell when exactly the Earth was born by studying meteorites that reach Earth from the asteroid belt. They have been able to date the remains of meteors. They date back to 4,600 million years ago and that was when the Solar System was formed.

The Origin of Earth
The Universe was formed 13.7 billion years ago. At an age of 4,600 million years, the Solar System is relatively younger. Though no one knows for sure how the Earth was formed, many astronomers believe that Earth was formed from spinning clouds of dust and gas left after the birth of the Sun.

Stages in the formation of Earth
1. Hot clouds of dust and gas circle the forming Sun.
2. A small cloud of dust clumps together and whirls round near the centre of the Solar System.
3. The forming Earth is bombarded with excess gas and dust blown off by the Sun.
4. Earth starts to cool down and volcanoes throw gases, forming clouds.
5. Rain falls and forms oceans and seas.

In the beginning

When the Earth was newly formed, a gravitational field was produced around it because of its mass. The force of gravity forced the Earth to take the shape of a sphere. When gravity acted upon it further, the planet compressed and the constituents changed into molten state. Soon the planet cooled. The gases emitted by the volcanoes created the first atmosphere.

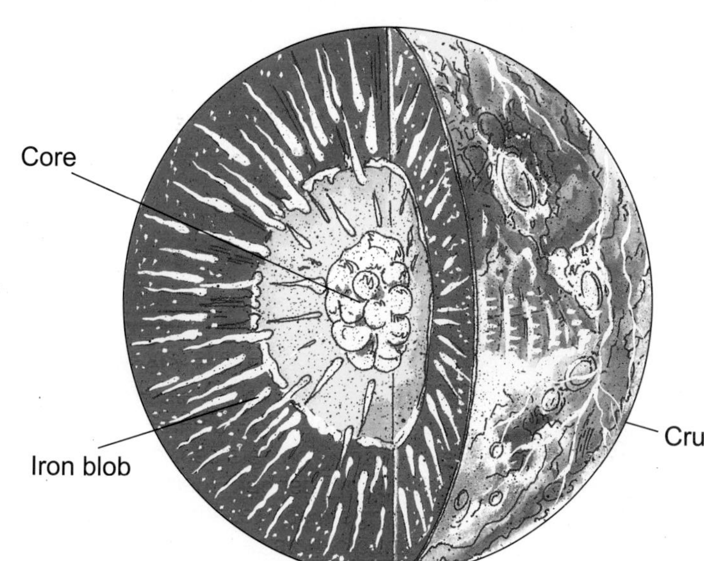

The metal core
When the Earth was just an 'infant', it was made up of molten material. As the Earth cooled, the heavier metals sank to the core while the lighter materials stayed afloat. Iron and metal formed the core while silica-rich magma floated and formed the rocks in the crust and mantle.

Giant magnet
The molten material in the outer core keeps boiling and churning all the while and keeps moving. With motion, it produces electricity that makes the Earth behave like a giant magnet. The Earth's magnetic field extends far into space. The magnetic field protects the Earth from the charged atomic particles that come out from the Sun in the form of the solar wind. The particles, however, enter the atmosphere at the poles and create a visual spectacle of shimmering lights in the sky called northern lights (aurora borealis) and southern lights (aurora australis).

Bar magnet
The shape of the magnetic field makes it look as if there were a huge bar magnet inside Earth.

The Blue Jewel

It was only when Earth was caught on a single photograph frame did we realise that our planet was a unique planet in the entire Solar System. The big, round ball whirls in the dark, star-studded expanse like a blue jewel. The blueness is because of the presence of water. The colour is in stark contrast to the other planets which are lifeless and barren. Earth is the only planet in the Solar System that is known to support life.

Land
The total surface area covered by land is 152,024,880 sq km. The seven continents make up a major part of the land surface. The continents are Asia, Africa, North America, South America, Antarctica and Europe. With an area of 44,391,200 sq km, Asia is the biggest continent.

Watery Planet
71 percent of the Earth's surface is covered with water. The rest makes up the land. Most of the water is contained in oceans and seas. The total volume of the water contained in the large water bodies is 1,321,000,000 million cubic km!

Clouds
Satellite pictures show swirling white puffs above the surface. They are clouds. The clouds bring rains that ensure that we get a steady supply of water.

Oceans
There are five major oceans — the Pacific, the Atlantic, the Indian, the Antarctic and the Arctic. The Pacific Ocean is the largest of all. It covers an area of 181,300,000 sq km! On the map, the world seems one ocean, broken by continents.

Layer of gases
Besides water, it also has a blanket of air that does not let the harmful rays of the Sun reach Earth. It helps to keep a constant surface temperature. This is important for the survival of all living things on the planet. The air contains gases like carbon dioxide and oxygen. Carbon dioxide is essential for plants, while oxygen is important for the existence of animals and human beings.

Structure of the Earth

While spending all our time on the surface of the planet, little do we realise that a different world exists in the Earth's interior. At a temperature of 7,500°C, the centre of the Earth is hotter than the Sun's surface (5,000°C). Natural phenomena like earthquakes and volcanoes help us understand a lot about the Earth's structure. The Earth is made up of four layers — the crust, mantle, outer core and inner core.

Crust
If the Earth were reduced to the size of an apple, the crust would be like its peel. The Earth's crust is similarly thin. It has an average thickness of 40 km. The crust is thickest under the continents (about 70 km) and thinnest under the oceans (about 8 km). Oxygen, silicon, calcium, aluminium and sodium are the chief elements that make up the crust.

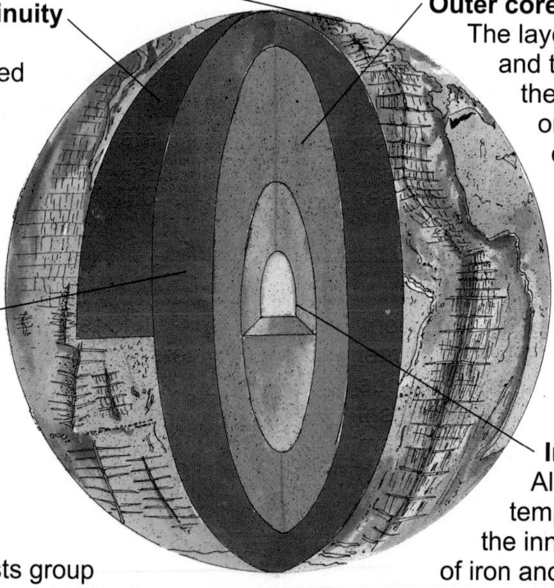

Mohorovicic continuity
The crust and the mantle are separated by a boundary called the Mohorovicic continuity. It is named after a Croatian scientist.

Mantle
The layer that lies immediately below the crust is the mantle. The upper layers of the mantle are just as hard as the Earth's surface. So scientists group the crust and the upper layer of the mantle and call it the lithosphere. The mantle is about 2,900 km thick. The lower layers of the mantle are entirely molten rock. Temperature varies between 2000°C and 4,000°C.

Outer core
The layer between the mantle and the inner core is called the outer core. It is the only layer that is completely liquid. It is made entirely of molten metal, chiefly iron with a small amount of nickel. The temperature of this hot layer is 4,000–5,500°C.

Inner core
Although at a temperature of 7,500°C, the inner core is a solid ball of iron and nickel. Metals do not remain solid at such great temperatures, but the pressure of the above layers of Earth is so immense that the metals in the inner core do not melt. The core is metallic because the heavy metals sank towards the centre.

Atmosphere

The blanket of air that envelops the Earth is called the atmosphere. It is vital for the survival of all living things. It absorbs or reflects most of the harmful rays coming from the Sun. The gases in the atmosphere absorb the warmth of the Sun and do not let it radiate into space. This helps to maintain a constant surface temperature on the planet. Otherwise Earth would have been a frozen, barren planet like the rest of the planets in the Solar System.

Mixture of gases
The atmosphere is made up of a mixture of gases. It contains 71 per cent nitrogen, 28 per cent oxygen and 1 per cent of various gases that are present in traces like argon, ozone, carbon dioxide and water vapour.

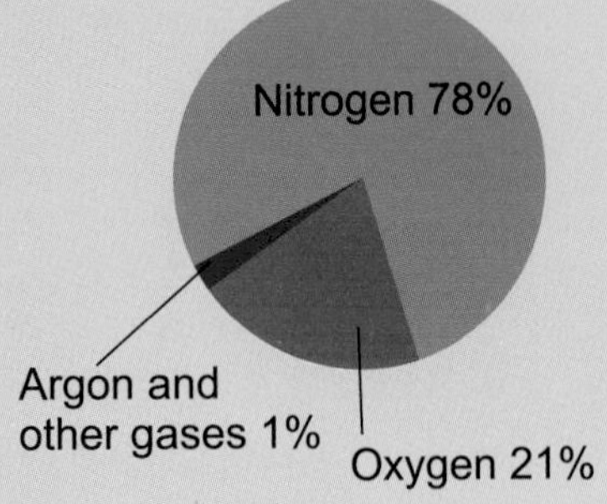

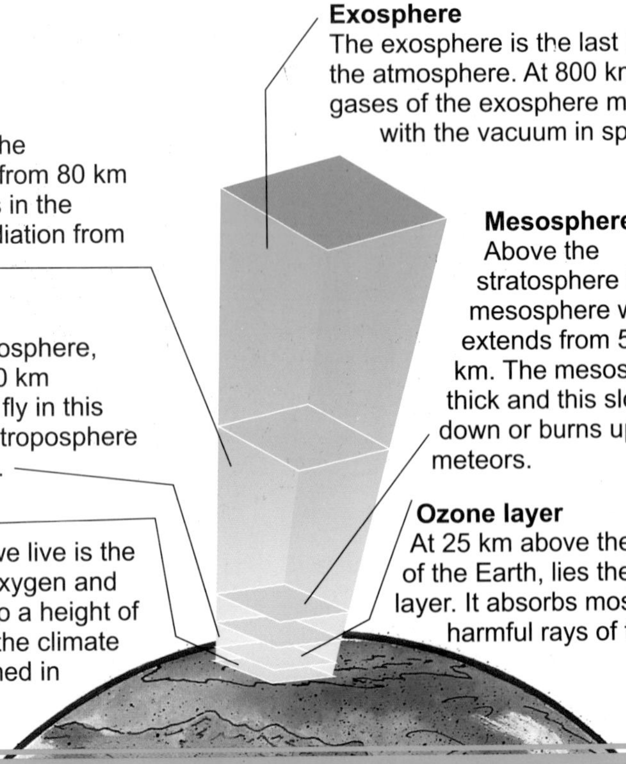

Exosphere
The exosphere is the last layer of the atmosphere. At 800 km, the gases of the exosphere merge with the vacuum in space.

Thermosphere
Above the mesophere is the thermosphere. It extends from 80 km to 500 km. The thin gases in the thermosphere trap the radiation from the Sun.

Mesosphere
Above the stratosphere is the mesosphere which extends from 50–80 km. The mesosphere is thick and this slows down or burns up falling meteors.

Stratosphere
The next layer is the stratosphere, which extends from 10–50 km upwards. Planes and jets fly in this layer as the clouds in the troposphere obstruct their movements.

Ozone layer
At 25 km above the surface of the Earth, lies the ozone layer. It absorbs most of the harmful rays of the Sun.

Troposphere
The layer of air in which we live is the troposphere. It is rich in oxygen and water vapour. It extends to a height of 10 km. This layer affects the climate on Earth. Clouds are formed in this layer.

The Ozone Layer

Ozone is a kind of oxygen that occurs as a layer in the stratosphere. The ultraviolet rays coming from the Sun react with the oxygen in the atmosphere and form ozone. Had the ozone layer not been there, all life forms would have perished because of the heat and the harmful radiation emitted by the Sun.

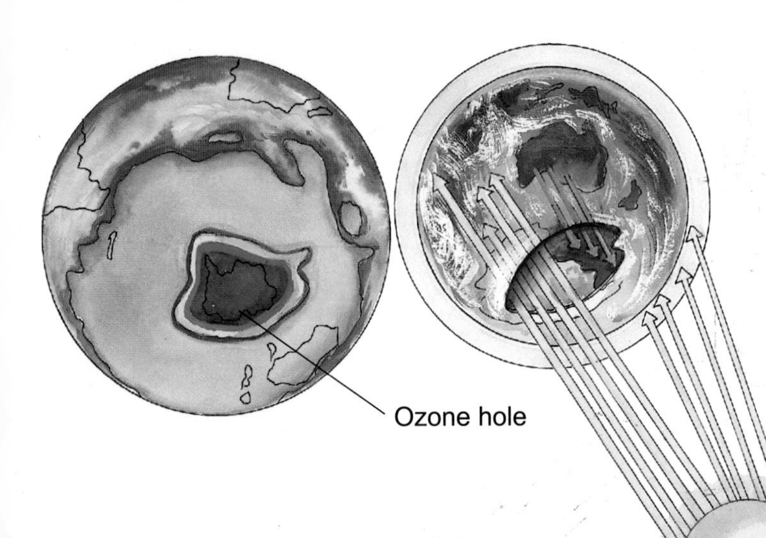

Thinning shield
Due to the release of harmful chlorofluorocarbons (CFCs), the ozone hole is getting thinner. Every year in October, the ozone layer over Antarctica thins by almost half. This has created a hole in the layer. The hole admits harmful rays of the Sun.

Global warming
There has been an increase in the level of greenhouse gases in the environment. Some are released when volcanoes erupt, but many more are released because of the burning of fossil fuel in industries. Fertilisers, forest fires and vehicular pollution are also increasing the levels of greenhouse gases in the environment. These gases are trapping the heat of the Sun more than what is required. This is leading to an increase in the Earth's surface temperature, thereby causing the phenomenon called global warming. If it continues unabated, it could cause melting of the polar icecaps and flooding of the low-lying regions.

Greenhouse effect
Carbon dioxide, nitrous oxide and methane are greenhouse gases. They trap the Sun's warmth and help to maintain a stable surface temperature of 15°C. Without the greenhouse gases, the temperature would have been –23°C, enough to turn Earth into a frozen planet.

Weather and climate

Because of the tilt of the Earth's axis, the heat of the Sun warms up the places along the Equator faster than those at the Poles. This causes the hot air at the Equator to rise. As the hot air rises, the cool air of the surroundings moves in to fill the space. This phenomenon is happening all the time and produces the weather and climate on Earth.

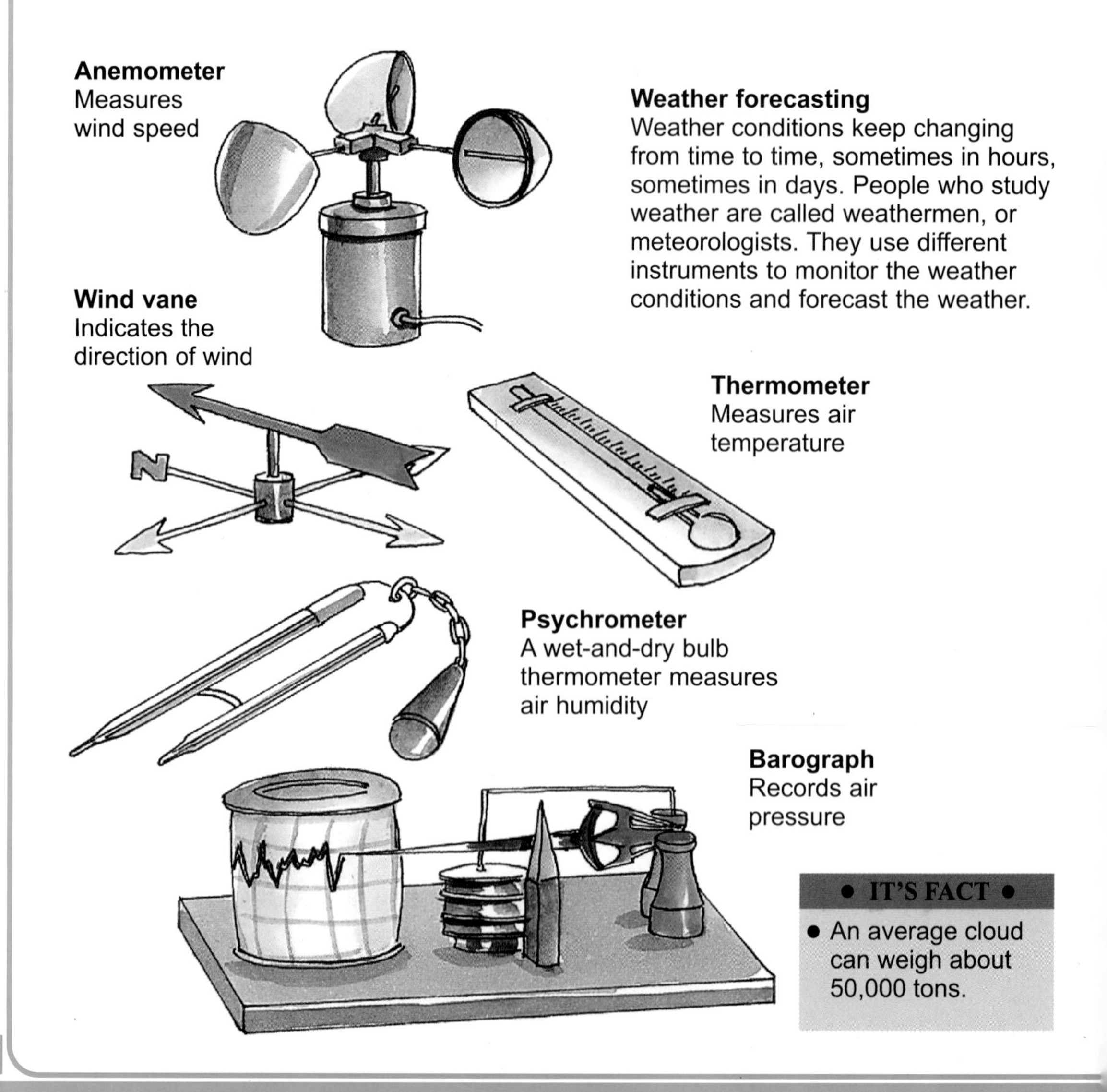

Weather forecasting
Weather conditions keep changing from time to time, sometimes in hours, sometimes in days. People who study weather are called weathermen, or meteorologists. They use different instruments to monitor the weather conditions and forecast the weather.

• IT'S FACT •

- An average cloud can weigh about 50,000 tons.

Cirrostratus are clouds at heights above 6,000 m. These are like thin sheets and are made up of ice crystals.

Altocumulus clouds are white and fluffy. They sometimes occur as layers or rolls at heights between 3,000 and 6,000 m.

Cumulus clouds are big, white and fluffy.

Stratus clouds are grey and flat. They are formed at low level.

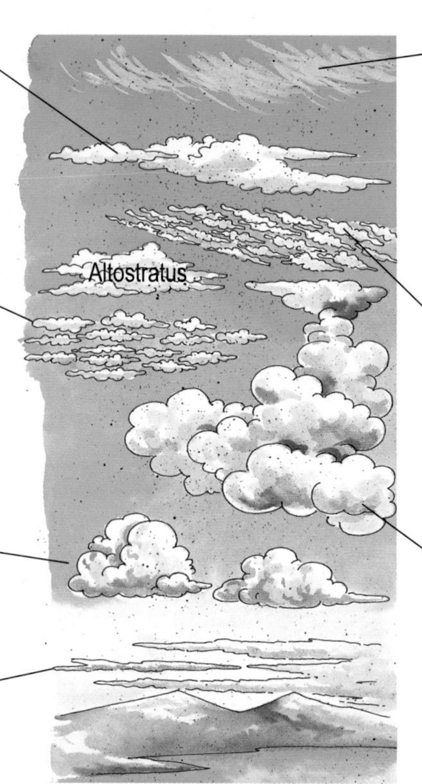

Cirrus clouds are found at the height of 12,000 m. They are entirely made up of ice crystals and are in the form of long, thin wisps.

Cirrocumulus clouds occur at levels above 9,000 m. They are made up of ice crystals and are in the shape of puffs.

Cumulonimbus clouds are dark rain clouds. They can be over 10 km in diameter.

How are clouds formed?

Clouds are formed when the warmth of the Sun heats up the water bodies on the surface of Earth. The heat causes the water to evaporate and form water vapour. The water vapour rises up through the air and condenses into tiny droplets. A number of such tiny droplets collect to form a cloud. When the cloud becomes laden with water droplets, it cannot stay afloat. So it comes down as rain, drizzle, snow or hail. These are forms of precipitation. Sometimes when the weather is too hot, droplets of rain can evaporate in mid-air instead of falling on the surface. Weather conditions inside the cloud determine whether we get the precipitation in the form of rain, hail or snow. In summer, we usually get rains because the ice crystals, if any in the cloud, melt as they fall.

Snow crystals

A snow crystal has six sides. When water freezes, its molecules form crystals. When crystals join together, they form snow. No two snow crystals are the same. Thousands of snow crystals join together to form a snowflake. They fall out of the cloud when they are heavy enough.

Hailstones

Hail is formed inside a cloud. Hailstones begin to form around an ice crystal or raindrop as it is carried up and down a cloud by warm air currents called updraughts. Alternating layers of clear and milky ice build around a crystal to form hailstones. Some hailstones can be as big as tennis balls.

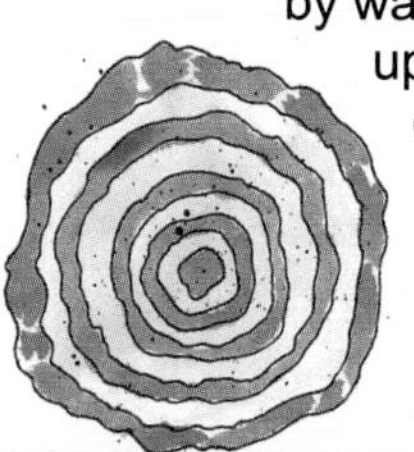

Living in harmony

Man has, since the dawn of civilisation, exploited the Earth's natural resources mercilessly, giving little thought to the fact that Earth is our home planet. By polluting the planet, we are putting the lives of all life forms, including humans, in peril.

Industrial pollution
Factories and industries have played a major role in the progress of man. But they have also contributed largely to the pollution in the environment. Factories all over the world emit millions of tonnes of harmful gases into the atmosphere every year.

Bicycles to the rescue
For going to smaller distances, bicycles can be used. It does not cause any pollution and helps keep fit.

Vehicular traffic
Transport has helped to conquer distances but the vehicles are known to cause atmospheric pollution. Over the years, the number of vehicles on the roads has increased. This has made it necessary to build more roads or broaden the existing ones. This means that more land is being used up for making roads. As transport has reached the remotest parts of the world, this is to mean that many areas under woodland have been destroyed to construct roads.

Acid rain
Rain is naturally acidic, but when it combines with the toxic gases like nitrogen oxides (from vehicular traffic) and sulphur oxides (from industries), it falls on Earth as acid rain. The winds carry the harmful gases away from the site of release of gases. So where acid rain falls, it harms plants and animals.

Destruction of rainforests

An area of about 41,000 sq km (almost the size of Switzerland) of rainforests is cleared every year. The land is cleared to make way for farmlands, to provide trees for timber or for construction of houses. Environmentalists estimate this loss contributes to the extinction of about 27,000 species of plants and animals every year.

Afforestation

Once it was understood that major floods and landslides were caused as a result of deforestation, many countries have taken initiatives to reclaim the denuded lands. During the rains, saplings are planted along slopes and hills by volunteers and the local people. The locals are educated about the need to plant more trees. Scientists have also developed fast growing species of timber in an attempt to replace the denuded forests.

River pollution

Household sewage and industrial effluents are thrown into rivers, seas and oceans untreated. This threatens the life forms in these waterbodies. When the polluted river ends up in the world's seas and oceans, they also become polluted. Polluted water should be treated before it is released into the rivers and oceans, to check water pollution.

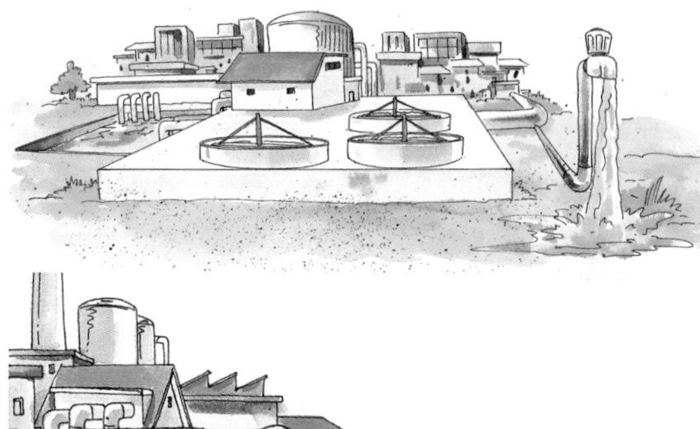

• IT'S FACT •

• Water Pollution

Chemical waste from factories is dumped or washed into seas, lakes and rivers, where it kills fish and plants. The Mediterranean Sea is one of the most polluted areas of water on Earth. In some places, the surface is now covered with a thin film of oil spilled from ships, and it is not safe to swim.

NATURAL

PHENOMENA

Moving plates

The Earth's crust is not continuous. It is broken into six major plates and about a dozen small plates. If we lay the map of the world flat on a table, it would look like a jigsaw puzzle with the edges of the plates fitting snugly into each other. Due to movements within the Earth, the plates on the crust keep moving. Major geographical changes, like drifting of continents, formation of mountains, volcanoes and earthquakes are the result of moving plates.

Continental drift

Some plates hold the continents while some plates hold the oceans. As the plates move, they carry the continents and the oceans around the world. The movement of the plates which made the huge landmasses drift apart is called the continental shift. Over millions of years, the plates moved and carried the continents to the present location.

200 million years ago

100 million years ago

Today

The Earth moves.

The rocking Earth

Every year, around one million earthquakes strike the world, but only few cause damage, the others are hardly felt. Most earthquakes occur where two plates on the Earth's crust meet. The movement under the Earth's crust causes the plates to slide. At most times, the movement between the plates is smooth, but at times they get jammed. Tension gets built up and is released with a great force in the form of waves. This produces earthquakes on the Earth's surface.

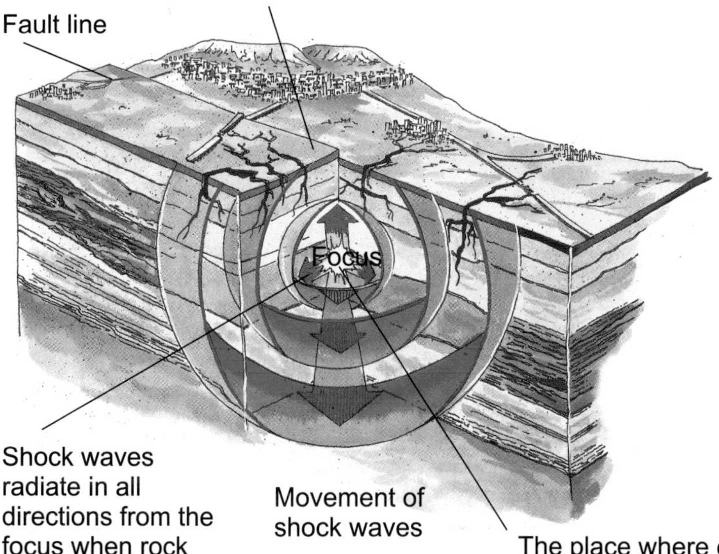

Epicentre – The point on the Earth's surface just above the focus which is the source of shock waves

Fault line

Shock waves radiate in all directions from the focus when rock fractures in the lithosphere

Movement of shock waves

The place where earthquakes emanate is called the focus or hypocentre

Focus and the epicentre

The point within the Earth at which the earthquake originates is called the focus. The point on the surface of Earth just exactly above the focus is called the epicentre. Damages are heavy at the epicentre. Places away from the epicentre incur lesser damages. This is because as the waves travel further away from the focus, they get weaker.

San Andreas fault

Most earthquakes occur along cracks on the Earth's surface. The cracks are called fault lines. The building up of tension between two plates causes the rock to crack producing a fault line. This is the San Andreas Fault that runs across the Mojave Desert in California, America. It is the most active fault line on Earth.

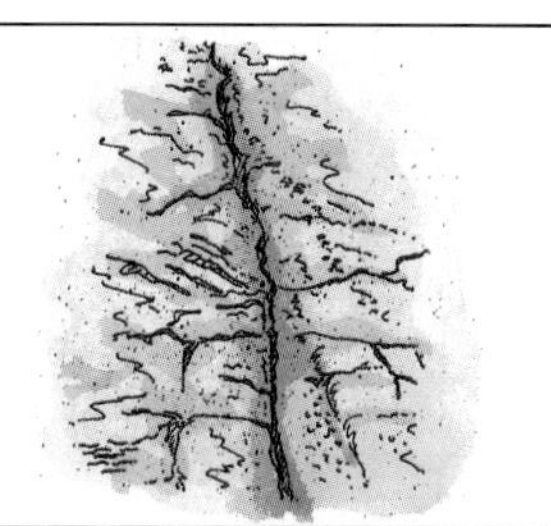

Volcanoes — Spewing fire

Volcanoes are cracks or fissures through which lava, ash, smoke and rocks come from deep below the Earth to the surface. When the plates on the Earth's surface rub against each other, some places become weak. And through such places, the hot magma is forced upwards through a vent and reaches the surface. The hot magma also brings with it ash, hot gases, rocks and steam.

A dog preserved in its final moments

Lost city
When Mt Vesuvius erupted in Italy in AD 79, the people of the Roman city of Pompeii were buried instantly. The remains of the city, almost perfectly buried under the ash, were discovered in the 18th century.

Kinds of volcanoes
Vulcanologists, people who study volcanoes, have classified volcanoes into three kinds:

Active : Volcanoes that emit molten material at regular intervals are called active volcanoes. There are about 800 active volcanoes in the world. Most of them line along the Pacific Ocean. The world's largest active volcano is Mauna Kea. Much of it lies under the sea.

Extinct : Volcanoes that have not emitted any lava for hundreds of years are said to be extinct. Mt Fujiyama of Japan is an example of such a volcano.

Dormant : Volcanoes that are dormant are 'sleeping'. Sometimes the vent is plugged by solidified lava so the volcano doesn't erupt. Such volcanoes can erupt at any moment. The Roman cities of Pompeii and Herculaneum were buried under the lava and volcanic ash of Mt Vesuvius which was a dormant volcano.

Ingredients of an eruption

A volcanic eruption sends out three kinds of material apart from steam and gas — clouds of ash, solid fragments of the volcanic plug called tephra, or volcanic bombs, and lava.

Main cone — Consists of layers of lava and cinders

Caldera — A broad crater formed when a volcano explodes or collapses

Lava flow

Vents — In a composite volcano, several vents lead molten rock and gases to the surface

Magma Chamber

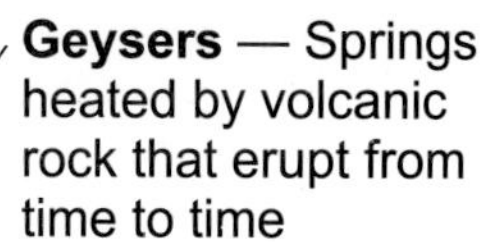

Geysers — Springs heated by volcanic rock that erupt from time to time

Fumaroles — Volcanic openings that leak only sulphurous gas or steam

Volcanic cone

Side vents — Minor lava channels lead to craters around main volcano

Pressure vent

The biggest eruptions are powered by a combination of steam and bubbles of carbon dioxide gas. Extreme pressure normally keeps them dissolved in the magma, but as the eruption begins, the pressure drops and bubbles begin to form in the magma and swell rapidly.

Kinds of eruptions

Volcanoes are determined by the chemical composition of the magma and temperature. Different volcanoes give off different kinds of eruptions.

Plinian eruption: Named after Pliny volcano that erupted in AD 79, a Plinian eruption throws volcanic ash and rock to great heights.

Hawaiianerupti on: The magma thrown out of a Hawaiian eruption is runny. The magma flows gently and creates a wider base.

Strombolian eruption : Volcanoes that erupt regularly giving off fluidy lava and ash are said to have a Strombolian eruption like the Strombolic volcano on an island near Sicily.

Vulcanian eruption: A volcano that gives off by an eruption throws out almost solidified magma. It is named after a volcano called Vulcano.

Pelean eruption : Volcanoes that erupt with a loud explosion are called Pelean volcanoes. The lava is thick and the clouds are made up of glowing particles.

Formation of mountains

A mountain is any piece of high ground that has a height of over 300 m. A mountain is taller than a hill. Hills are sometimes the remains of mountains that have borne the brunt of the weather. The Earth's surface is always in motion. At places, where two continental plates collide, pressure and strain is built which causes the rocks to break, thrust or fold up. This leads to the formation of mountains. It takes millions of years for mountains to be formed and is an ongoing process.

Old mountains
Mountains that have long stood the ravages of times and survived to this age are worn out by the action of wind, water, ice and snow. They have rounded and smoothened out edges. Such mountains are called old mountains. Examples of old mountains are the Welsh and Cambrian range in the UK and the Appalachians in the US. The Appalachians were formed some 250 million years ago. Mt Mitchell is the tallest peak in the mountain range and it is just 2,037 m tall.

Young mountains
Mountains that are 'born' recently are tall and have sharp edges. This is because they have not been eroded by snow, ice, wind and rain. The Himalayas and the European Alps are examples of young mountains.
Mt Everest is the tallest peak in the Himalayan mountain range (8,848 m).

Folded mountains
Mountains that are formed when the Earth's crust rises like waves in the sea are said to be folded. They appear as folds on the surface.

Rift valley
Sometimes when two plates slide against each other, a piece of land may be pushed downward to create a rift valley.

Block mountains
When two plates slide against each other, a piece of land that falls between them may be pushed upward. This piece stands out as a block, so this is called a block mountain.

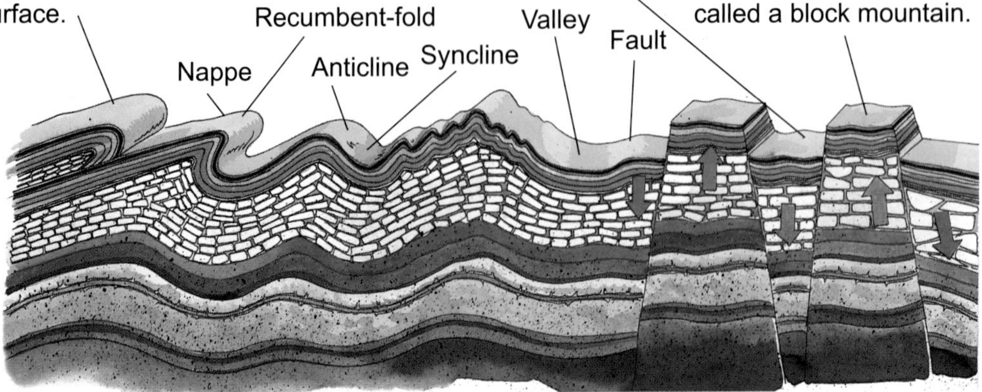

The Himalayas

India was once an island! Some 135 million years ago, the Indian plate moved north towards the Eurasian plate. When the Indian plate rammed into the Eurasian plate, the former rose up forming the Himalayas. The Indian plate is still pushing the Eurasian plate.

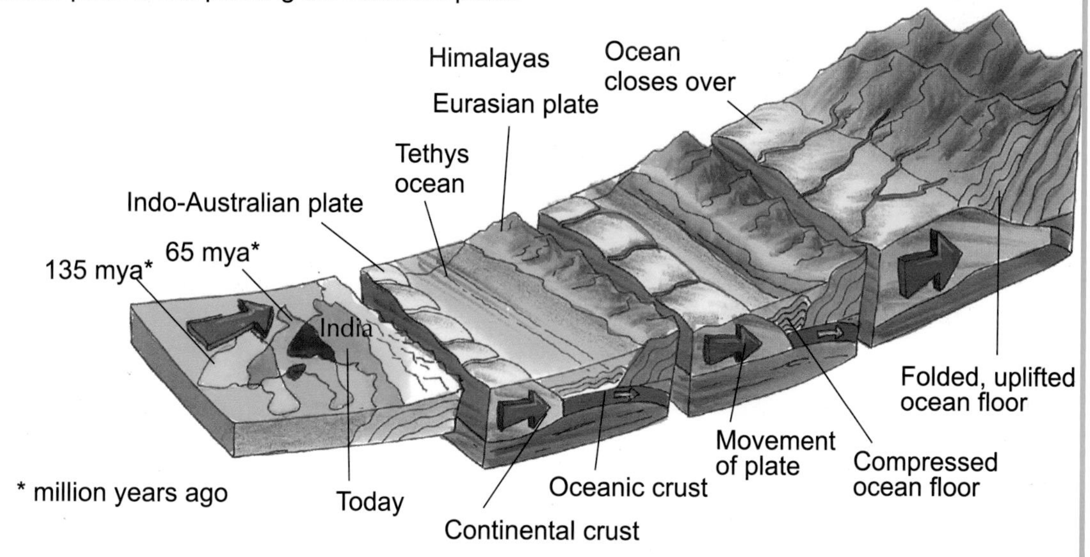

Rocks

Rocks are huge masses of mineral that occur naturally on the planet. Rocks are basically of three types — Igneous, Sedimentary and Metamorphic. Rocks are classified according to their formation.

Metamorphic rocks

Heat and pressure from the above layers sometimes change igneous and sedimentary rocks into metamorphic rocks. Marble and slate are forms of metamorphic rocks.

Igneous rocks

Rocks that are formed when the lava cools down are called igneous rocks. The word 'igneous' means fire. Granite, basalt and pumice are igneous rocks.

Granite

Marble

Slate

Sedimentary rocks

Rocks that are made from sediments are called sedimentary rocks. Sediments are pieces of rock and pebbles and grains of sand and mud. When a layer of sediments is subjected to pressure from the above layers, it turns into sedimentary rock. Limestone and sandstone are sedimentary rocks.

Sandstone

Basalt

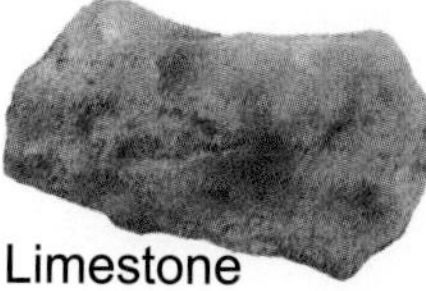

Limestone

Glaciers

A glacier is a slow-moving river of snow and ice. A glacier begins its life when it receives the new snow called the neve. Over the years, as more and more snow gets deposited, it turns into tick, white glacier ice.

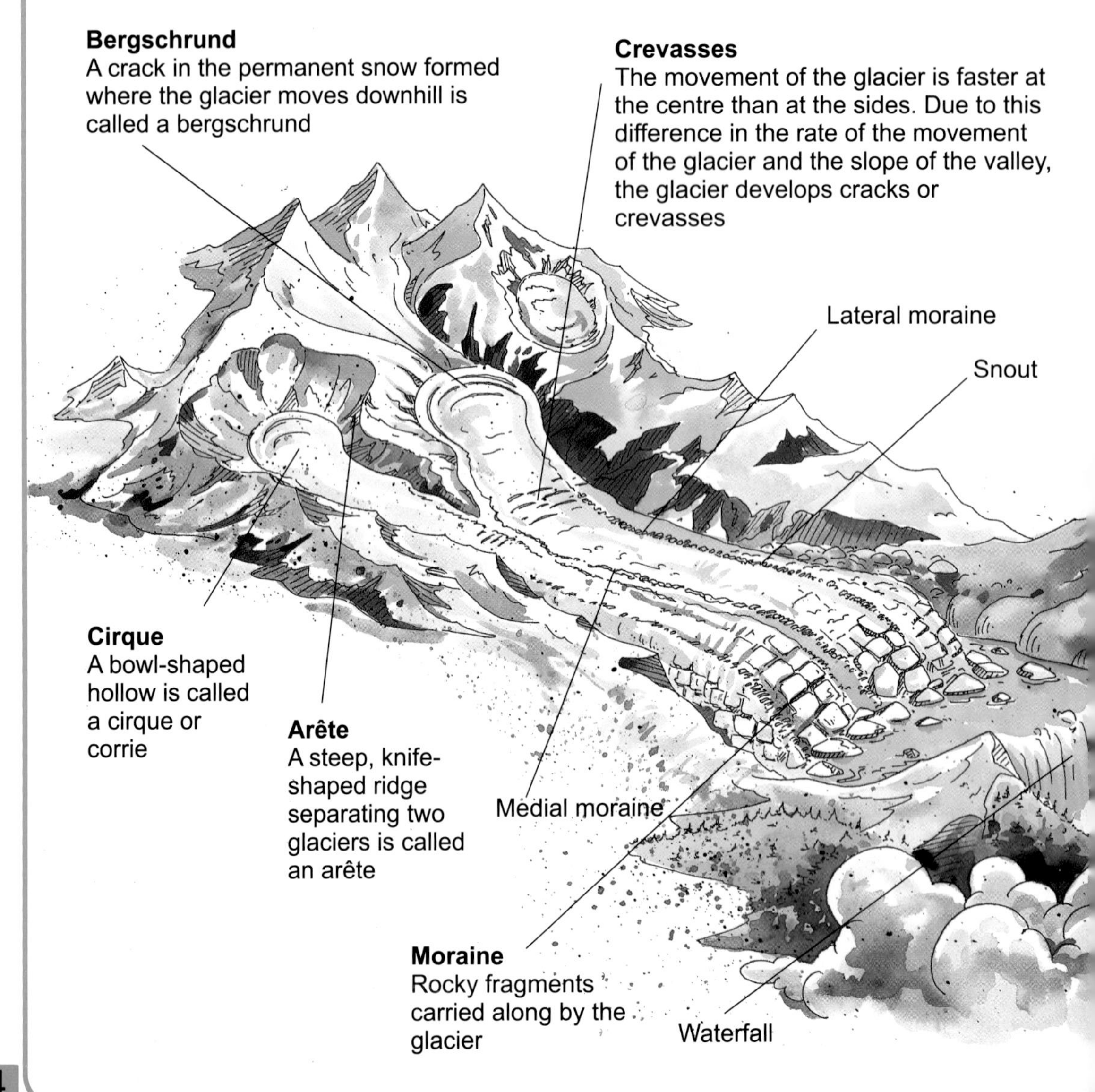

Rivers

Rivers start in high ground where there is lots of rainfall or melting snow or ice. From the hills or mountains of the river's source come the many small, fast-flowing streams that are the beginning of almost all rivers in the world.

First stage
The river moves quickly and fiercely, all the while carving a path between mountains and creating a valley. It carries the sand, gravel and pebbles strewn along its path, downhill.

Second stage
The river's flow becomes slow and it flows in giant loops called meanders. It deposits most of the sediments it carried with it in the first stage at the riverbanks. This process is called sedimentation.

Third stage
At the end of its journey, the river deposits the remaining sediments at the mouth before entering the sea. Over the years, the deposition of sediments causes the river to break up into a number of branches before emptying itself into the ocean. Then it is said to form a delta.

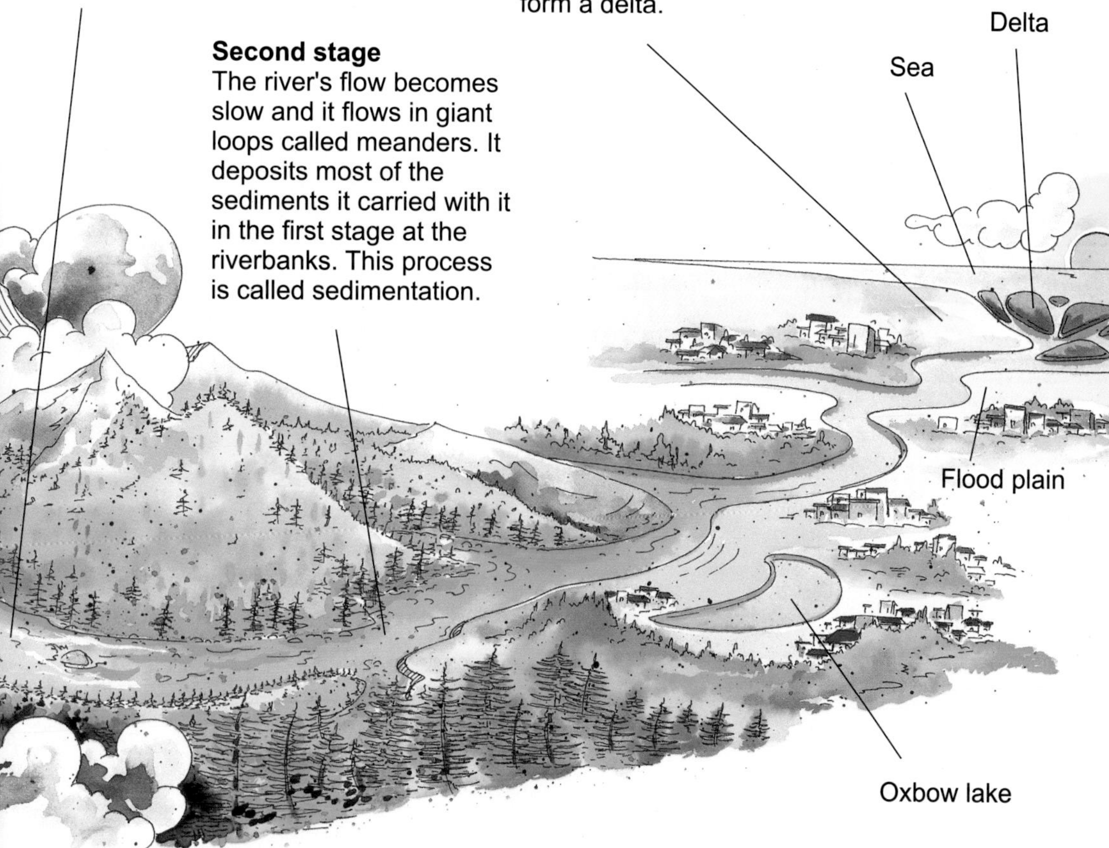

Moving Rivers of Ice And Snow

A glacier begins its life when it receives the new snow called the névé. Over the years, as more and more snow gets deposited, it turns into thick, white glacier ice. The ice in glaciers are pulled slowly downhill by gravity. Then it begins to flow downhill slowly, almost 1 m each day.

Icebergs

All glaciers carry sediments, rocks and even boulders along with it downhill. It deposits them at the snout where it begins to melt. The water of a melting glacier feeds rivers. Sometimes glaciers do not melt, especially those at the poles. Then large chunks of ice break off and float into the sea or ocean. These large chunks are called icebergs.

Largest and fastest glaciers

The world's largest glacier is the Lambert Glacier in Antarctica. It is 514 km long. The fastest glacier is the Quarayac Glacier in Greenland. It flows at the rate of 20 m per day.

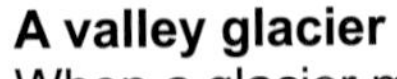

A valley glacier

When a glacier moves downhill, it erodes the sides through which it moves. It tends to straighten out the curves because the mass of ice is too heavy and stiff to bend easily around the curves. So a glacier carves out U-shaped valleys.

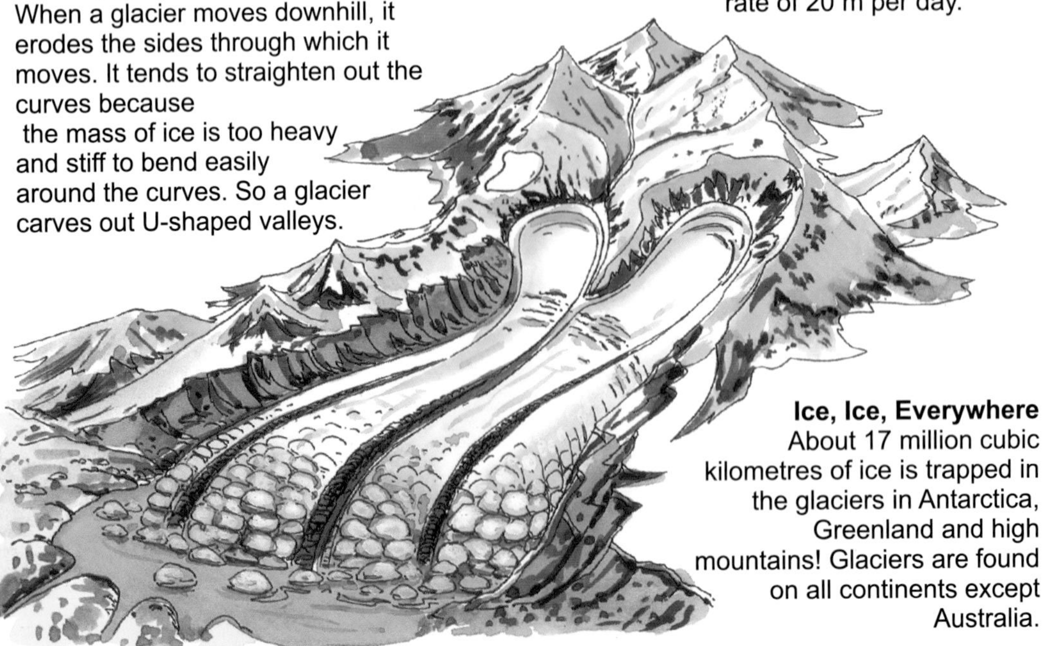

Ice, Ice, Everywhere

About 17 million cubic kilometres of ice is trapped in the glaciers in Antarctica, Greenland and high mountains! Glaciers are found on all continents except Australia.

Flowing Water Bodies

Rivers are water bodies that flow constantly. Most rivers start their journey from high up in the mountains and end up in large water bodies like seas and oceans. They play a vital role in water cycle. They also erode the landscape.

Water cycle
Water level on the surface of Earth is maintained by a process called the water cycle. Water on the surface of Earth gets evaporated from the water bodies and forms water vapour. This water vapour rises and goes up into the atmosphere and forms clouds. When these clouds become saturated, i.e., they cannot take any more water vapour, the clouds come down as rain or snow. The cycle of water forming water vapour, then clouds and then coming down as rain is called water cycle.

Tumbling gracefully
A waterfall is a place where a river plunges vertically over a ledge of rock. During the first stage of the journey of a river, it skips and leaps as it flows downhill. The fierce river erodes the portions of soft rock along its path and creates a sharp vertical descent. Over the years, the sharp fall of water over the ledge takes its toll on the soft rock beneath and creates a waterfall. The world's highest waterfall is the Angel Falls in Venezuela. It plunges 978 m deep!

Oceans and Coastlines

More than two-thirds of the Earth's surface is covered by oceans, yet we do not know much about it. This is because the average depth of the ocean is 3,730 m below sea level. Such depths are difficult to explore because the pressure of the layers of water weighs heavy on humans as well as machines.

From the edge of the ocean to around 500 m into the ocean, the land slopes. This part of the ocean is called the continental shelf

Continental slope
The land slopes further into the ocean from the continental shelf to make the continental slope

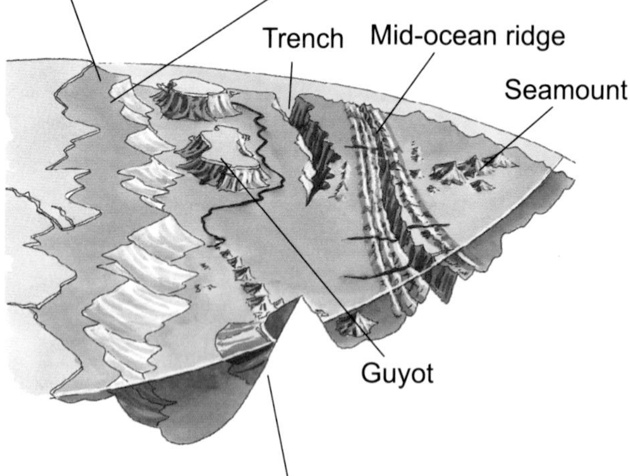

Marianas trench
The deepest point on the Earth's surface is the Challenger Deep in the Marianas Trench in the west Pacific. It is 10,920 m deep!

Ocean floor
The underwater landscape looks no different from the landscape on the continents. It is interspersed with mountain ranges, towering volcanoes and vast plains called the abyssal plain.

Pacific ocean
The Pacific Ocean occupies almost half the surface of Earth. It covers an area of almost 181,300,000 sq km! The Pacific-centred map of the world will help you guess how large the water body is.

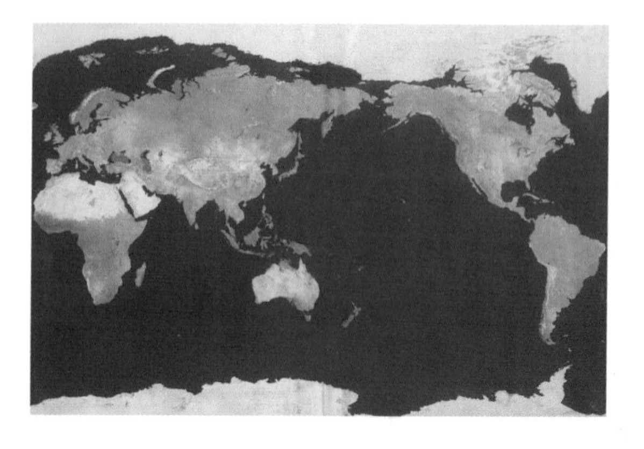

Waves
The wind whips up the surface of the sea into waves. A wave's height, length and speed is controlled by the wind speed, the length of time that the wind blows and the distance that the wind blows over the water.
The water within each wave stays in almost the same place, moving in circles. Near the shore, some of this water catches against the seabed. This slows the wave down, so the top curves over the breaks.

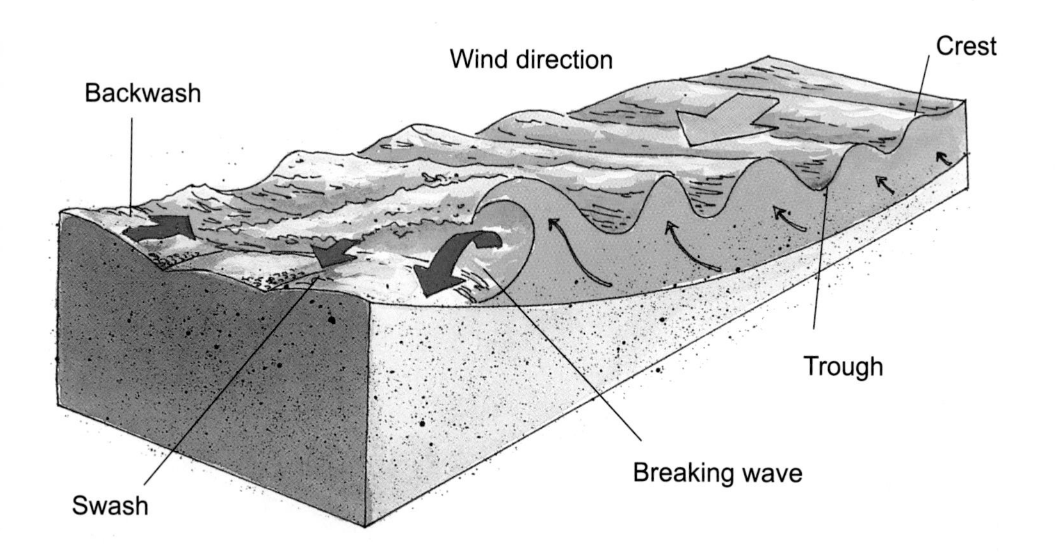

Tsunamis
An underwater disturbance can sometimes cause a disturbance on the surface of water. An earthquake or volcanic eruption on the ocean floor can cause huge waves on the surface. Such tidal waves are called tsunamis. When the Krakatoa volcano erupted in 1883 in Indonesia, it caused such a large disturbance that tsunamis up to the height of 35 m were raised in the ocean.

Eroding Coastlines

The constant pounding of the waves against the coasts changes coastlines of the world. That is why we have different types of coastlines, narrow or broad. Narrow beaches are sandy or rocky and have a steep cliff at the back. Broad beaches are rocky and gently slope into the sea.

Rock arch
The waves batter the beaches with rocks, sand and gravel that they carry along with them. As a result, it sometimes weakens the base of the cliff to create a natural arch, if the high portion of the cliff remains intact.

Changing coastlines
Wave erosion of headlands creates cliffs, which may have sea caves cut by waves in weak rock. If waves cut away caves on both sides of a headland, a rock arch forms. If the top of the arch collapses, a tall pillar of rock called a stack is left just off the coast.

Battered coasts
Coasts are constantly being shaped by waves, currents and tides. Soft rocks wear away faster to form bays. Hard rocks form headlands. Paradoxically, the shape of the shoreline has an effect on the tides. The highest tidal range occurs where there are long bays and inlets, forcing the rising water into narrow gap.

Blowhole
The pressure of a breaking wave may sometimes force water up a crack and emerge as a fountain above the cliff. This is called a blowhole.

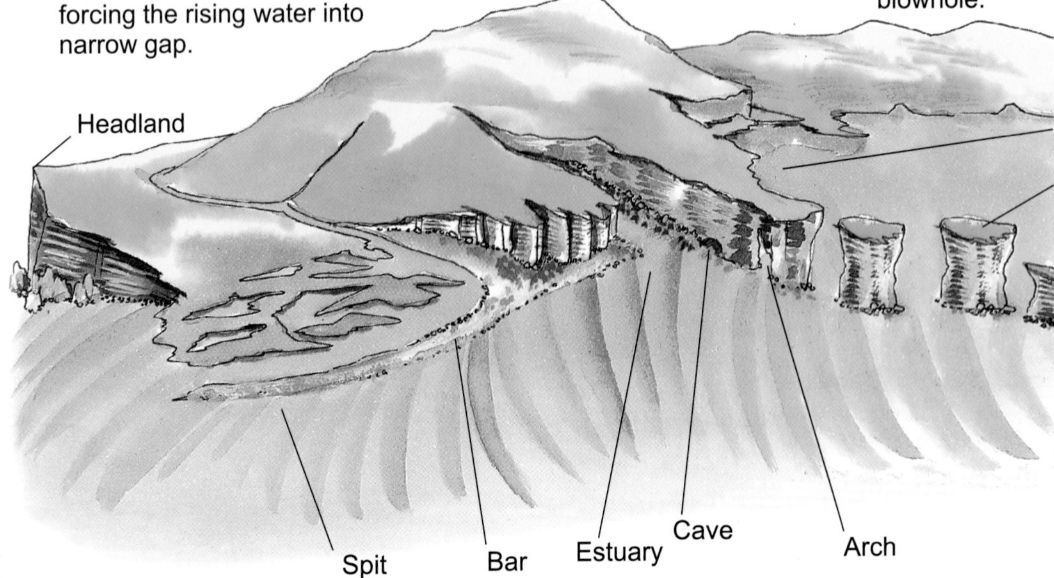

A fringing coral reef
Sometimes a volcanic island comes up above the surface of the ocean. The coral reef builds along the edge of the island.

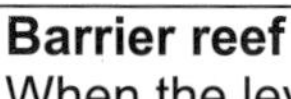

Barrier reef
When the level of the water goes up or the island sinks, a barrier reef grows quickly enclosing a lagoon between it and the island.

Coral atoll
The island eventually sinks leaving behind a coral atoll enclosing a lagoon. When the water level rises or the ocean floor sinks, the reef sinks.

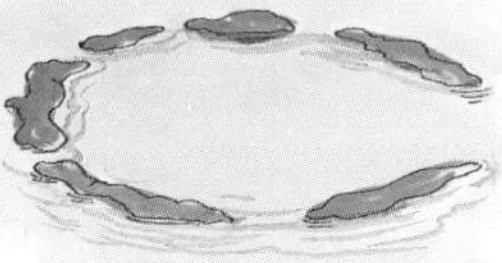

Underwater ridges
When the two plates pull themselves apart, they create a ridge. Molten material from the inner layers wells up and fills the gap. The material solidifies and forms a chain of mountains parallel to the ridge.

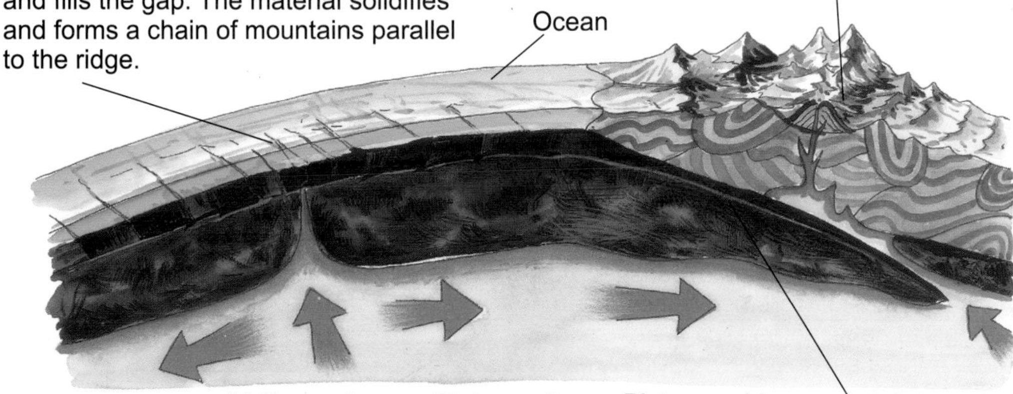

Stack
Over the years, the weathering of the base may cause the arch to widen and finally break off from the cliff. It then drifts seaward like a column called stack.

Underwater trenches
At trenches, old plates are being destroyed. When a continental and an ocean plate collide, the latter, being weaker, is forced down resulting in the formation of a trench. This is called the subduction zone. When the plate is pushed down, the heat melts the rocks and they emerge as lava through volcanoes that erupt near the trenches.

Weathering

Landscapes are formed and destroyed because of weathering or erosion. The action of wind, water, snow, ice and the heat of the Sun erode the landscape. Weathering causes huge mountains to erode. It breaks them into boulders and then rocks. Over the years, the rocks break into fragments and pebbles and finally into soil. Erosion takes millions of years to manifest itself. But weathering does not put an end to mountains. New mountains are being formed all the time.

Strange shapes
In many desert regions, rocks have been worn away over millions of years by the effects of heat and wind. Many deserts are full of strange-shaped, dramatic rock forms.

Rock arches
The Delicate Arch of the Monument Valley has been sculpted by the winds over a period of time. Dust-laden winds help to carve strange shapes on the rocks. The heat of the Sun plays a role in the erosion. It expands the rocks during daytime. At night, the rock shrinks thereby producing cracks in it.

Sea arches
These arches have been formed as a result of the constant lashing of the waves against the rocky beaches. The pounding waves initially produced caves in the soft porous rocks, which later gave way to form these arches.

Rock erosion
The rocks are eroded to form pebbles, which then get converted into tiny fragments and finally into sand.

Water erosion

The Colorado River has carved a marvellous landscape as it snaked through the Colorado Plateau over millions of years to form the Grand Canyon in Arizona, America. The naturally-sculpted valley is about 1.6 km deep and 350 km long. It exposes the various layers of rock that have taken about 600 million years to form.

Caves

Chemical action of rainwater and limestone leads to the formation of caves. The carbon dioxide in the atmosphere dissolves in rainwater and falls on Earth. This reaction produces a weak acid that reacts with limestone and dissolves it. A limestone cave starts off from a small crack that eventually gets wider as more rainwater trickles into it and eats away the limestone. Horizontal caves are formed this way.

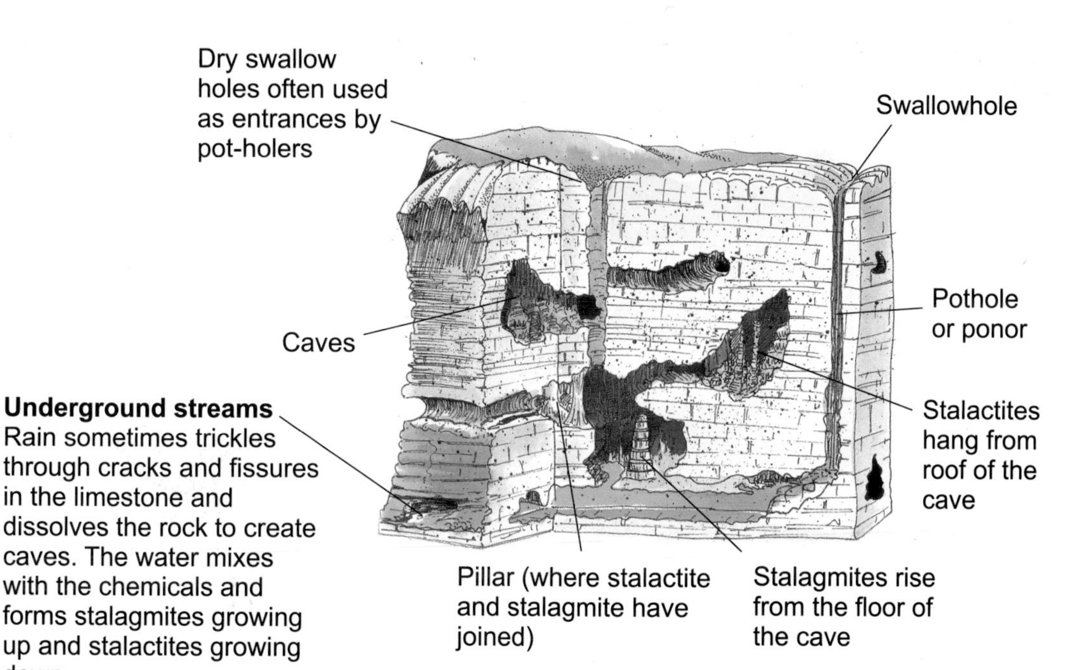

Underground streams

Rain sometimes trickles through cracks and fissures in the limestone and dissolves the rock to create caves. The water mixes with the chemicals and forms stalagmites growing up and stalactites growing down.

CLIMATIC

REGIONS

Clouds and Storms

Black clouds indicate a heavy downpour. Clouds can come down on Earth as rain, snow or hail, but this depends on the temperature inside the clouds. You know that water freezes at 0°C. If the temperature inside the cloud is above the freezing point, we have rains. If the temperature is below freezing point, water droplets in the clouds freeze into crystals. A number of crystals join together and come down as snow. Hailstones grow from frozen ice crystals swept up and down inside tall storm clouds. The water droplets surrounding the hailstones freeze on them and make them heavier. Then they cannot hold themselves to the clouds and fall on Earth.

We get to see lightning before thunder because light travels faster than sound.

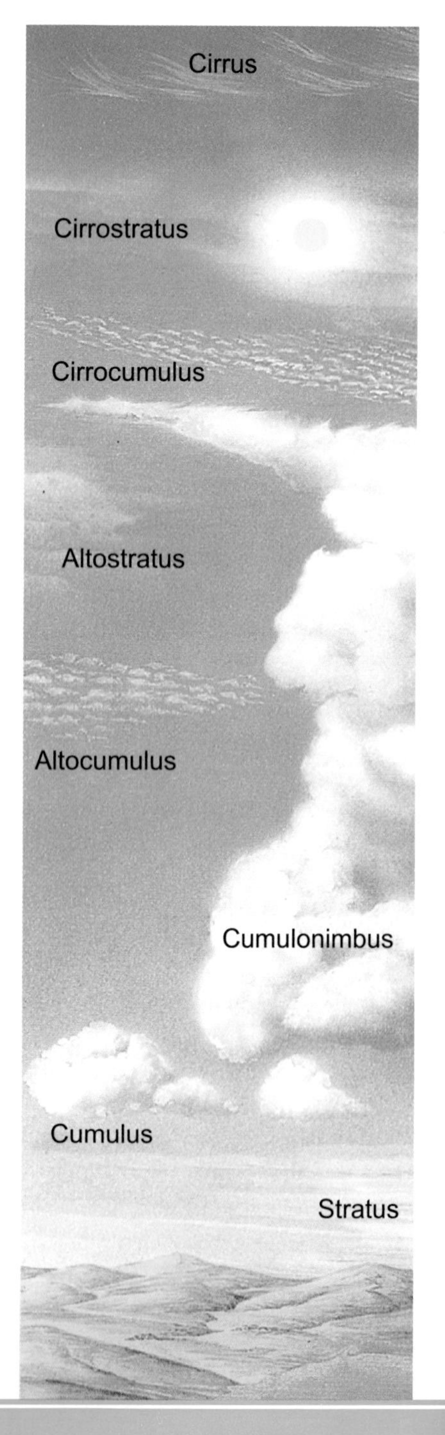

High-level clouds are made of ice-crystals. Medium-level clouds are made of water droplets and ice crystals. Lower level clouds are made of just water droplets. Shown alongside are the different types of clouds.

Polar Regions and Tundra

The Arctic region and the Antarctic are called the polar regions because they lie around the North Pole and the South Pole respectively. Together they contain about 90% of the world's water reserves in their icecaps. The thickness of ice in the largest island of the world, Greenland, could be 1500 m thick, while that in Antarctica could be 2000 m thick. The area below the Arctic Circle is called the tundra region. The region is restricted only to the northern hemisphere.

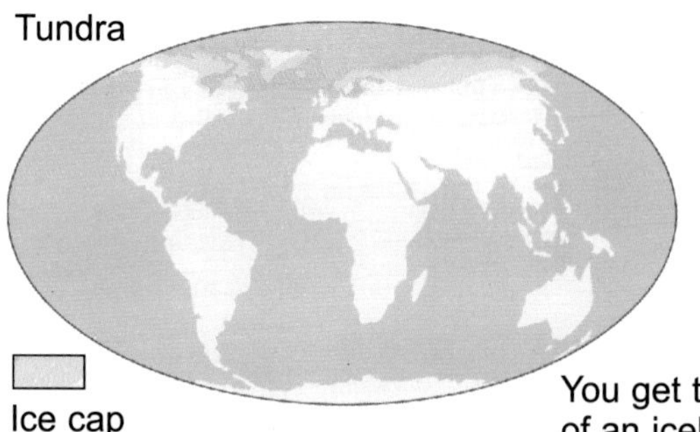

You get to see only the tip of an iceberg above water. In the northern hemisphere, icebergs break off from the Greenland ice sheet while in the southern hemisphere. They break off from the Antarctic ice sheet.

Here the emperor penguin keeps his young one warm in the Antarctic cold.

There is no land at the North Pole. The regions that lie above the Arctic Circle and below the Antarctic Circle are known as the Polar Regions.

Temperate Woodland and Grassland Regions

The temperate woodlands are regions that lie south of the coniferous forest zone. During the Ice Age that existed about 16,000 years ago, the area was covered under thick snow. But as the planet grew warmer, the ice retreated. The warm climate encouraged the growth of plants and they covered the rocky area. Soon conditions became appropriate and the area became covered by thick forests. Grasslands lie between the deserts and the broad-leaved forests.

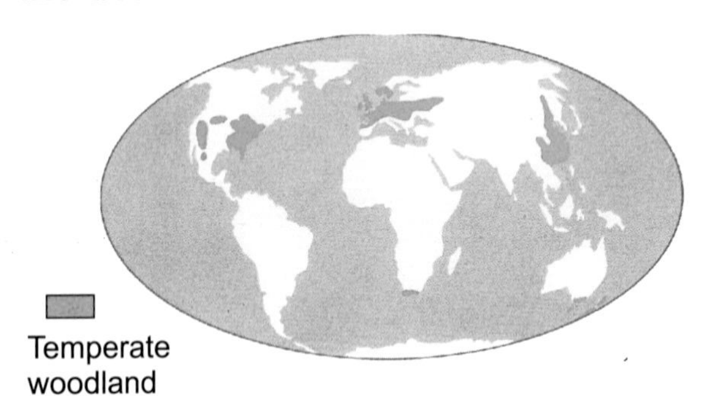

Temperate woodland

Most grasslands are being burnt during the dry season when the grasses have withered to clear them for cultivation.

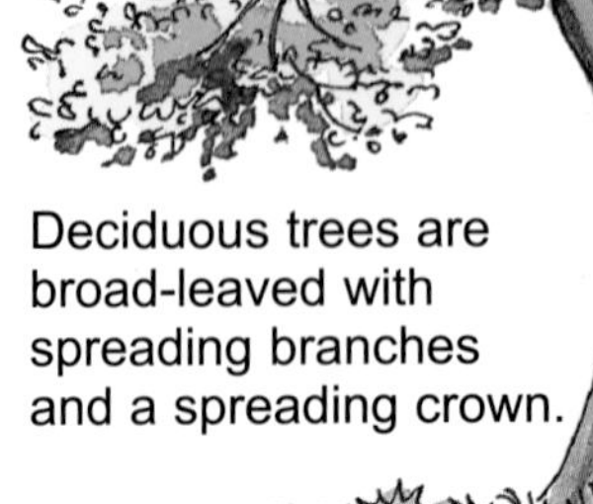

Deciduous trees are broad-leaved with spreading branches and a spreading crown.

Deserts

Deserts are those parts on the Earth's surface, which do not get more than 2.5 cm (250 mm) of rain in a year. Whenever we think of a desert, we think of a vast expanse of sand dunes with little or no vegetation. But actually, most deserts are stony or rocky. Temperatures in the Gobi Desert remain below freezing point for almost half the year.

The dry, arid land does not support rich vegetation. Prickly pears have thick, fleshy stems and its leaves are reduced to spines to conserve water.

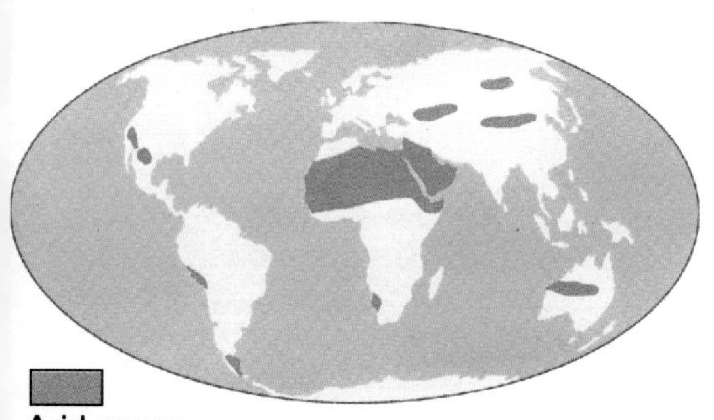

These hills of sand are called dunes. They are never static. Strong winds carry the sand and deposit it elsewhere to make new dunes.

• IT'S FACT •

- The Sahara is the biggest desert in the world. It covers an area of around 9,065,000 sq km!
- Oases are natural desert features where underground water comes to the surface and supports vegetation like date palms. Oases can also be man-made.
- Only 11 per cent of the Sahara Desert is sandy, rest is rocky.
- A dromedary is an Arabian camel which is used for racing.
- The Sahara also has an antelope called the addax.

CHAPTER TWO

PLANTS

PLANTS

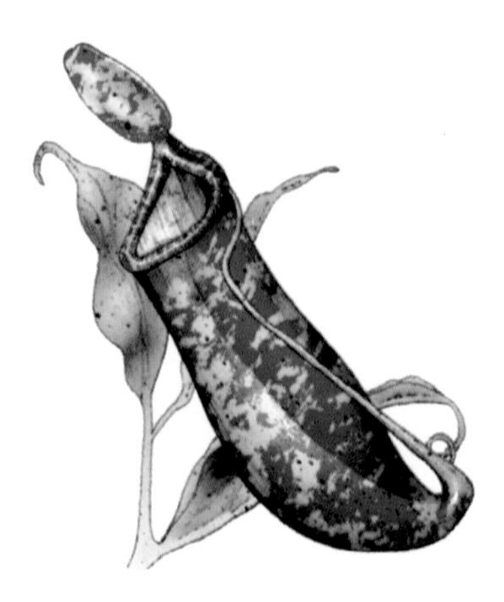

TREES

FRUITS

FLOWERS

PLANTS

What are plants?

Plants are found everywhere. Any member of the Plant kingdom which goes through a process named Photosynthesis, in which they make food for themselves, is called a plant.

There are plants, for example, that do not produce their food by photosynthesis but rather are parasitic on other living plants; other plants are saprophytic, obtaining their food from dead organic matter.

Plants grow old as surely as do animals; however, a generally accepted definition of age in plants has not yet been realized.

Some plants are carnivorous. A plant which traps animals, usually insects and small invertebrates, and secretes digestive enzymes which break down the prey, allowing the resulting products to be absorbed; also known as an insectivorous plant. Carnivorous plants grow in nutrient-poor habitats, and food obtained from prey, especially organic nitrogen, augments that is produced by photosynthesis.

The pitchers are often brightly and attractively colored, and bear honey glands on the inner surface to entice animals towards a smooth, glossy 'slip zone.

Pitcher plant

Parts of a plant

As we have several body parts, a plant is also made of several parts. Each part has a different function to perform.

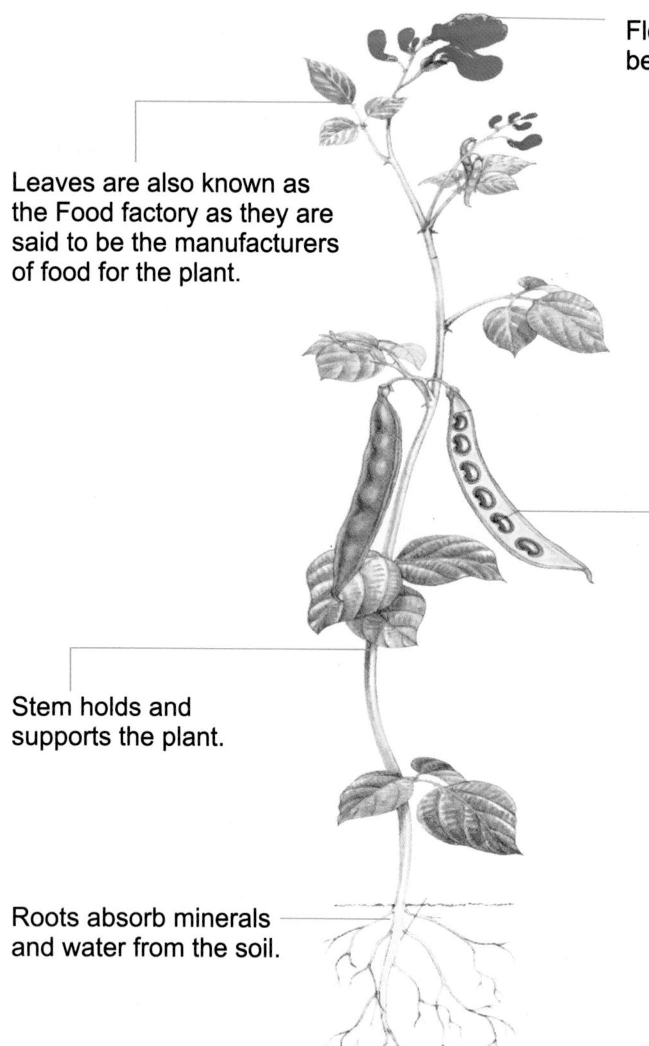

• IT'S FACT •

- Few plants can live in the bitter Arctic cold. Two that do are the yellow poppy and Arctic willow.
- The most leaves counted on a clover is 14
- The largest of all flowering plant families is the grass family.

Growth of a plant

A plant needs many essentials to grow, such as sunlight, water, minerals etc. to make its food in order to carry out the process of photosynthesis.

A plant is sown as a seed. The seed is then watered. A small bud appears on the surface of soil. Then it grows into a plant.

Types of plants

Plants may be of many types. Some of them are : Herbs, shrubs and trees.

A herb is a plant with a distinctive smell or taste, used to enhance the flavor and aroma of food. Herbs are usually grown in temperate climates.

Shrubs are woody perennial plants, usually differentiated from a tree by being smaller and having a trunk.

Trees are woody plants that renew their growth every year. Most plants which are classified as trees have a single self-supporting trunk containing woody tissues, and in most species the trunk produces secondary limbs, called branches.

The shape of a tree is an ecological construct as well, since its form is dependent on the habitat and the stresses of the environment.

Thyme, a herb

Aloe, a shrub

Water plants

Water plants are supported by their buoyancy in water and do not need a rigid stem; flotation devices which enable them to grow towards the water surface and obtain sufficient sunlight for photosynthesis.

Even in aquatic plants, water is seldom the true medium of pollen dispersal.

Water plants are readapted to an aquatic environment. They are not woody.

Most water plants, including even the large water lilies, do well in still water two to five feet deep.

Desert plants

Deserts are extremely dry areas of land with sparse vegetation. It is one of the Earth's major types of ecosystems, supporting a community of distinctive plants and animals specially adapted to the harsh environment.

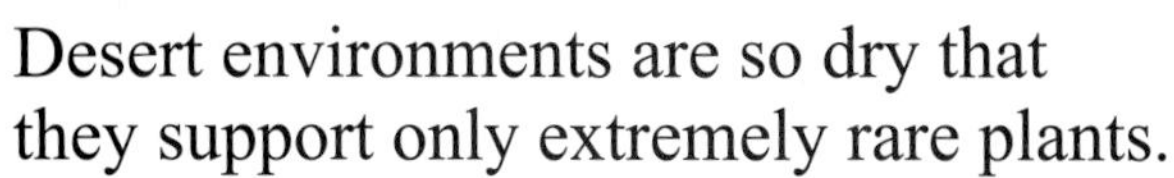

Desert environments are so dry that they support only extremely rare plants. Trees are usually absent and, under normal climatic conditions, shrubs or herbs provide only very incomplete ground cover.

Extreme aridity renders some deserts virtually devoid of plants. However, this barrenness is believed to be due in part to the effects of human disturbance, such as heavy grazing of cattle, on an already stressed environment.

Other desert plants survive dry periods through underground organs such as bulbs, tubers, or rhizomes. These structures are inactive, requiring and using little water until triggered to grow by rain soaking into the soil.

• IT'S FACT •

- Most deserts are the Equator, the imaginary line that runs around the center of the Earth. These deserts are hot and dry and few plants, the cactus, stores water in its thick, fleshy stems.

Cold region plants

Arctic plants grow in a harsh environment including low temperatures, continuous daylight in summer, infertile and often mobile soil and permanently frozen ground, and in many areas strong, dry winds and blowing snow.

The species that survive are few and are frequently dwarfed. Many plants grow in compact cushions for maximum protection from the climate.

Arctic plants have a rapid seasonal life cycle. Spring growth often begins when snow is on the ground and there are still heavy frosts.

At first sight, many parts of the polar regions are deserts without soil or vegetation. Closer inspection shows that some plant life is always present, and even on permanent ice there are often algae, lichens and some moss.

These plants are the source of food for the northern grazing mammals but contain few foods of direct value to man.

The sudden blooming of flowers is spectacular, particularly along the southern edges of the Tundra.

The growing season is so short that annuals are rare and perennials reproduce by shoots or runners.

The Temperate zone

The temperate zone is characterized by dry and wet forests, temperate mixed woodlands, savanna woodlands, with areas of alpine vegetational complexes and temperate rain forests.

In marked contrast to the tropical rain forests, the predominant trees throughout the majority of the temperate zone communities are either eucalyptus or acacia.

Much of the many shrubs have adapted themselves similarly to the arid conditions, so that in their vegetative state many representatives of different families look alike. Acacia, eremophila, and casuarina are examples of genera that tend to displace eucalyptus as the dominant tree or shrub. Much of this vegetation is badly degraded.

Temperate zone vegetation has been cleared for agricultural purposes, leaving only the vegetation communities of infertile or inaccessible localities.

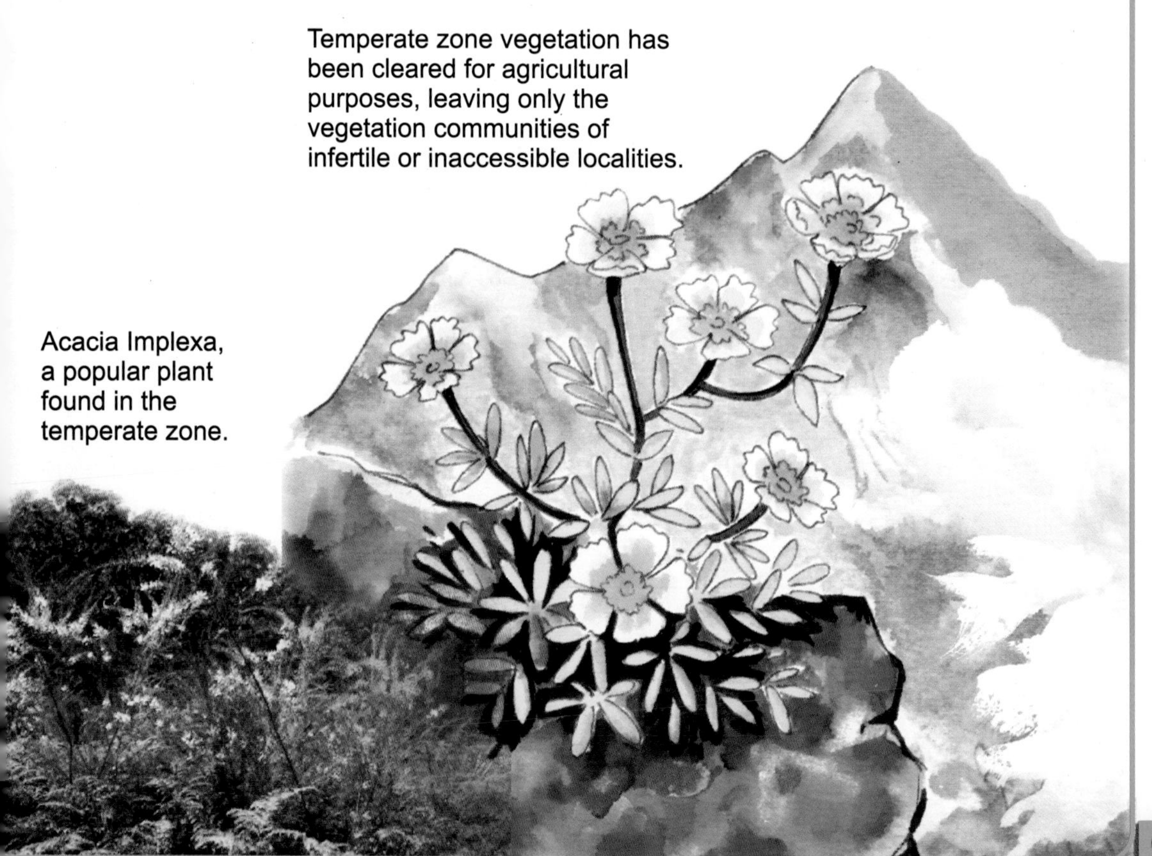

Acacia Implexa, a popular plant found in the temperate zone.

TREES

What are trees?

A tree is the biggest of all plants. Perhaps a general definition would describe a tree as a perennial woody plant that develops along a single main trunk to a height of at least 4.5 meters at maturity. This may be contrasted with a shrub, which might be loosely defined as a woody plant with multiple stems that is, in most cases, less than three meters tall.

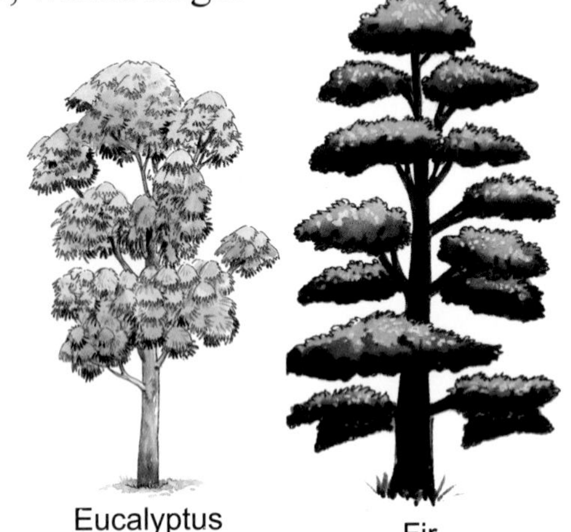

However, a species fitting the description of either in one area of the world might not necessarily do so in other regions, since a variety of stresses shape the habit of the mature plant. Thus, a given woody species may be a tree in one set of habitats within its range and a shrub elsewhere.

A tree root is the mineral store of the tree. The vast trunks and root systems store carbon dioxide and water and respire oxygen into the atmosphere.

Many small creatures live in the roots of trees. They take all their nutrition from the tree's root itself.

Importance of trees

Trees are of immense importance in soil stabilization and erosion control, especially in mountainous and hilly regions. They also protect and conserve water supplies and prevent floods. Small groups of trees and even single trees have a similar role locally in preventing washouts and in holding stream banks.

Many tree products other than wood are important. Edible fruits produced by trees include guavas, apples, cherries, peaches, pears, avocados, figs, coconuts, jackfruit, mangoes etc. which are eaten with great pleasure.

Guavas are native to the tropics of America but are now cultivated throughout the world.

Primitive people were dependent on trees for many materials in addition to wood. They even lived in houses made of wood. Fruits and nuts of many kinds were important foods for both humans and animals. Leaves of palms and other trees were used for thatching roofs.

Modern civilizations are no less dependent on trees. Although substitutes are now commonly used for some tree products, the demand for trees remains strong, as in the manufacture of newsprint and other papers as well as cardboard and similar packaging. The plywood industry converts immense numbers of trees into building materials.

• IT'S FACT •

- Trees contribute significantly to nutrient recycling, carbon dioxide absorption, and oxygen generation.

Tallest tree and smallest tree

The tallest trees are the Pacific Coast redwoods (Sequoia sempervirens) which exceed 105 meters in height in an impressive grove along Redwood Creek Valley, California, USA.

The next tallest trees are the Australian mountain ash (Eucalyptus regnans) found in Victoria, Australia. They exceed 90 meters, the greatest heights known for non-coniferous trees. The giant sequoia attains heights in excess of 90 meters and may have a trunk diameter of about 7.5 meters.

Smallest tree

The world's smallest trees probably are also conifers: the natural Bonsai cypresses and shore pines of the pygmy forests of the northern California coasts.

On the sterile, hardpan soils of these astounding forests, the trees may reach full maturity at under 0.2 meter in height, while individuals of the same species on richer, deeper soils can grow to more than 30 meters.

Other conifers, such as the pygmy pine of New Zealand, the smallest conifer, are always shrubby and may mature as shorter plants and grow up to 5 centimeters.

• IT'S FACT •

- The shape of a tree is an ecological construct as well, since its form is dependent on the habitat and the stresses of the environment.

Trees of special interest

Mangroves spread out into the water by sending from their branches roots that reach into the mud and develop into sturdy supporting props.

A distinctive feature of mangroves is their large fruits, the seeds of which germinate and grow into strong seedlings before they leave the parent plant.

The Traveler's tree of Madagascar has a palm-like trunk up to 9 meters tall. The leaves have hollow bases from which, it has been reported, travelers could obtain potable water.

The Talipot palm of tropical Asia may live as long as 75 years before it flowers and fruits just one time, then dies.

Gardening trees

Trees are the most permanent features of a garden. The range of tree sizes, shapes, and colors is vast enough to suit almost any gardening scheme, from shrubby dwarf trees to giant shade trees, from slow to rapid growers, from all tones of green to bronzes, reds, yellows, and purples.

A balance between evergreen trees, such as pines and spruces, and deciduous trees, such as oaks, maples, and beeches, can provide protection and visual interest throughout the year.

Forests at risk

Forests constitute natural habitats for wildlife. Unfortunately, today people are destroying forests in a large number to get timber and to make way for farmland. This is an evil practice.

Cutting down of trees is known as deforestation. Much of the remaining forests are being cut down for fuel and building materials.

We should understand the importance of plants and stop destroying forests. Trees take a long time to grow but it takes a few minutes to cut them. It is our duty to take care of them.

The conservation of forest trees involves three fundamental principles.

The first is protection of the growing tree crop from fire, insects, and disease. Fire, however, once regarded as a destroyer of forests, is now recognized as a management device when carefully employed. Some important timber trees require fire for successful regeneration.

Conifers

Conifer trees are so called because of their cone-like shape. Conifers take a long time to mature. When they open, the winged seeds inside drift away in the breeze. Conifers have needle-shaped leaves. Most of such trees do not shed their leaves in winters so they are called evergreen.

There are two types of conifers; the pinales and the taxales. Conifers have been studied from fossils more than 290 million years old. Although more species of conifers once existed, they are still a widely distributed group and are one of the world's most important renewable resources.

Most conifers contain highly flammable resins. The flammability of these trees increases during hot, dry weather, when the water content of the living needles is drastically reduced. Few adult conifers can withstand a conflagration.

Most conifer leaves, whatever their shape, minimize water loss. The reduced surface area of the scale- to needle-shaped leaves is an obvious example, but even the broader forms often have a thick, waxy coating that makes them waterproof.

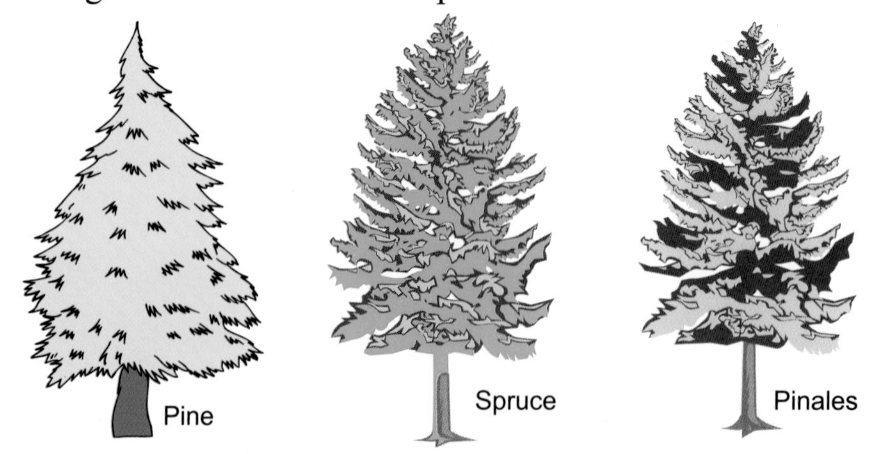

FRUITS

What are fruits?

Fruits are the fleshy or dry ripened ovary of a plant, enclosing one or many seeds. A fruit is a mature ovary and its associated parts. It usually contains seeds, which have developed from the enclosed ovule after fertilization.

Banana

The individual **bananas** are grouped in clusters of 10 to 20. The ripe fruit contains 22 percent of carbohydrate and is high in potassium, low in protein and fat, and a good source of vitamins C and A.

Apple

Apple is the fruit in which the ripened ovary becomes fleshy and edible. Apples at harvest, vary widely in size, shape, color, depending upon cultures and environment.

Orange

Oranges are rich in vitamin C and also provide some vitamin A. The usual shape of the sweet-orange fruit is round and the color of its pulp orange, but there are variations.

Mango

Mango is also known as 'The king of fruits.' There is a single large seed which is flattened, and the pulp that surrounds it is yellow to orange in color. Mangoes are a rich source of vitamins A, C, and D.

Grapes contain such minerals as calcium and phosphorus and are a source of vitamin A. All grapes contain sugar. They may be eaten as table fruit, dried to produce raisins, or crushed to make grape juice or wine.

The fruit is an oval berry within the juicy pulp of which lie the seeds.

Grapes

Common fruits

Some fruits are commonly eaten worldwide with great ecstacy. Some of them are :

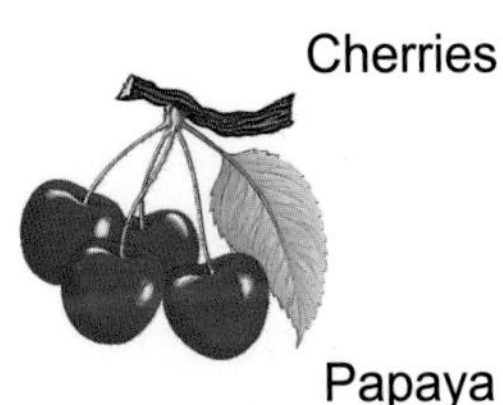
Cherries

Cherries are small fruits that are mainly found in bunches. They are dark red in color. Three types of cherry are mainly grown for their fruit.

Papaya

The **papaya** is slightly sweet, with a musky tang. It is a popular breakfast fruit in many countries and is also used in salads, pies, sherbets, juices, and confections. The unripe fruit can be cooked like squash.

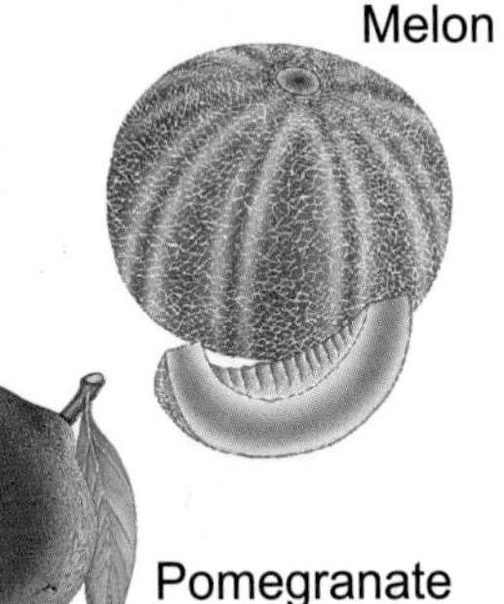
Melon

Pomegranate

Melons are juicy fruits whose pulp is eaten without skin. They weigh from 1 to 4 kilograms.

A **pomegranate** is the size of a large orange, obscurely six-sided, with a smooth, leathery skin that ranges from brownish yellow to red. Inside, it is divided into several juicy parts which contain reddish seeds.

Peach

Peach is about 87 per cent water and has fewer calories than either apples or pears. Yellow-fleshed varieties are especially rich in vitamin A. Peaches are widely eaten fresh as a dessert fruit, often with cream. Thousands of varieties of the peach have been developed.

Pear

Pears are generally sweeter and of softer texture than apples. The fruit is distinguished by the presence of hard cells in the flesh, the so-called grit, or stone cells.

Juicy fruits

Some fruits are juicier than others. They are seasonal and mostly used as desserts. Some of them are :

Watermelon contains vitamin A and some vitamin C. It is usually eaten raw. The rind is sometimes preserved as a pickle. The sweet, juicy flesh may be reddish, white, or yellow. Weight varies from 1 to 2 kg to 20 kg.

Watermelon

Blueberries are sweet, juicy fruits, which provide a source of vitamin C and iron. Blueberries are eaten fresh, often with cream, as a dessert fruit, or baked in a variety of pastries.

Blueberries

The **strawberry** is not a berry and is much more than a single fruit. Rich in vitamin C, the strawberry also provides iron and other minerals. It is eaten fresh as a dessert fruit, used in a pastry or pie filling, and may be preserved in many ways. The strawberry shortcake, made of fresh strawberries, sponge cake, and whipped cream, is a traditional American dessert.

Strawberries are produced commercially both for immediate consumption and for processing as frozen, canned, or preserved berries or as juice.

• IT'S FACT •

- Fruit life can be extended further by both refrigeration and controlled atmosphere.
- After fresh fruit, one of the most common fruit products is fruit juice. Fruit juice can take on many forms including a natural-style cloudy product, a fully clarified juice, juice concentrate, and fruit drinks.

The **plum** has long been recognized as one of the most delicious fruits. It is widely eaten fresh as a dessert fruit, cooked as delicacy or jam, or baked in a variety of pastries. Plums are the most extensively distributed of the stone fruits.

Plum

Fleshy fruits

Some fruits are fleshy. Let us know about some of them : The **coconut** fruit grows close to the seashores. The soft and mushy fruit is covered with a hard shell and thick husk. The fruit may also be grated and mixed with water to make coconut milk, used in cooking or as a substitute for cow's milk. Coconut oil is the world's ranking vegetable oil.

Besides the fruit and the drink obtained from coconut, the husk yields coir which is used in manufacture of ropes, mats, baskets, brushes, and brooms.

Water chestnut is sometimes called singhara nut and is native to India. The fruit is 2.5 to 5 cm in diameter and usually has four spiny angles. It has floating leaves, about 5 to 8 cm long and hairy petioles which are 10 to 15 cm in length. The fruit is covered with thick green peel. It is cultivated in most of East Asia.

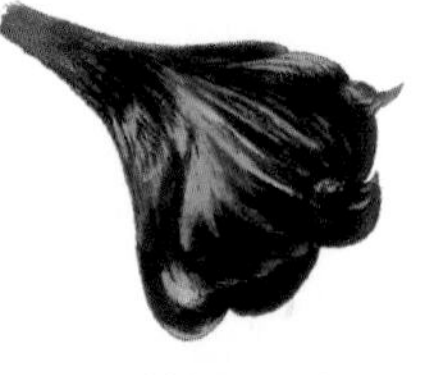

Water chestnut

The skin of the common **custard apple** or bullock's heart of the West Indies, is green and dark brown in color and marked with depressions giving it a quilted appearance. Its pulp is reddish yellow, sweetish, and very soft. The kernels of the seeds are said to be poisonous of some varieties.

Custard apple

The **pineapple** has become a characteristic ingredient in meat, vegetable, fish, and rice dishes of what is widely termed as Polynesian cuisine, a blend of various Oriental styles of cooking. The fruit is eaten fresh where available and in canned form worldwide. In the United States and in Europe, it is sometimes used as a pastry filling or in baked desserts.

A pineapple has nothing to do with a pine or an apple.

Dry fruits and nuts

Dry fruits are those fruits in which the entire pericarp becomes dry at maturity. This category includes the legumes, cereal grains, capsulate fruits, and nuts.

Cashew nut is shaped like a large, thick bean and is sometimes more than 2.5 cm long. The edible fruit is known as the Cashew apple which is used in making beverages, jams, and jellies.

Cashew nut

Beetle nut

Beetle nut is also known as Supari in India. They are mostly used by Indians for chewing.

Cardamom is used as a spice consisting of dried fruit or seeds. The seeds have a warm, slightly pungent and highly aromatic flavor. **Cardamom** may be bleached to a creamy white color in the fumes of burning sulphur.

Cardamom

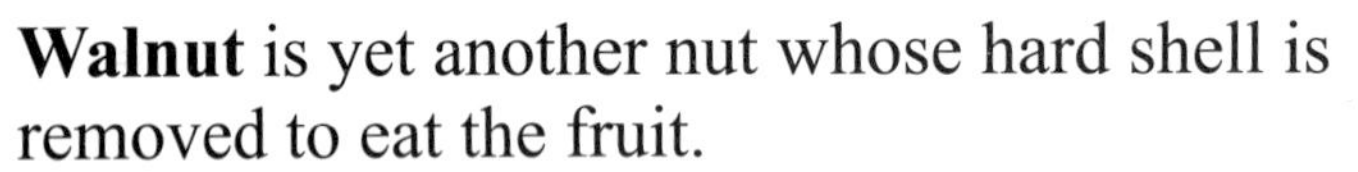

Walnut is yet another nut whose hard shell is removed to eat the fruit.

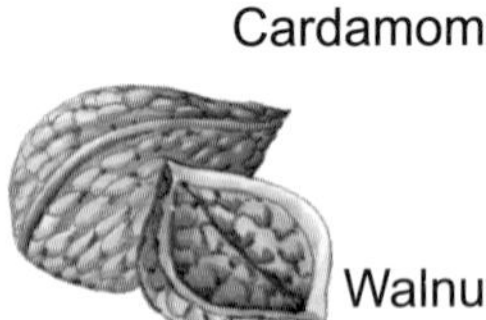

Walnut

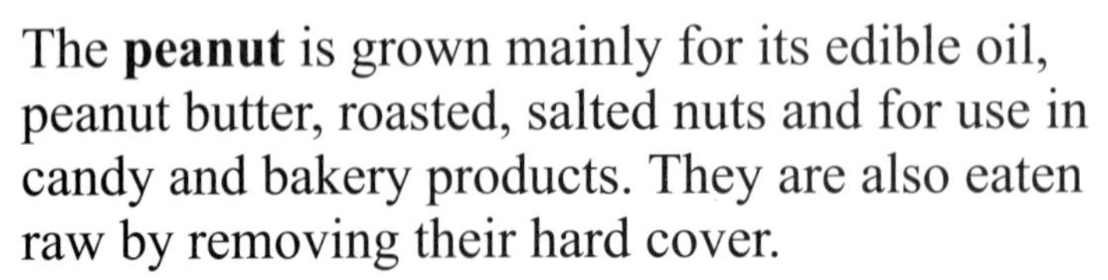

The **peanut** is grown mainly for its edible oil, peanut butter, roasted, salted nuts and for use in candy and bakery products. They are also eaten raw by removing their hard cover.

Peanut

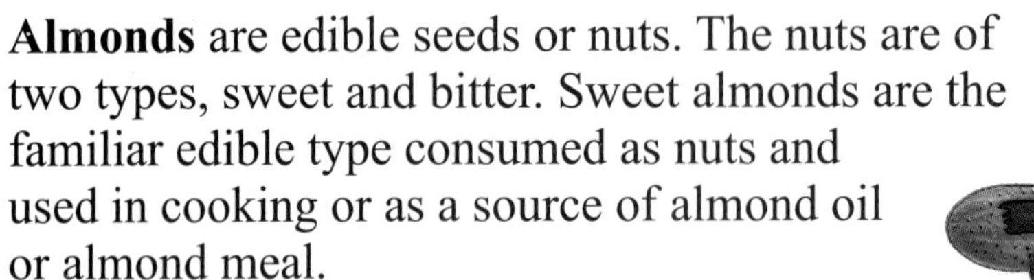

Almonds are edible seeds or nuts. The nuts are of two types, sweet and bitter. Sweet almonds are the familiar edible type consumed as nuts and used in cooking or as a source of almond oil or almond meal.

The growing fruit resembles the peach until it approaches maturity.

The **date** is a one-seeded fruit, usually oblong, but varying in shape, size, color, quality, and consistency of flesh. The fruit is more than 50 per cent sugar and about 2 per cent of protein, fat, and mineral matter. It is a rich source of iron.

Dates

FLOWERS

What are flowers?

Flowers are the reproductive portions of any plant. As popularly used, the term 'flower' especially applies when part or all of the reproductive structure is distinctive in color and form.

Aster

In their range of color, size, form, and anatomical arrangement, flowers present a seemingly endless variety of combinations. They range in size from minute blossoms to giant blooms. In some plants, such as poppy, magnolia, tulip, and petunia, each flower is relatively large and showy.

Magnolia

Regardless of their variety, all flowers have a uniform function, the reproduction of the species through the production of seed.

Basically, each flower consists of a floral axis upon which are borne the essential organs of reproduction and usually accessory organs. The latter may serve to both attract pollinating insects and protect the essential organs. The floral axis is a greatly modified stem; unlike vegetative stems, which bear leaves, it is usually contracted, so that the parts of the flower are crowded together on the stem tip.

Harebell

Bellflower

Hibiscus

Carnation

Common flowers

Some flowers are usually used as decorative materials at home. Some of these commonly known flowers are daisy, daffodil, geranium, fuchsia and dahlia.

Daisies are distinguished by a flower composed of 15 to 30 white ray petals surrounding a bright yellow disk flower. Some varieties of the English daisy have double flowers, others may have pink or red ray flowers.

Daisy

The beautiful **daffodil** has five or six petals that grow from the bulb. The stem bears one large yellow blossom that is frilled at its edges. This 'trumpet' shape contains the stamens.

Daffodil

Geranium flower is of great value. The oil is colorless to pale yellow-brown or greenish and has an odor like that of roses. It is used chiefly in perfumes, soaps, ointments and powders.

Geranium

Fuchsia are valued for their showy pendulous flowers, tubular to bell-shaped, in shades of red and purple to white. The hanging growth habit and flared shape of the flower gave rise to the popular name ladies' eardrop.

Dahlia flowers may be white, yellow, red, or purple in color. Dahlias grow well in most garden soils. They flower late in the summer and do so until interrupted by frost in the autumn.

Dahlia

Fuchsia

Sepals and petals

Sepals and petals together make up the floral envelope. The sepals are usually greenish and often resemble smaller leaves, while the petals are usually colorful and showy.

Holly

The male parts of the flower, comprise the stamens, each of which consists of a supporting filament and an anther, in which pollen is produced. The female parts of the flower, comprise the pistils, each of which consists of an ovary on the top of which rests the stigma, the pollen-receptive surface.

The ovary encloses the ovules, or potential seeds. A pistil may be simple, made up of a single carpel, or ovule-bearing modified leaf; or compound, formed from several carpels joined together.

A flower having sepals, petals, stamens, and pistils is complete; lacking one or more of such structures, it is said to be incomplete.

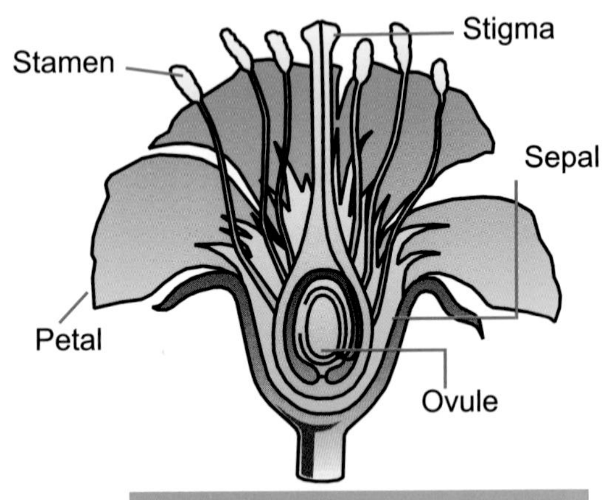

Willow

Stamens and pistils are not present together in all flowers such as holly, willow and carrion.

• IT'S FACT •

- Sepals and petals that are indistinguishable, as in lilies and tulips, are sometimes referred to as petals.

Symbols of beauty

Roses

Flowers have been symbols of beauty in most civilizations of the world, and gifting flowers is still the most popular tradition at social functions. As gifts, flowers serve as expressions of affection for spouses, other family members, and friends; as decorations at weddings and other ceremonies; as tokens of respect for the deceased; as cheering gifts to the bedridden; or as expressions of thanks to hostesses and other social contacts.

Most flowers bought by the public are grown in commercial greenhouses and then sold through wholesalers to retail florists.
No other flower is so universally known and admired as the rose. Its blossoms range in color from white through various tones of yellow and pink to dark crimson and maroon. Many varieties have been bred with beautiful blends of color.
Roses have a delightful fragrance, which varies according to the variety and to climatic conditions.

Jasmine

Tulip

Amaryllis

Lilacs

• IT'S FACT •

- Roses can become infected by a number of diseases, most of them are caused by fungi.
- Many countries have their national symbols as flowers. The most popular flower is white lily which is the national symbol of nearly 10 countries.

Pollination

Pollination is the transfer of pollen grains from the stamens, the flower parts that produce them, to the ovule-bearing organs or to the ovules.

In flowering plants, however, the ovules are contained within a hollow organ called the pistil, and the pollen is deposited on the pistil's receptive surface, the stigma. There the pollen germinates and gives rise to a pollen tube, which grows down through the pistil toward one of the ovules in its base.

Pollination is essential to the production of fruits and seeds and plays an important part in programs designed to improve plants by breeding. In flowering plants, these are insects, wind, birds, mammals, and water act as external agents for pollen transport.

When a honey bee or any other insect sits over a flower, some of its pollen grain gets stuck to its feet. After that when it goes to another flower, it brushes off the pollen grain on it. This way it helps in pollination.

Pollination by insects probably occurred in primitive seed plants, reliance on other means being a relatively recent evolutionary development.

VEGETABLES

What are vegetables?

Vegetables usually refer to the fresh edible portions of a plant, for example roots, stems, leaves, flowers, or fruit. These plant parts are either eaten raw or cooked in a number of ways. Most fresh vegetables have a water content in excess of 70 per cent, with only about 3.5 per cent protein and less than 1 per cent fat. Vegetables, however, are good sources of minerals, especially calcium and iron, and vitamins, mainly A and C.

Vegetables are usually classified on the basis of the part of the plant that is used for food. The root vegetables include beets, carrots, radishes, and turnips. Stem vegetables include lotus stem, asparagus and kohlrabi.

Among the edible tubers, or underground stems, are potatoes. The leaf and leafstalk vegetables include Brussels sprouts, cabbage, celery, lettuce, rhubarb, and spinach. Among the bulb vegetables are garlic, leek, and onion. The head, or flower, vegetables include artichokes, broccoli, and cauliflower. The fruits that are commonly considered vegetables by virtue of their use include beans, cucumbers, eggplant, okra, sweet corn, squash, peppers, and tomatoes.

Vegetables may be washed, sorted, graded, cut, and packaged for sale as fresh products.

Modern farming

Modern vegetable farming ranges from small-scale production for local sale to vast commercial operations utilizing the latest advances in automation and technology.

Most vegetables are planted by sowing seeds in the fields where they are to be grown, but occasionally they are germinated in a nursery or greenhouse and transplanted as seedlings to the fields.

During the growing season, herbicides, pesticides, and fungicides are commonly used to inhibit damage by weeds, insects, and diseases, respectively.

Harvesting operations are usually mechanized in well-developed nations, but the practice of harvesting by hand is still employed in some areas or is used in conjunction with machine operations. Another concern of the vegetable farmer is post-harvest storage, which may require refrigerated facilities.

Vegetable farming requires special skills and techniques. The crop is not ready for harvest until the edible portion of the plant reaches the stage of maturity; it must be carried through further stages of growth. Special techniques are applied during the stage of flowering and seed development and also in harvesting and threshing the seeds.

As urban centres grew, agricultural production became more specialized and commercial farming developed, with farmers producing a sizable surplus of certain crops.

Nutrition

The four quality factors of vegetables are color, texture, flavor, and nutritive values. Fresh vegetables are purchased on the basis of color and texture, but repeated purchases are made on the basis of flavor and nutritional content. The major nutrients contributed by vegetables to the human diet are dietary fiber, minerals, and vitamins.

Certain vegetables contribute lipids to the diet, mostly in the form of unsaturated oils. Roots and legumes can be important contributors of dietary proteins.

Fresh vegetables are subject to quality and vitamin losses during transportation and storage, whereas processing before these losses occur can yield a nutritionally superior vegetable. Research has shown that a major cause of nutrient loss in vegetables is in the usage of cooking or processing liquids.

It is a common misconception that fresh vegetables are always superior in nutritional value to processed vegetables. Several investigations have shown frozen or canned vegetables can actually have higher nutritional value than fresh products.

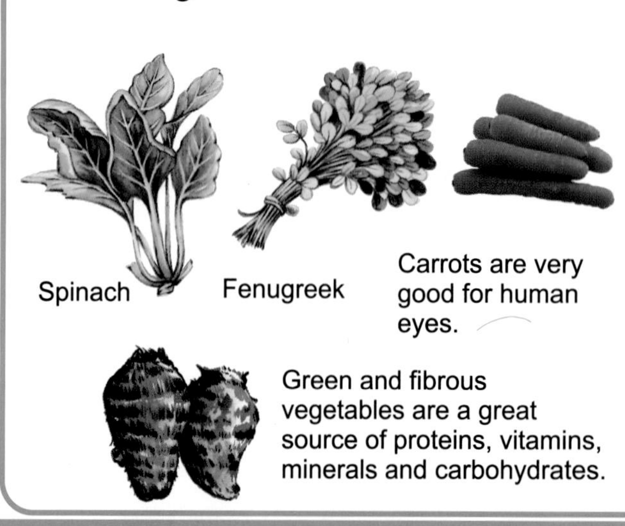

Spinach

Fenugreek

Carrots are very good for human eyes.

Green and fibrous vegetables are a great source of proteins, vitamins, minerals and carbohydrates.

• IT'S FACT •

- Most vegetable proteins are low in one of the eight essential amino-acids, however, if proteins are obtained from a proper mixture of vegetables, there will not be a nutritional problem.
- Processed vegetables that are intended for inclusion in prepared foods should be frozen if they are to be stored for a long duration.

Capsicum, tomato and cucumber

Capsicum comprises all the varied forms of fleshy-fruited peppers, the red, green, and yellow peppers that are rich sources of vitamins A and C are being used in seasoning and as a vegetable food. Capsicums are used as relishes, pickled, or ground into a fine powder for use as spices.

Yellow capsicum

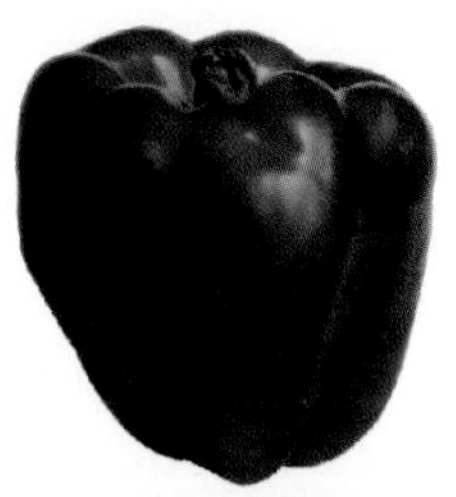

Green capsicum

Capsicums have larger, variously colored but generally bell-shaped, furrowed, puffy fruits that are used in salads and in cooked dishes. These varieties are harvested when they become bright green in color.

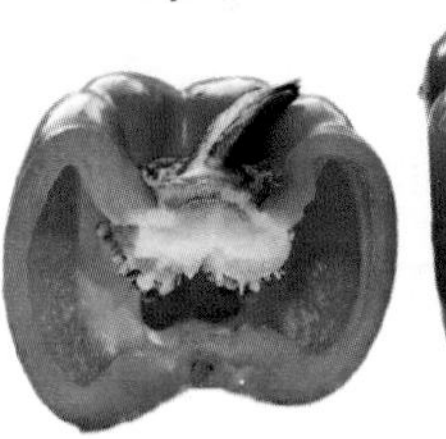

Red capsicum

Tomatoes are bright red colored vegetables which are widely used across the whole world.

The tomato is eaten raw in salads, served as a cooked vegetable, used as an ingredient of various prepared dishes, and pickled. The fruit is a soft, succulent berry, containing from two to many cells of small seeds surrounded by jelly-like pulp. Most of the tomato's vitamin C is found in this pulp.

The food value of **cucumber** is low, but its delicate flavor makes it popular for salads and relishes. Fresh cucumbers should be firm, well-shaped, and bright green in color. They may be kept in refrigerated storage for about two weeks.

Red tomato

The large-fruited cucumber having white spines are used primarily for slicing and pickling.

Leafy vegetables

Some leafy vegetables are eaten raw or cooked. All varieties of asparagus, broccoli, spinach, cabbage and fresh herbs come under this classification.

Asparagus

The garden **asparagus** is cultivated as a green vegetable for its succulent spring stalks. As a vegetable, it has been most commonly served cooked, either hot or in salad.

In case of asparagus, it is necessary to cover the plant portion with soil.

Broccoli

Fresh **broccoli** should be dark green in color, with firm stalks and compact bud clusters. As a vegetable, it can be served raw or cooked.

Spinach is served as a salad green and as a cooked vegetable. Spinach can be made into various soups, soufflés, and mousses and is used as an ingredient in various prepared dishes.

Spinach

Cabbages have succulent leaves free of hairs and covered with a waxy coating; in most of them the waxy coat gives the leaf surface a gray-green or blue-green color. Edible portions of these plants are low in caloric value. They are an excellent source of ascorbic acid and also supply minerals and necessary nutrition in the diet.

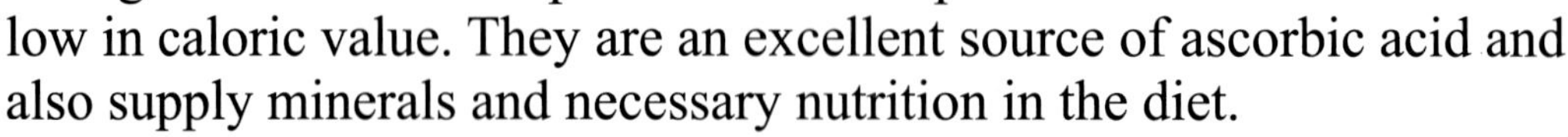

These plants grow best in mild to cool climates and light frost, and some of them tolerate hard freezing at certain periods of growth.

• IT'S FACT •

- The true turnip probably originated in middle and eastern Asia and by cultivation has spread throughout the temperate zone.

Head cabbage, generally designated simply cabbage, is a major table vegetable in most countries of the temperate zone.

Onions and shallots

Onions are among the world's oldest cultivated plants. The common onion has one or more leaf-less stalks in a cluster of small greenish white flowers. The leaf bases of the developing plant swell to form the underground bulb that is the mature, edible onion.

Onions

Green onions, also called scallions and spring onions, are young onions harvested when their tops are green and the underdeveloped bulbs are 13 mm or less in diameter. Their flavor is mild, and the entire onion, including top, stem, and bulb, is used raw in salads and sauces, as a garnish, and also as a seasoning for cooked dishes.

The **shallot** is a hardy, bulbous vegetable which is closely related to onion and garlic. Its leaves are short, small, cylindrical, and hollow. The flowers are lavender or red, in a compact umbel. The bulbs are small, elongated, and angular and develop in clusters on a common base, much like the garlic plant.

Leafy Stalks

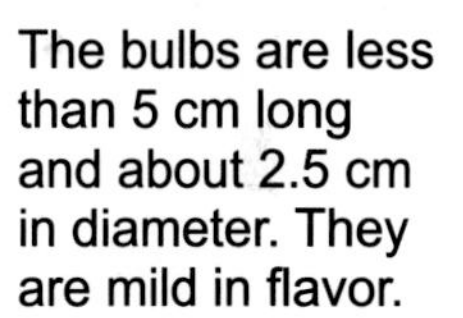

The bulbs are less than 5 cm long and about 2.5 cm in diameter. They are mild in flavor.

Most commercially cultivated onions are grown from the plant's small black seed, which is sown directly in the field, but onions may also be grown from small bulbs or from transplants.

Onions are used widely in cooking. They add flavor to such dishes as stews, roasts, soups, and salads, and are also served as a cooked vegetable.

Beans and peas

Most edible-podded beans produce relatively low yields of mature seeds, or seeds that are of low-eating quality. Seed colors range from white through green, yellow, tan, pink, red, brown, and purple to black in solid colors and countless contrasting patterns. Seed shapes range from nearly spherical to flattened, elongated, and kidney-shaped. Pods are of various shades of green, yellow, red and purple and splashed with red or purple; pod shapes range from flat to round.

The pea plant is a hardy, leafy plant with climbing stems. Each leaf has three pairs of leaflets. The vegetable is a many-seeded pod that grows to 10 cm long, splitting in half when ripe. It is mostly found in green color.

Widely grown varieties of peas include dwarf, half-dwarf, trailing, smooth-seeded, wrinkled-seeded, and black-eyed. Some varieties, called sugar peas, produce pods that are edible. The pods are picked before the seeds reach maturity and are eaten raw or cooked like green beans.

Dried peas are sometimes ground into flour.

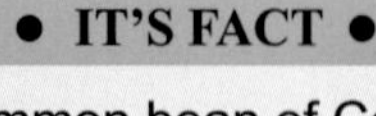

• IT'S FACT •

- The common bean of Central and South American origin is second to the soybean in importance. It is known as French bean.
- Shallots are planted early in spring and grow in any good garden soil; the bulbs are harvested in the autumn.

Cauliflowers and carrots

Cauliflowers and carrots are the two most common vegetables. Cauliflower is frequently served as a cooked vegetable, and the florets are also used in salads and as relishes in raw form. It belongs to the cabbage family consisting of a compact, greatly thickened and partially developed flower structures, together with their subtending fleshy stalks.

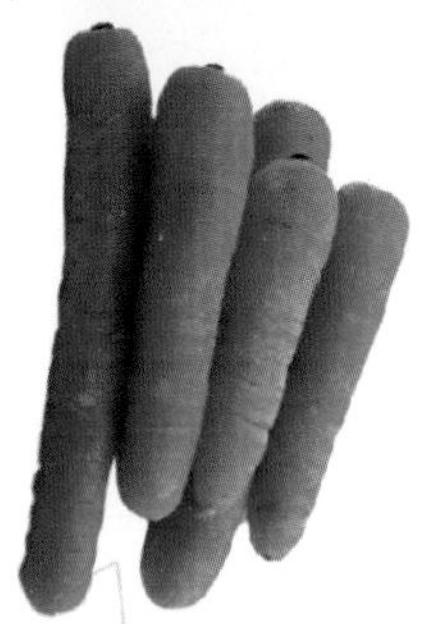

Fresh carrots should be firm and crisp, with smooth and unblemished skin. Bright-orange color indicates high carotene content; smaller types are the most tender. Carrots are used in salads and as relishes and are served as cooked vegetables and in stews and soups.

• IT'S FACT •

Important Cauliflower Nutrition Facts:

- The chemical called 'Allicin', present in cauliflower helps in maintaining heart health. It has also been found to reduce the risk of strokes in heart patients.
- The presence of vitamin C and Selenium in cauliflowers help in strengthening the immune system of the body.
- Regular consumption of cauliflower can help in maintaining the cholesterol level of the body.
- Cauliflower is rich in a nutrient called folate. Folate helps in improving cell growth and cell replication mechanism. Overall, it aids tissue growth.
- Cauliflower contains a substance called Sulforaphane, which can effectively remove chemicals that cause cancer in the body! This substance also aids in preventing the spread of cancerous cells, that is metastasis, even in advanced stages of cancer! This chemical is released when you chop or chew cauliflower.
- Very recently, it was found that a chemical called 'indole-3-carbinol', found in cauliflower can effectively prevent the development of breast cancer, because it works as an anti-estrogen agent!
- Consumption of cauliflower regularly can aid patients afflicted with diseases like asthma, arthritis, kidney and bladder disorders, constipation and high blood pressure.
- A regular and high intake of cauliflower reduces the risk of prostrate cancer!

Potatoes and turnips

Potatoes are frequently served whole or mashed as a cooked vegetable and are also ground into potato flour, used in baking and as a thickener for sauces. Potatoes are highly digestible.

The potato is one of the world's major food crops, differing from others in that the edible part of the plant is an underground stem. The skin varies in color from brownish white to deep purple.

Young turnip roots are eaten raw in salads or pickled, and the young leaves may be cooked and served. The roots are also cooked and served whole or mashed and are used in stews.

• IT'S FACT •

- The vitamin-C present in potatoes can help prevent this dreaded deficiency disease, caused due to lack of vitamin-C. It is characterized by cracked lip corners, spongy and bleeding gums, frequent viral infections like cold etc.
- You can get 50 percent of the recommended daily dosage of vitamin B6 and vitamin C for adults in just 7 ounces of baked potato with the skin intact. There is also plenty of potassium and nearly 5 grams of fiber. You get all these for zero grams of fat and only 220 calories.

Ginger and garlic

Ginger has a slightly pungent taste and is used, usually dried and ground, to flavor breads, sauces, curry dishes, confectionaries, pickles, and ginger ale. Fresh ginger is used in cooking. Ginger is also used to treat many common diseases.

Ginger contains about two per cent essential oil; the principal component is zingiberene and the pungent principle of the spice is zingerone. The oil is distilled from rhizomes for use in the food and perfume industries.

Garlic is native to central Asia but also grows wild in Italy and southern France. The membranous skin of the garlic bulb encloses up to 20 edible bulblets called cloves. Flower stalks sometimes arise bearing tiny bulblets and blossoms without seeds. Garlic is propagated by planting cloves or top bulblets. Garlic contains about 0.1 per cent essential oil.

Garlic bulbs are used either sliced or ground to flavor tomato sauces, stews, and salad dressings.

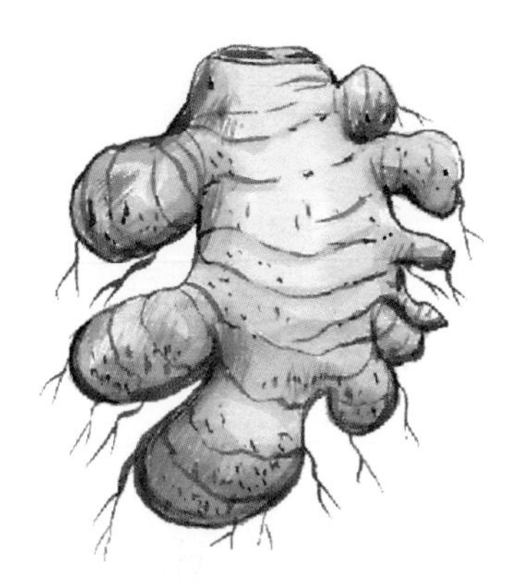

Ginger rhizomes are irregular in shape, branched or palmate. Their color varies from dark yellow through light brown to pale buff.

In ancient and medieval times, garlic was prized for its medicinal properties and was carried as a charm against evils. Garlic is also believed to have anti-ageing properties.

OTHER

PLANTS

Ferns

Ferns are a diverse group of plants. Although they are found worldwide, ferns are more common in tropical and subtropical regions. They range in size and complexity from small floating aquatic plants that are less than 2 centimeters long to tall tree ferns up to 20 meters high. Fern stems never become woody since all tissues of the plant body originate at the stem apex. Fern leaves are either whole or variously divided. Fern leaves often have prominent epidermal hairs and large chaffy scales.

Fern leaves are coiled when they are immature. As they become mature, they unfold and the little brown pores underneath fall on the ground.

Coiled tree fern tendril

Ferns are nonflowering vascular plants that possess true roots, stems, and complex leaves and reproduce by spores. The number of fern species is usually placed at approximately 12,000. The number varies because certain groups are as yet poorly studied and new species are still being found in unexplored tropical areas.

Ferns constitute an ancient division of vascular plants, some of them as old as 360 million years and perhaps older.

Their type of life cycle which is dependent upon spores for dispersal, long preceded the seed-plant life cycle. Ferns, which come in a wide variety of forms, provide many popular houseplants. Among the best smaller parlor ferns is the sword fern with bushy rosettes of leafy fronds.

Mosses

Mosses are any of at least 10,000 species of small, spore-bearing land plants distributed throughout the world except in salt water.

Mosses existed as early as the Permian period (286 to 245 million years ago), and more than 100 species were present during the Tertiary period (66.4 to 1.6 million years ago).

Mosses are commonly found in moist, shady locations and are best known for those species that carpet woodland and forest floors. Mosses may range in size from microscopic forms to plants that are more than one meter. They differ primarily in the structure and specialization of their spores.

Mosses reproduce by branching and fragmentation, by regeneration from tiny pieces of leaves or stems, and by the production of spores. The spore, under favorable conditions, germinates and grows into a branching, green thread.

Mosses break down and release nutrients for the use of more complex plants that succeed them.

They help in checking soil-erosion by providing surface cover and absorbing water, and they are important in the nutrient and water economy of some vegetation types.

Because the peat mosses are very absorbent, they are widely used to improve soil texture.

Lichens

Lichens are any of about 15,000 species of plants that consist of algae and fungi.

Lichens have been used by humans as food and as sources of medicines and dyes. They also provide two-thirds of the food supply for the reindeer that roam the far northern ranges.

The composite body of a lichen is called a thallus.

Lichens grow relatively slowly, and there is still some question as to how they propagate. Most botanists agree that the most common means of reproduction is vegetative; that is, portions of an existing lichen break off and fall away to begin new growth nearby.

Lichens that form a crust like covering that is thin and tightly bound to the substrate are termed crustose. Squamulose lichens are small and leafy with loose attachments to the substrate.

Foliose lichens are large and leafy, reaching diameters of several feet.

It is not certain when fungi and algae came together to form lichens for the first time, but it was certainly after the mature development of the separate components. The basis of their relationship is the mutual benefit that they provide each other.

Lichens were once classified as single organisms until the advent of microscopy, when the association of algae and fungi became evident.

Algae

Algae are members of aquatic, photosynthetic organisms. They range in size from a micrometer in diameter to giant kelp that grows in the sea and can reach up to 60 meters in length. Algae provide much of the Earth's oxygen. They are the food base for almost all aquatic life. They are an original source of petroleum products, and they provide foods and industrial products for humans.

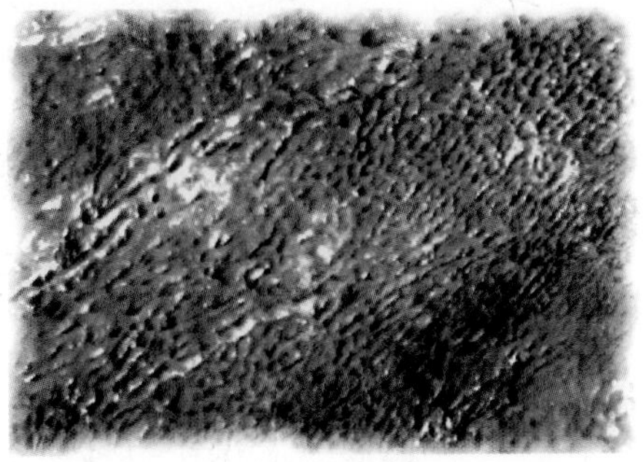

Beginning in the 1830s, algae were classified into major groups based on color.

The algae have many types of life cycles, from simple to complex. The photosynthetic pigments in algae are more varied than those of plants, and their cells have features not found among plants and animals. Some algae are ancient, while other groups have evolved more recently.

Plants always have multicellular reproductive structures where the fertile, gamete-producing cells are surrounded by sterile cells; this never occurs in algae. Algae lack true roots, stems, and leaves.

Thus, some algae have a closer evolutionary relationship with the protozoa or fungi than they do with other algae, and the converse is also true--some protozoa or fungi are more closely related to algae than to other protozoa or fungi.

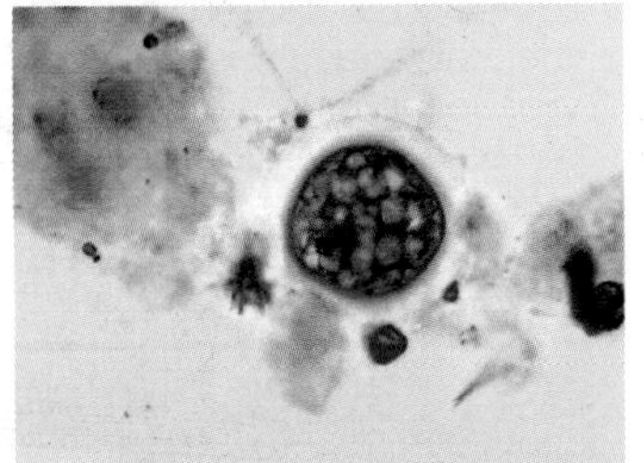

At one time, it was believed that algae with specialized green-absorbing accessory pigments out-competed green algae and plants in deeper water.

Some know algae as green sheens on pools and ponds. The algae are the base of the food chain for all marine organisms since most plants do not live in the oceans. Because the oceans occupy about 71 per cent of the Earth's surface area, the role of algae in supporting aquatic life is very vital.

Grass and fungi

Grass is the most important of all flowering plants because of their nutritious grains and soil-forming function. They also have the most widespread distribution and the largest number of individuals. Grasses provide forage for grazing animals, shelter for wildlife, construction materials and food for man. Some species are grown as garden ornamentals, cultivated as turf for lawns and recreational areas, or used as cover plants for erosion control. Most grasses have round stems that are hollow between the joints, blade-like leaves, and extensively branching fibrous root systems.

Fungi are distinguished from other organisms by the nature of their body and reproductive structures and by the mode of nutrition they use. They include yeasts, rusts, smuts, mildews, molds, toadstools and mushrooms. They are among the most widely distributed organisms on Earth and are of great importance.

Puffball is a type of globular fungi that grows in moist humus or on decaying tree stumps. The mature fruit becomes leathery and dry and, when disturbed, emits puffs of powdery spores through an opening at the top.

The mushrooms are the most numerous of the fungi. They are the most conspicuous members of the group.

The garden mushroom is a common fungi found in grassy areas during summers.

Herbs, spices and endangered plants

Herbs are dried plants cultivated for their aromatic, pungent, or otherwise desirable tastes. Spices and herbs consist of rhizomes, bulbs, barks, flower buds, stigmas, fruits, seeds, and leaves. They are commonly spoken of loosely as spices, spice seeds, and herbs. Herbs are the fragrant leaves of such plants as marjoram, mint, rosemary, and thyme. In medicine, spices and herbs have not entirely lost their reputation. In India and other Asiatic countries, their curative virtues enjoy respect.

Spices are the highly esteemed, fragrant or pungent plant products. The dominant species of the trade include cardamom, cinnamon, cloves, ginger, and pepper.

Endangered plants

A part from cutting of trees, there are other factors like fires and pollution which are destroying the plants around us. Slowly and gradually, some plants have come on the verge of extinction. If we do not take care of them, they will disappear from our world forever.

Some of the endangered plants are Venus flytrap, corn cockle, chickweed wintergreen, geissorhize radians, dwarf birch, eucalyptus, fir etc.

Hence, we must stop at once picking flowers, cutting down trees or doing anything that damages the plants. We must remember that by destroying plants, we are ultimately destroying ourselves.

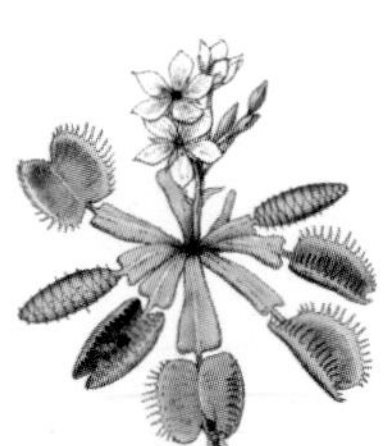

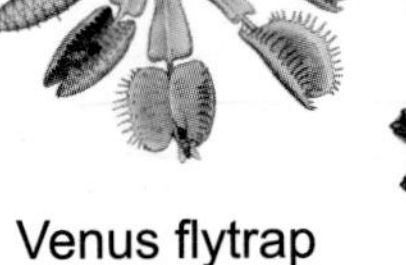

Venus flytrap

Fir

Shrubs

Shrubs are woody plants that have several stems and are usually less than three meters tall. When much-branched and dense, it may be called a bush. There are some shrubs, such as lilacs and honeysuckles that, under especially favorable environmental conditions, grow to the size of a small tree. Some specimens of shrubs may take a tree form.

Lemon shrub

A shrub is far from a tree. Some large shrubs are essentially small trees. Many shrubs are very small, and woody only at the very base, and can easily be mistaken for herbs; but they do not die back to ground level in winter.

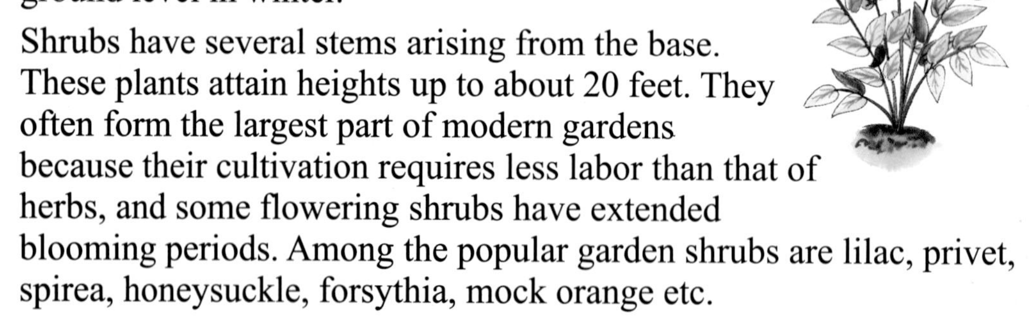

Shrubs have several stems arising from the base. These plants attain heights up to about 20 feet. They often form the largest part of modern gardens because their cultivation requires less labor than that of herbs, and some flowering shrubs have extended blooming periods. Among the popular garden shrubs are lilac, privet, spirea, honeysuckle, forsythia, mock orange etc.

The soil beneath shrubs is several times more fertile than it is between shrubs. Shrub roots contribute to this process by retrieving nutrients from the deep soil and depositing them in litter on the soil surface beneath the shrub canopy.

• IT'S FACT •

- Shrubs provide useful cover for wildlife, especially birds and small mammals.
- Shrubs are multiple-stem plants that grow from 2 to more than 20 feet high.
- Use shrubs for screening, privacy, windbreaks, wildlife habitats, and landscape color and texture.

Thorny plants

Some plants have thorns on their stems to protect themselves from being eaten. Cactus, Holly, Nettle and Carrion are examples of such plants.

All species of cactus are succulents and store water, sometimes in the roots but usually in stems which may be of huge capacity and capable of sustaining the plant over several years without rain. The plants are leathery with a thick waxy cuticle.

Some cacti have large flowers of many colors. Flowers are red, white, or yellow, on tubes up to 38 cm long and often fragrant. They are among the largest in the cactus family.

The spines can be very intricate, ranging from simple prongs to parasols and long, soft hairs; they shade or insulate the cactus, protect it from animals, reflect light, and collect and absorb droplets of dew–an important source of water. Cacti show a wide range of flowers, often large and conspicuous, pollinated by bees, hawk-moths, hummingbirds, and bats.

Cacti are widely cultivated as ornamentals. In addition, various species, notably prickly pears and chollas are cultivated as food. Some cacti are also used as living fences and some are a source of water in emergencies.

Flowers of cactus are often large and colourful. They are usually solitary.

PLANT

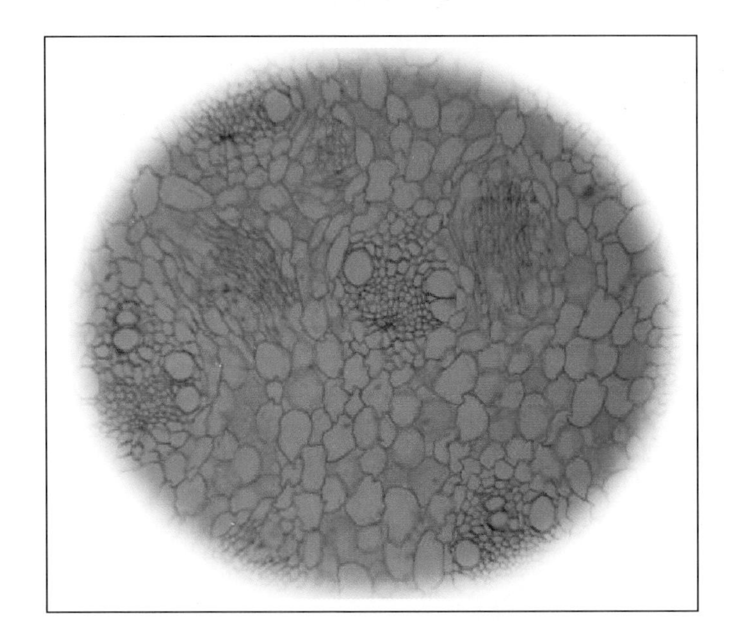

STRUCTURE

Plant cell

Cell is the basic unit of all plants. It comprises of a nucleus and cytoplasm that is enclosed within a cell membrane.

The plant cell wall is a specialized form of extracellular matrix that surrounds every cell of a plant. This is responsible for many of the characteristics distinguishing plant from animal cells. Although often perceived as an inactive product serving mainly mechanical and structural purposes, the cell wall actually has a multitude of functions upon which plant life depends.

The main functions of a plant cell are :

a. Providing the protoplast, or living cell, with mechanical protection

b. Providing a porous medium for the circulation and distribution of water, minerals, and other small nutrient molecules

c. Providing rigid building blocks from which stable structures of higher order, such as leaves and stems, can be produced

d. Providing a storage site of regulatory molecules that sense the presence of pathogenic microbes and control the development of tissues.

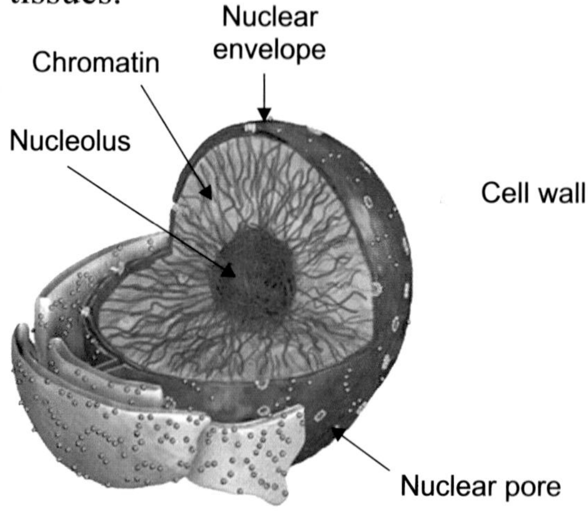

Nucleus is the dark structure inside the cell that controls the cell's activities and contains material such as DNA.

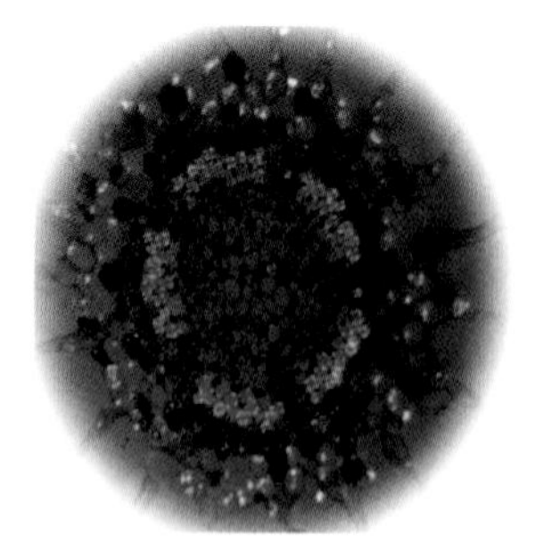

Many cells are more complex, and contain other specialized structures, such as mitochondria, chloroplast, Golgi bodies.

Vascular plants and vascular tissues

Vascular plants differ from the nonvascular in that they possess specialized supporting and water-conducting tissue, called xylem, and food-conducting tissue, called phloem.

The ability of vascular plants to flourish in so many different habitats is a key factor in their having become the dominant group of terrestrial plants.

The ferns, gymnosperms, and flowering plants are all vascular plants. Because they possess vascular tissues, these plants have true stems, leaves, and roots.

In vascular plants, leaves are supported by the stem which helps in trapping sunlight for use in photosynthesis.

Vascular tissues

The conducting tissues, both xylem and phloem, which distribute water, minerals, and sap throughout a plant, and help provide internal support. It forms thin strands called vascular bundles, with xylem to the inside and phloem to the outside. They are separated by a cambium layer which provides for secondary growth of the conducting tissues.

These bundles are scattered throughout the stem or arranged in a ring. In trees and shrubs, the bundles eventually join to form a band.

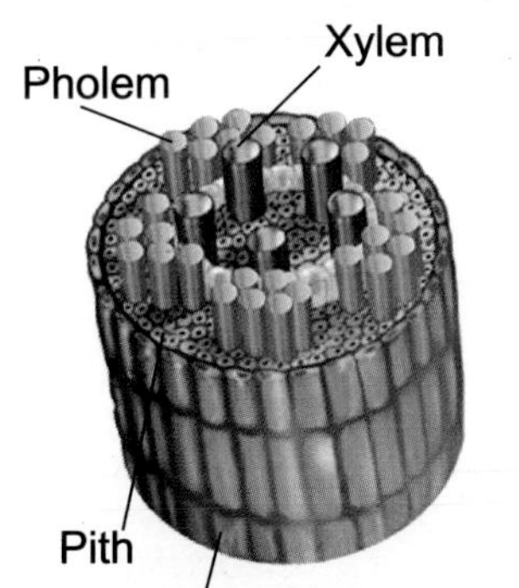

These two types of vessels run side-by-side, extending from roots to leaves. Xylem conducts water and dissolved minerals and phloem conducts food and other organic substances.

DIFFERENT

PLANTS

Cereals, oils, sugar and honey

Cereals form the main course of our meals. Normally, we consume their seeds which are popularly known as grains. Some grains are ground to make flour by which bread and chapatis are baked. Farmers feed some grains to their animals.

The fruits and seeds of some of the plants provide cooking oils. These oils contain a number of nutrients required by our body. Oil is obtained by crushing of their seeds.

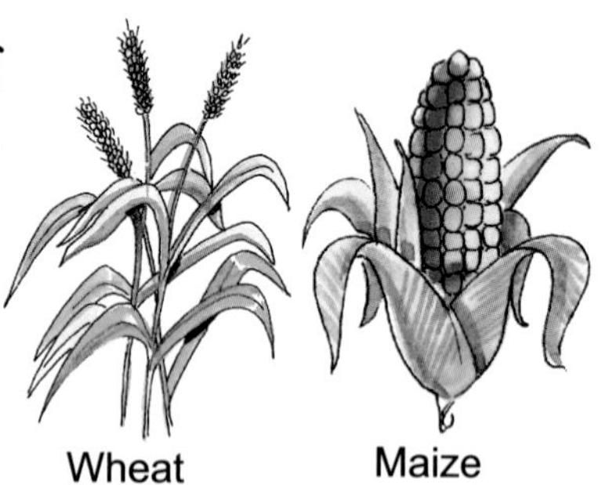

Wheat

Maize

Bread is made of flour

Sugar and honey

Sugar also comes from the plants. It comes from the root of sugar beet. Sugar can also be obtained from sugar cane. The stems of sugar cane are cut down and crushed, and their juice is used to make sugar.

Rice

Sunflower oil

Mustard oil

Bees collect nectar from flowers and convert it into honey. They feed on this honey throughout the winters. Once when the honey is taken from the hive, it is treated under special conditions to make it eatable and free from impurities.

Bees collect nectar and store it in their hives.

Plants to drink

Sometimes, plants are used to prepare juices. For this purpose, fruits are blended with milk and ice-cream to get a mouth-watering milkshake.

Coffee is obtained from the beans that grow on coffee plant. Coffee is one of the most popular drinks of the world.

The Arabs were the first people to drink coffee.

Coffee beans

A popular brand of coffee

Black coffee

Coffee powder

Tea is made from the leaves of tea plant. The young tips of tea leaves are neatly plucked by tea pickers, who are mostly ladies.

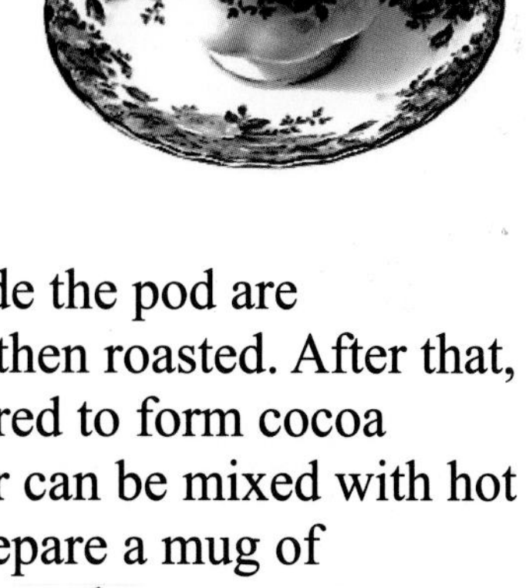

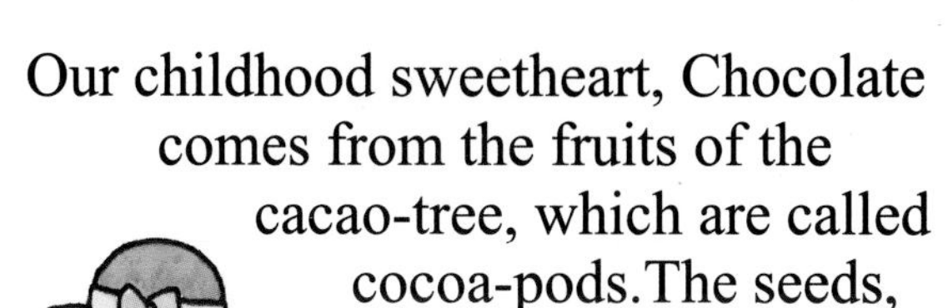

Our childhood sweetheart, Chocolate comes from the fruits of the cacao-tree, which are called cocoa-pods.The seeds, or cocoa-beans, inside the pod are extracted, dried and then roasted. After that, the beans are powdered to form cocoa powder. This powder can be mixed with hot milk and sugar to prepare a mug of delicious drinking chocolate.

New plants

Now-a-days, many people plant new kinds of plants in their houses. Children have become very fond of gardening. Here the child is helping a plant propagate.

Propagation means replacing an old plant by using parts of it to grow new ones. The spider plant can grow young plants on the end of long stems. These plantlets can then be planted again. Some plants can be produced by placing a leaf in the soil.

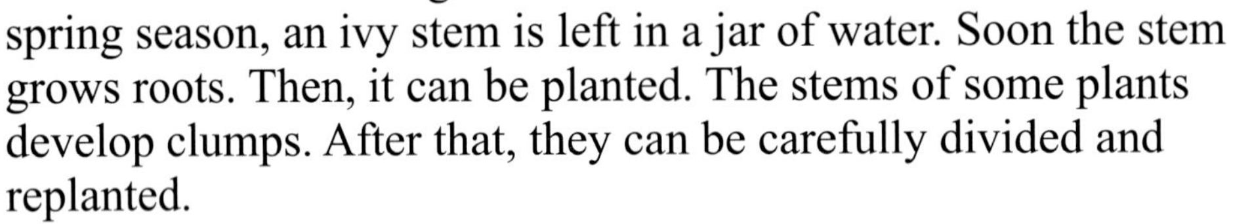

There are many ways of growing new plants. One of these processes is known as leaf cutting. In the spring season, an ivy stem is left in a jar of water. Soon the stem grows roots. Then, it can be planted. The stems of some plants develop clumps. After that, they can be carefully divided and replanted.

While planting a new plant, it is very important to prepare the right soil in which it has to grow.

Decorative plants

Ornamental horticulture consists of floriculture and landscape horticulture. Each is concerned with growing and marketing plants and with the associated activities of flower arrangement and landscape design.

Floriculture has long been an important part of horticulture, because flowers and pot plants are largely produced in plant-growing structures in temperate climates.

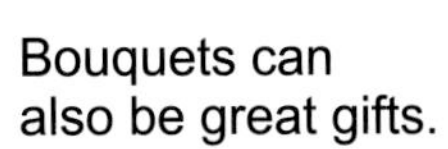

Bouquets can also be great gifts.

Decorative display of plants in its ornamental sense needs a certain level of civilization before it can flourish.

Many people decorate Christmas tree on Christmas Eve.

CHAPTER THREE

BIRDS

SHAPED FOR FLIGHT

FLIGHT AND FEATHERS

TYPES OF BIRDS

SHAPED

FOR FLIGHT

What are Birds?

Any animal that has feathers is a bird. Feathers help a bird to fly. Feathers have also made them the most successful of all animals. So you will find them in scorching deserts and even in biting cold temperatures of the Antarctic. Because of their ability to fly, birds have always fascinated man.

Hummingbird

There are about 9,000 species of bird on Earth.

Mallard duck

Sparrow

Penguin

Parrot

Bald eagle

Bird of paradise

What makes a bird unique?

Every time we see a bird flying by, we are fascinated by its ability to fly. Birds are unique. They are the only creatures with wings covered with feathers. With their wings, they can take off, fly with twists and turns, soar, dive and land on a perch.

Birds have been flying for thousands of years but we have understood the intricacies of flying only a couple of centuries ago. Everything about a bird is uniquely designed for flight. They have light weight bones. They have wings that are covered with feathers. Their heart beats faster and their body temperature is higher than any other animal in the vast animal kingdom. Their digestive system works faster. And their breathing is faster.

Scientists are not sure whether this ancient bird could fly.

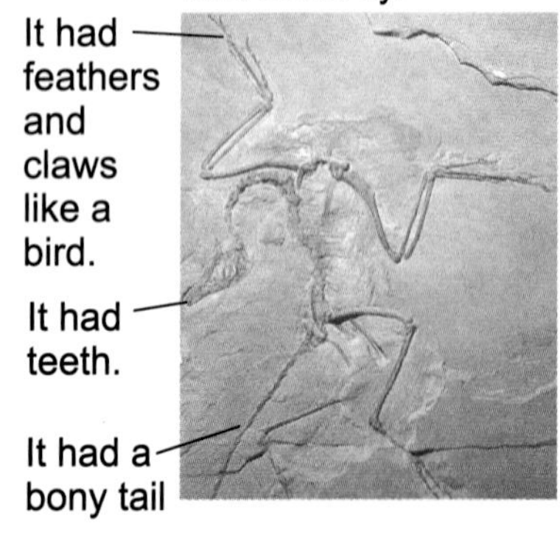

Scientists believe that birds evolved from reptiles. The archeopteryx was an animal that lived about 140 million years ago. It had the characteristics of birds as well as reptiles.

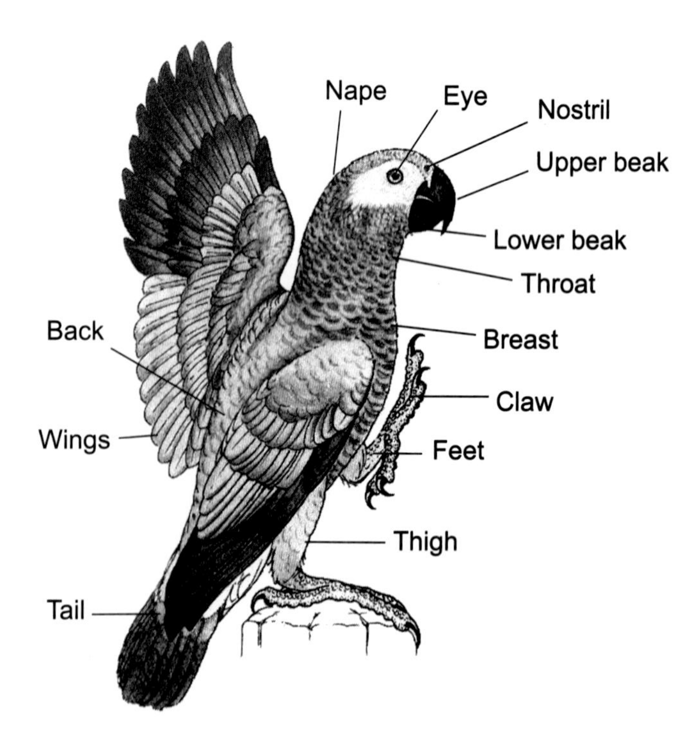

A typical bird's body is covered with feathers. It has a pair of wings and a pair of feet. It also has a bill.

Skeletal system

The best way to fly is to be light. So birds have light feathers and light bones. The avian skeleton is hard but thin. Birds in fact have less bones than most animals. The reason for lightness is that many bones in a bird's skeleton are hollow. The hollow bones are honeycombed with air spaces.

The skull of a bird also plays a part in streamlining a bird's body. It usually makes up just one per cent of its total body weight. This is because a bird does not have teeth, jaws or jaw muscles.

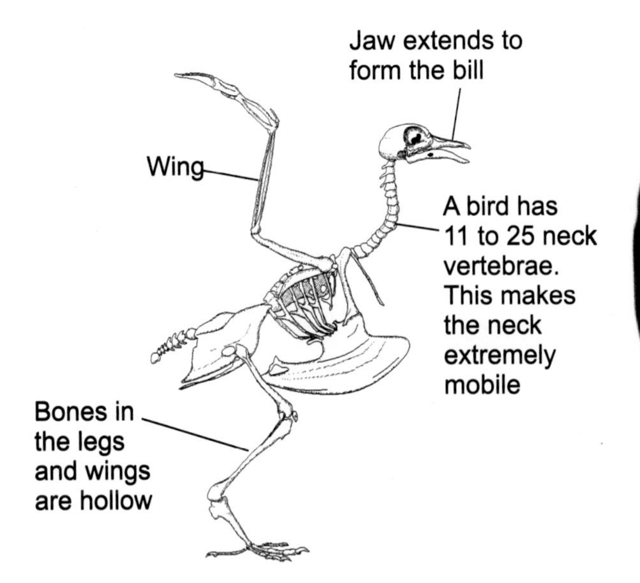

The avian skeleton is a combination of remarkable lightness with strength, that is essential for flight. The skeleton is strong enough for flight because many of the bones are fused.

Large gliding and soaring birds, like the albatross, have the most hollow bones. The biggest bones in their bodies are the breast bone and the shoulder bones.

• IT'S FACT •

- Wheatears living in Greenland are lager than those found further south. Being larger helps the birds to survive cold and longer migration flights to central Africa. the farther north a bird lives, the larger it tends to be.

Respiratory and circulatory system

Getting into the air needs a lot of energy. And a bird's body is well-designed for supplying energy to its body while maintaining lightness.

To create energy, birds must burn food. Oxygen is required to burn food. Oxygen is taken into the body through the lungs where it passes into the bloodstream. Birds also have two air sacs next to the lungs. So they never run out of breath.

The blood circulation in birds functions more efficiently than that of mammals. The heart is relatively larger and the rate of heartbeat is higher than that of a mammal. So a greater quantity of blood is pumped through within any given period. This is because vast amount of energy is needed by a bird when flying.

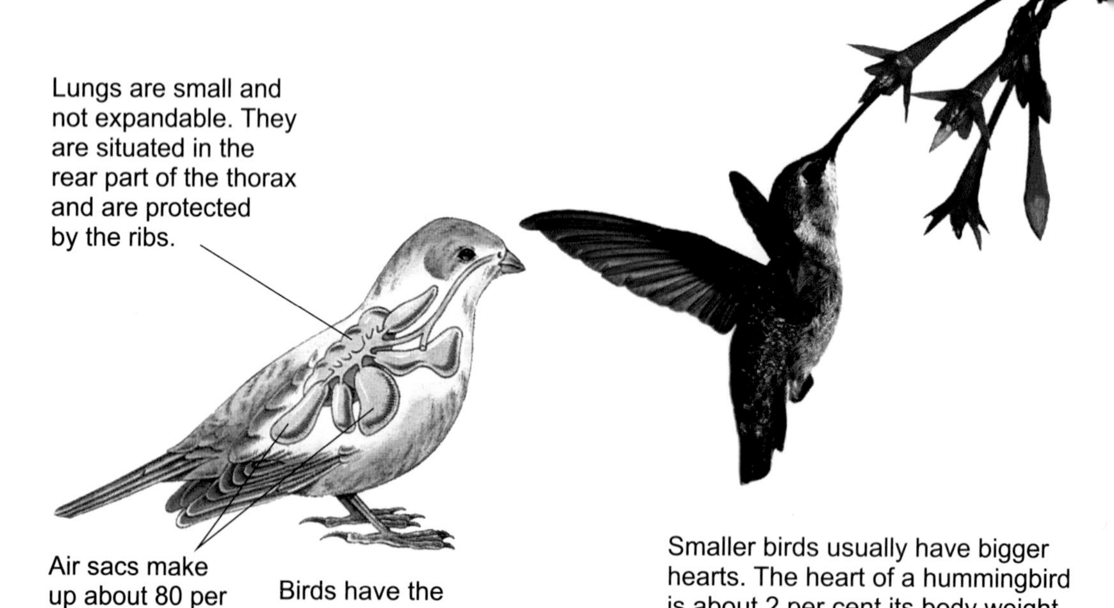

Lungs are small and not expandable. They are situated in the rear part of the thorax and are protected by the ribs.

Air sacs make up about 80 per cent of the volume of the lungs

Birds have the most efficient respiratory systems of all vertebrates.

Smaller birds usually have bigger hearts. The heart of a hummingbird is about 2 per cent its body weight.

Digestion

Birds do not have teeth. So they swallow their food, and digestion begins in the stomach of the bird. Once food reaches the lower part of the stomach, called the gizzard, strong digestive juices begin the process of digestion. Since food is not chewed in the mouth, the strong, muscular walls of the gizzard mix and crush the food.

Since birds do not have teeth, they swallow their food. When an owl eats small animals, it swallows it whole. The owl's stomach is not able to digest the animal's fur and bones. So this is thrown out and later coughed out by the owl in the form of pellets.

Some birds like owls, swallow small stones and shells to help the gizzard grind the food!

Owl

Birds fill up the crop and bring it up for their chicks.

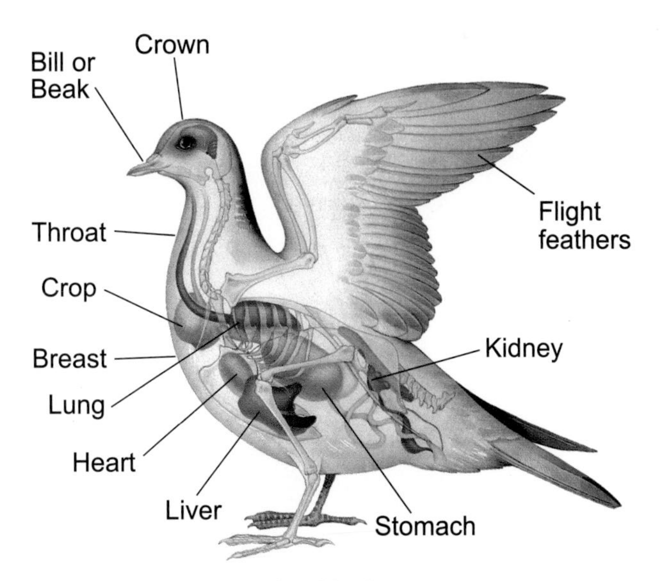

Birds can store food in the crop. This allows them to feed quickly and digest at leisure.

The pellet is a tightly packed lump of unwanted leftovers.

Muscle system

Because a bird is adapted for flying, it possesses a muscular system that is highly developed, particularly at the front of the body, so as to enable it to move its wings powerfully and rapidly.

A bird has about 175 muscles in its body. These muscles control the movements of its wings, legs, feet, tongue, eyes, ears, skin, neck and lungs. Breast muscles, or pectorals, are the largest of all muscles in a bird's body. These support the bird when in flight.

The supracoracoid, or antagonistic muscle raises the wing, while the large pectoral muscle is used for lowering the wings and are therefore the most important muscles in a bird's body. Together with the pectorals, the supracoracoid muscle makes up about 25 to 35 per cent of a bird's weight.

Taxonomists recognize four groups of muscles in a bird's body, for purposes of classification – the tracheal muscles, the mandibular muscles and the muscles of the front and hind limbs.

The most unique flying bird is the hummingbird. It can hover in one place for long periods of time. So both its flight muscles are large. They make up 30 per cent of its total body weight!

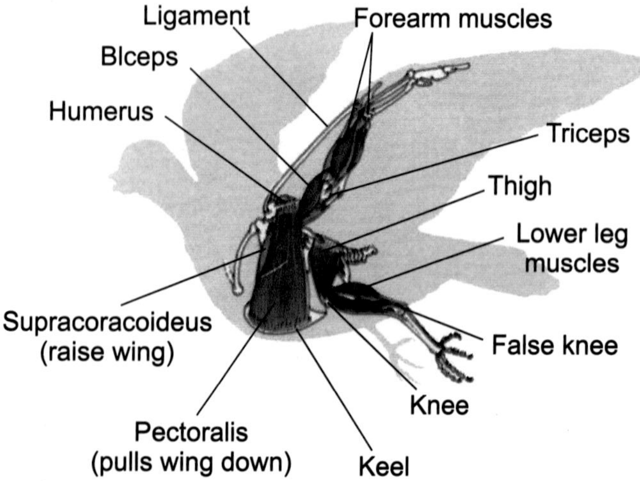

Migration

The migration journey of birds are highly spectacular. It is a behavior that has evolved over many thousands of years. It can be defined as a behavior designed to adapt to the seasonal variations of the environment. Many birds rear their young in the temperate lends of the north, where food is plenty during the summer. When the weather becomes cold and food is scare, they migrate south to warmer places where food is available.

Arctic terns fly 37,800 km each year! In autumn, it migrates across the equator and flies to the Antarctic returning again in spring.

Dove

Birds find their way over enormous distances with astonishing accuracy. Swallows return unerringly from South Africa to the same nesting site in Europe each year

Birds, it seems use the sun, moon and stars to guide them. When there is no visible aid. They perhaps use the Earth's magnetic field as their guide.

FLIGHT

AND FEATHERS

Plumage

Birds get their beautiful coloration from feathers. Feathers in turn get their colors from the melanin present in keratin and from carotenoids. While melanins are produced in their bodies, carotenoids are acquired through their food. Some birds change their colors with changing seasons. A ptarmigan is white in winter, white with brown neck in spring, speckled brown in summer and brown and white in autumn. This is to blend itself with the vegetation and landscape so that hungry predators do not notice it easily.

A ptarmigan in summer plumage.

A ptarmigan in winter plumage.

The blues, greens and other variations in a peacock's feathers are because of the presence of minute structures on the surface of the feathers which reflect light of only one wavelength.

Scarlet macaw

The scarlet macaw is one of the many brightly colored parrots that are found in the tropical forests of Central and South America. They are collected for their brilliant plumages and some species have become endangered.

Feather Structure

Have you ever noticed a bird repeatedly running its beak through its feathers? It is preening itself and making its feathers smooth and glossy. Since feathers are crucial to flight, birds have to keep them in good condition.

A flight feather is made up of many tiny strands called barbs. The barbs are attached to the central shaft called quill. Each barb branches out into minute hooked strands called barbules. The barbules lock the barbs.

Feathers serve a variety of functions — for flight, heat conservation, waterproofing, camouflage and display.

A bird's survival depends upon the condition of its feathers. So a bird takes care of its feathers by cleaning them and oiling them. This process is called preening.

Bathing helps remove a lot of dirt that adds to the weight.

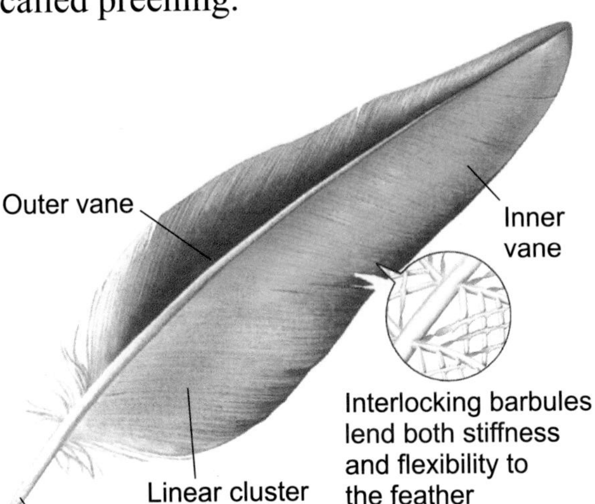

Tail feathers are often symmetrical but wing feathers are not.

Birds use their beaks and feet to arrange their feathers. Most birds have an oil gland near their tails. Birds use the oil to make their feathers shiny and waterproof.

Equipped for flight

Feathers play a crucial role in flying. Hence feathers are made up of a light yet strong protein that forms our nails and hair.

A flying bird has four types of feathers. Each serves a distinct function: wing feathers are for flying and manoeuvring, tail feathers act as rudders, down feathers are for warmth and contour feathers for streamlining.

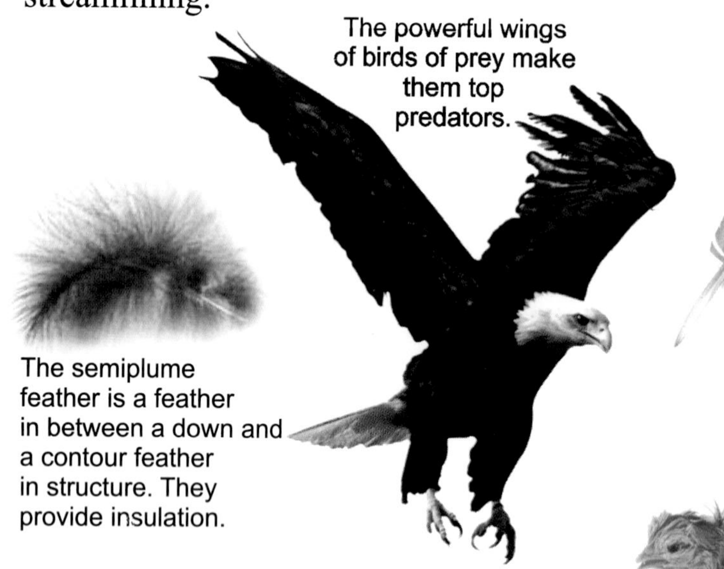

The powerful wings of birds of prey make them top predators.

The semiplume feather is a feather in between a down and a contour feather in structure. They provide insulation.

Outer vane

Inner vane

Wing feathers are long, firm but flexible and waterproof. Wing feathers are unevenly shaped. This is to allow air to escape through the wing as it beats.

In adult birds, down feathers form an insulating underlayer.

This young chick is covered with fluffy, fur-like down feathers to keep it warm.

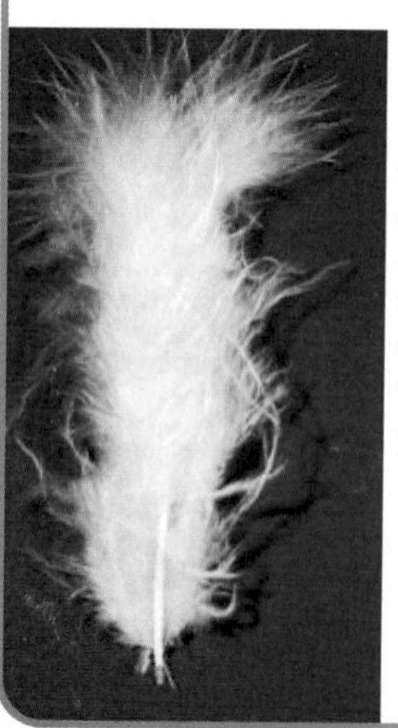

Down feathers do not look neat because they lack the barbules. But they are perhaps the most important feathers because they provide most of the insulation.

Flight feather is the feather on the wing of a flying bird.

Contour feathers streamline the bird's body. They are the most abundant feathers and cover the outer surface of the bird.

Wings

An eagle can stay aloft like a glider for hours, a hummingbird can hover in one place like a helicopter, a penguin can swim in water like a fish, all thanks to their wings. All birds have two pairs of wings. And the wings are covered with feathers. Each feather has around 400 tiny barbs. These barbs keep the feathers firmly interlocked with each other. So neither strong wind nor rain can cause them to fall out.

A bird's wings are perfectly crafted for flight. The feathers on the wings help the bird to control its flight. The feathers are arranged to make a light but strong wing.

The feathers are attached to the flesh on the bone in the wing.

These are the feathers on the wing of a pigeon.

Each outer flight feather is asymmetrical

Wing coverts

contour feathers

Inner flight feathers

Tail coverts form a smooth surface for air flowing over the tail

Tail feathers are symmetrical feathers used for steering in the air and for balance

Feathers are arranged together to make a light but strong wing. The feathers are attached to the flesh on the bone in the wing.

A crane in flight

How do birds fly?

Birds fly with the help of their wings. The wings of a bird are in many ways like the wings of an aircraft. The wing of an aircraft is more curved on the top than on the bottom. When air passes over the wing, it goes faster over the top than over the bottom. The difference in the speed of air above and below the wing, pushes the wing upwards. The same holds true for the wing of a bird.

All birds have wings. But it is not easy for some birds to fly. Ducks have to paddle along in the water a little way before they can get into the air. This is to overcome the drag of the water. And when they do so, it seems they are running on the water. Ostriches are on the other hand too heavy, so their wings cannot carry them.

Ostrich

A bird's wing

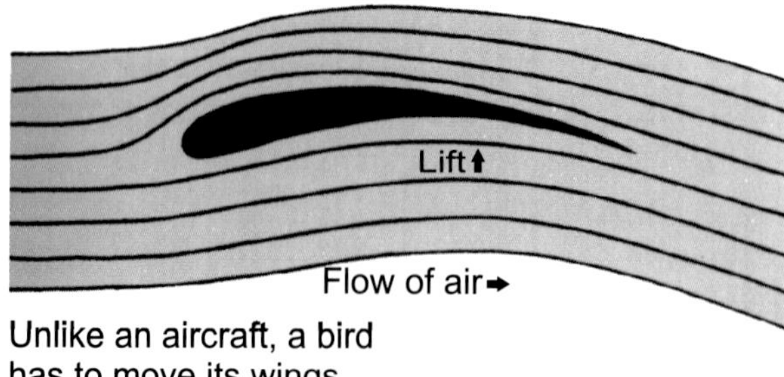

Unlike an aircraft, a bird has to move its wings through the air.

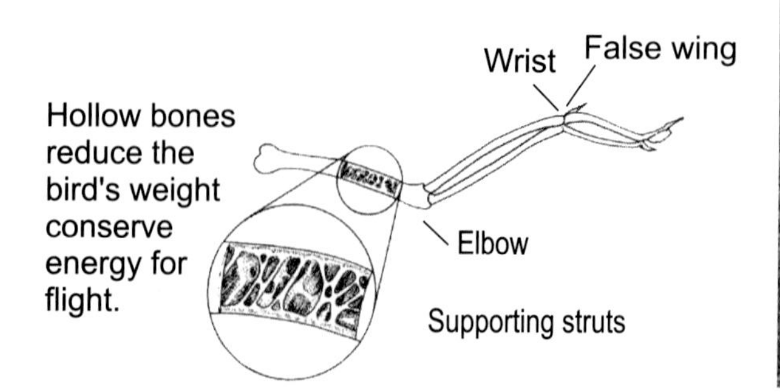

Hollow bones reduce the bird's weight conserve energy for flight.

Duck

TYPES OF

BIRDS

Flightless birds

All birds have wings, but not all birds can fly. Birds that cannot fly are called flightless birds. They usually have short, stubby wings that are covered with down feathers and not flight feathers. Flightless birds include ostriches, emus, kiwis and penguins.

Millions of years ago, there lived many flightless birds. They were found in all parts of the world. Now they are found only in Africa, Australia and New Zealand. The ostrich is the largest living bird, even bigger was the giant moa that lived in New Zealand.

The ostrich is the only bird to have a two-toed foot.

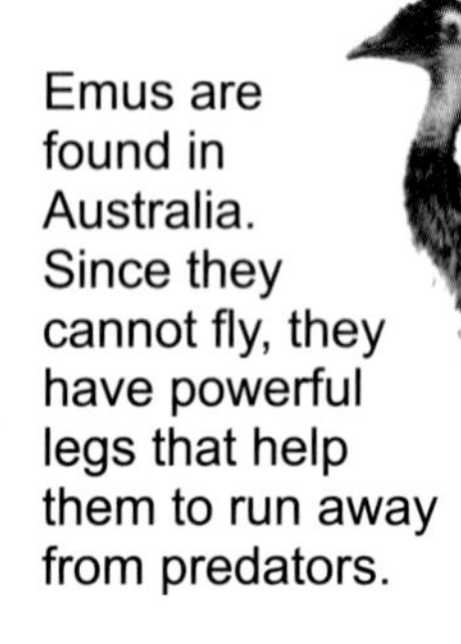

Emus are found in Australia. Since they cannot fly, they have powerful legs that help them to run away from predators.

Penguins have adapted their wings as flippers, making them excellent swimmers.

Rheas are found in the grass plains of central South America. On very rare occasions they can fly.

Kiwis are the size of chickens. The stout body is covered in soft, hair-like plumage. The slender curved bill is highly-touch sensitive.

The last dodo died in 1680. Dodos were turkey-sized birds that lived in Mauritius. When Europeans landed there in 1500s, their pets destroyed the eggs of dodos.

Perching birds

There are more than 5,000 species of perching birds, or passerines. Perching birds are called so because they usually live on trees and hop from one branch to another in search of food and to find places for making nests. Most perching birds are small like bulbuls, finches, weavers, sparrows, buntings, warblers, thrushes, larks, swallows, tits and wrens, but they range from the large ravens, up to 65 inches long to the short-tailed pygmy tyrant, only 3 inches long!

The male lyrebird of south east Australia can mimic the songs of other birds.

Crows, bowerbirds, lyrebirds, shrikes are large passerines. The crow group itself includes 100 species like rooks, jackdaws, jays, magpies and ravens.

Some of the fine songbirds are perching birds. They include the cuckoo, bulbul, thrush, warbler and nightingale. It is the male that sings and it is usually to attract a mate. The song is a sequence of sounds that seem musical. The song is produced by a vocal organ called the syrinx.

The male nightingale sings by day mainly to mark its territory and deter rivals and by night to attract females.

A robin's song augur the spring. But robins sing in autumn and winter too!

Ravens are the largest in the crow family.

Birds of prey

There are about 300 species of birds of prey. They are powerful hunters and the most feared in the bird world. They are powerful fliers and have a good eyesight which helps them pick out their prey on the ground when flying high in the air. Most birds of prey hunt during the day. Birds of prey include ospreys, eagles, hawks, falcons, vultures and condors.

Most birds of prey are now restricted to mountainous areas. Since some attack farm animals and birds, they are perceived as threats and killed.

A bird of prey has both eyes at the front of its head. This gives it the stereoscopic vision and allows it to judge distances accurately.

One of the most distinguishing feature of this group is the powerful, hooked beak to rip and tear the flesh off its prey.

Eagles build a nest of sticks, called an eyrie. They use the same nest each year but keep adding more sticks.

Night birds

Birds like owls, nightjar and frogmouths hunt by night. Although they are birds of prey, they prefer to hunt by night when the other big hunting birds are asleep. This helps to avoid competition for food and also keeps a check on the population of small insects and mammals that come out at night.

Owls rely on their powerful senses of hearing, sight and smell to hunt in the dark.

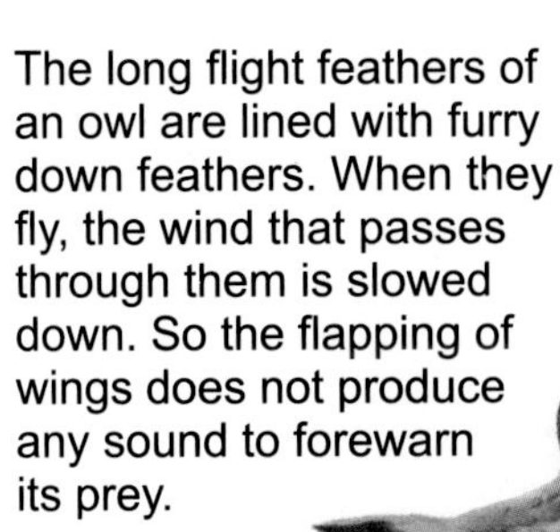

The long flight feathers of an owl are lined with furry down feathers. When they fly, the wind that passes through them is slowed down. So the flapping of wings does not produce any sound to forewarn its prey.

The ears are set at different heights on the owl's head. The owl can work out accurately where a sound is coming from.

Owls have binocular vision. The eyes are on the front of their rather flattened faces.

Nightjars hunt by night. During the day, they roost among dry vegetation or trees. Their grey, black and brown plumage serves as a camouflage.

Seabirds

Seabirds live by or on the sea. Seabirds include gulls, cormorants, gannets, auks, terns, skuas, frigatebirds, albatrosses, shearwaters and petrels.

Gulls can stay aloft without flapping the wings.

Auks are related to puffins but they resemble penguins. They dive into the water and chase the fish under water.

Albatrosses have the longest wingspan, more than 3 metres. They spend most of their lives gliding above the southern oceans. They come back to land only to breed.

Gannets are large, white birds. They have long, pointed, black-tipped wings which can be up to 1.8 metres in width. They spend most of the time at sea, coming to shore only to breed.

Cormorants are good divers and underwater swimmers. They feed mainly on fish. They dive down to catch their prey and then bring it to the surface to eat.

waterproofing on their feathers is not very effective. So they spread out their wings to dry after a diving bout.

Puffins have a rounded body with black and white plumage. In its large, brightly-coloured bill, it can hold up to a dozen sand-eels.

Waders

The avocet skims its strong, upturned beak from side to side while probing for food in the mud.

There are about 150 species of wading birds or shorebirds. They live along shores of seas, oceans, lakes, rivers and marshes. Waders include birds like oystercatchers, plovers, avocets, stilts, sandpipers, curlews, flamingoes, herons and storks.

Waders have long legs and long, pointed bills. The long legs and large feet support their rather ungainly bodies and also keep them from sinking deeply into the mud.

The long bills of waders help in searching food in shallow water. Many waders have beaks with sensitive tips to feel the food in the mud.

Herons, egrets and bitterns are freshwater waders. Herons have a slender body, long legs and neck and large, wide wings.

The stilt sandpiper has long, thin legs that help to wade in deep water. Its long bill helps it to find worms and small crustaceans in the wet mud or sand.

The oystercatcher uses its strong, chisel-like beak as a hammer to prise apart shellfish like oysters and mussels.

A heron may stand motionless on one leg for ages. But as soon as it spots a fish or other water animal, it snaps at its prey like lightning.

Waterbirds

Ducks, geese and swans are waterbirds. Ducks live in marshes, rivers, lakes and seas throughout the world, except in Antarctica. Geese are found mostly in Asia, North America and Europe. Swans are found in North America, Europe and northern Asia. Waterbirds are mainly vegetarians. They feed on grass and waterweeds. Some ducks eat shellfish.

Geese are powerful flies. They migrate over long distances. Flying north in the warm and south in the cold season.

All waterbirds have special characteristics for life in water, like broad bodies for easier floating, medium to long necks for catching food underwater and short legs with big, webbed feet for efficient swimming.

Duck

When geese and ducks fly, they make a V formation.

Swans are the largest waterbirds. Most swans have pure white plumage, except the black swan of Australia and the black-necked swan of South America.

Black-necked swan

Tropical birds

Hummingbirds, woodpeckers, hornbills, toucans, barbets, bee-eaters, rollers, kingfishers, honeyguides, swifts and jacamars are tropical birds.

Hummingbirds have a compact muscular body and relatively small body.

Tropical birds are small and colourful and spend most of their time on treetops, darting between branches in search of fruits, insects and grub. Most tropical birds have beaks that are larger than their body size.

Birds like hummingbirds and swifts spend most of their time in the air. So their long, narrow wings have made them good flyers, but their legs and feet have become quite weak.

Because of its weak legs, a swift usually rests on upright surfaces like cave walls, tree trunks and chimneys.

Kingfishers will sit out on the branch of a tree, above a stream, and see in it. Once a prey is spotted, they will drop like plummets, hitting the water hard. Then up they will come with the prey which they swallow whole.

Although the toco toucan has a large bill, it is light. So the large size of the bill does not interfere with its flying or balancing.

Polar birds

Being warm-blooded animals, birds are able to survive and thrive well even in polar regions of the Arctic and Antarctic, arguably the world's most difficult habitats. Some of the polar birds are skuas, penguins and Arctic owls.

The pure white plumage of the Arctic owl is a perfect disguise in its snowy Arctic habitat.

The Arctic tern makes one of the longest migration of any bird — a journey that may be as much as 37,800 km! Each autumn, it flies from its nesting place in the north to Antarctica and returning again in spring.

Penguins cannot fly. They use their wings as paddles and short legs and webbed feet as rudders for underwater swimming. Their short, glossy feathers protect them from the cold.

Skuas are powerful birds with hooked bills and webbed feet. They are scavengers but they sometimes make a kill too!

City birds

Over the last few decades, large cities and towns have grown, replacing countryside habitats. As a result many species of birds have disappeared from such areas, but a few birds have adapted themselves to the man-made environment and have survived very well indeed. The commonest city birds are the starling, sparrow, crow, dove and pigeon. They are very adaptable species. They have learnt to make nests on trees in parks and gardens, on terraces, roofs, window ledges and even in the chimneys of houses!

Even birds of prey like hawks and owls have become city-dwellers. They are never short of food. They eat rats and mice which live in human populated areas.

Crows are found in both the city and in the countryside. They are found all over the world, except for New Zealand, Antarctica, and South America. They now thrive on the trash we discard.

Swan

Water-loving birds like swans and ducks are often found in parks in cities.

Duck

The common town pigeons we see around us have descended from the wild rock dove found around the coasts, but the city birds have descended from domestic pigeons which escaped from medieval dovecotes.

The house sparrow was native to Asia but now resides from Britain, northern Scandinavia, and northern Siberia to northern Africa, Arabia, India and Burma.

Gamebirds

This group of birds live mainly on the ground. Some, like the chicken, provide an important food source and others like pheasants, grouse, partridges, quails, capercaillies, curassows and guineafowl and hunted for their meat. So they are called gamebirds. There are more than 240 species of gamebirds.

Red jungle fowl

All present day species of domestic fowl are derived from the jungle fowl.

Gamebirds are mostly large, stout-bodied, and heavily-built, with a small head and short, rounded wings. Their powerful flight muscles help them take to the air in emergencies.

Partridge

Turkeys were first tamed by the Aztecs about 1,500 years ago. Domestic turkeys descended from the common turkey.

Most female gamebirds have dull, mottled brown plumage that blends with their surroundings. Males usually have extremely striking coloration.

During courtship, the male Temminck's tragopan inflates his colourful throat wattle until it covers his breast and then female's attention.

The male peafowl, or the peacock, is one of the world's most spectacular gamebirds.

A long train of brilliant green tail feathers, each ending in a colourful 'eye'. When courting the peacock throws up his tail feathers into a gigantic fan.

BILL

ADAPTATIONS

Bills

Birds do not have teeth. Their jaws have evolved into a hard mouthpart called a beak or bill. Birds use their bills like hammers, chisels, nutcrackers, hooks, pincers, spears, needles and even strainers. Birds also use their bills to preen and defend themselves and for building nests. The shape and size of a bird's bill depends on the food it eats.

Bald eagle

Pelican

Hummingbird

Duck

Spoonbill

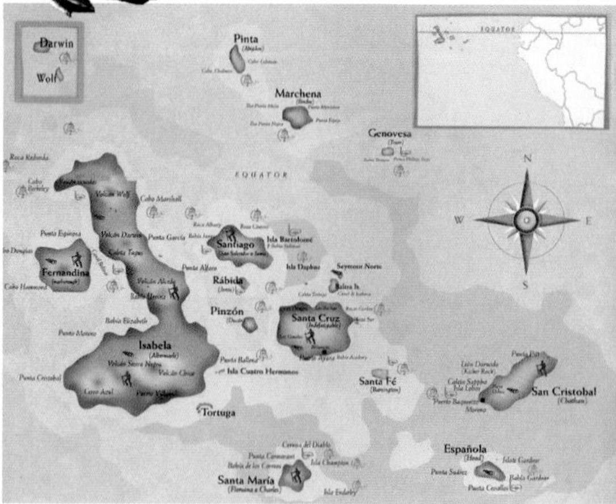

When Charles Darwin visited Galapagos Islands, he was surprised to find 13 species of finch. He later realised that these finches were descendants of the finch that originally came from South America. The descendants evolved different bills to adopt to different ways of life.

Parrot

The bill is one of the characteristics of a bird. Bird watchers can actually identify a bird by looking at its beak.

Toucan

Nutcracker

Small perching birds, like finches, sparrows, weaverbirds and waxbills, have short, strong, stubby, triangular beaks for feeding on seeds. Some of these birds have such powerful beaks that they can crack open seeds.

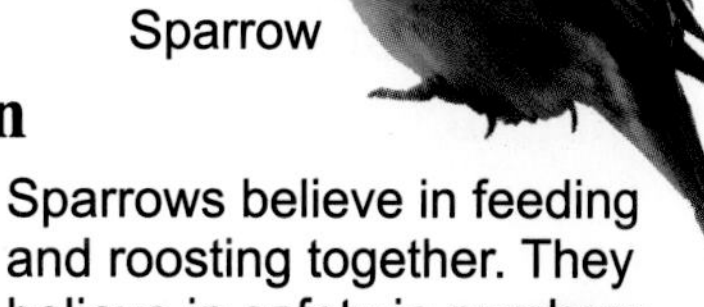

Sparrow

Sparrows believe in feeding and roosting together. They believe in safety in numbers.

Waxbill

The tips of the crossbill's beak actually cross over at the tip. This allows it to pick up seeds from pine cones.

Crossbill

Weaverbird

Hawfinch

With its thick, strong beak, the hawfinch can crack open nuts and even the seeds of fruits like cherries.

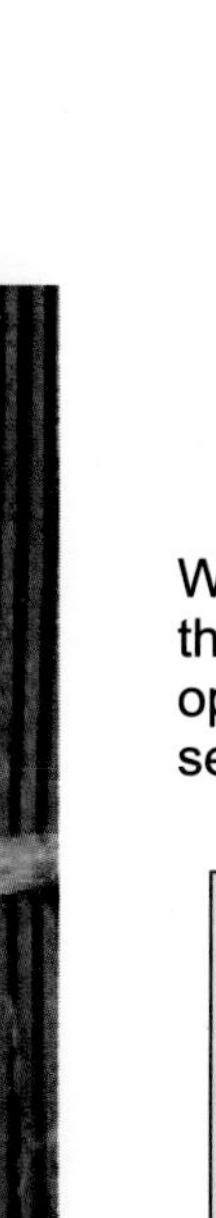

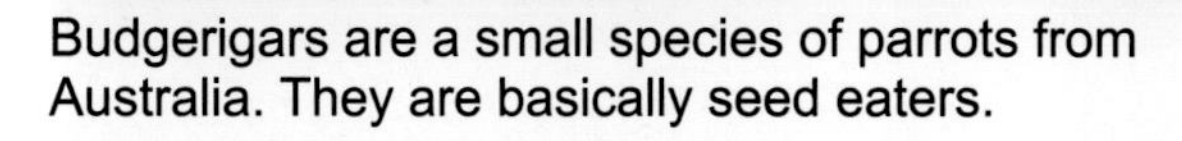

Budgerigars are a small species of parrots from Australia. They are basically seed eaters.

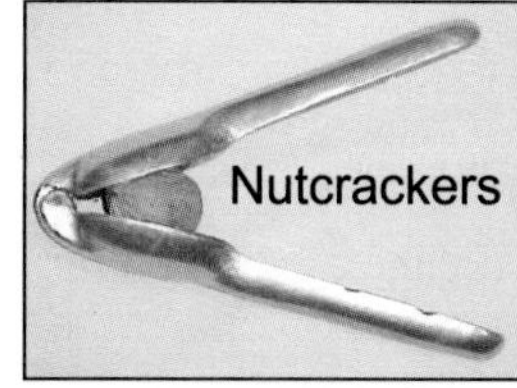

Nutcrackers

The powerful seed-cracking beaks of the small perching birds work like a nutcracker.

Spear-shaped

Birds like herons and kingfishers have narrow, pointed bills for spearing its prey. They spear fish, frogs and crayfish and gulp them down head first.

Spear-like bills are adapted for fishing.

Although a fish-eater, a pelican does not have a spear-shaped bill. Its beak has a stretchy pouch to scoop up a huge mouthful of water and fish. It then tips out the water and swallows the fish.

Large, webbed feet

The long bill of the mergansers with serrated edges and a hooked point allows it to grab fish.

Its slender body and snake-like neck, makes darter one of the most streamlined swimming bird. When it chances upon a prey,it delivers a stabbing peck with its dagger-like beak.

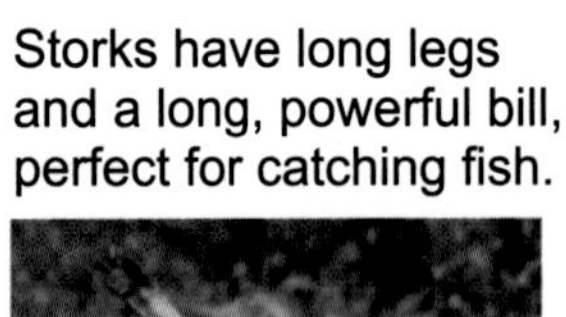

Storks have long legs and a long, powerful bill, perfect for catching fish.

Chisel-like bill

Downy woodpeckers, nuthatches, flickers and other tree-clinging birds have thin, powerful bills for drilling wood and feeding on grubs and insects under the wood. They also use their bills for drilling nesting holes in trees.

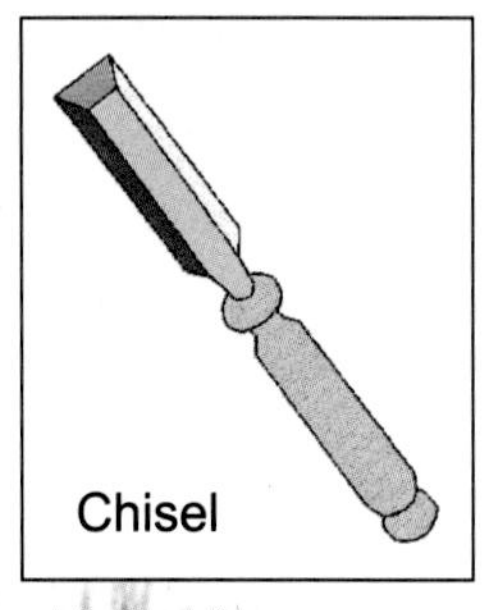

Nuthatches are found in North America, Europe, Asia and Australia. They make nests in holes in tree trunks and seal up the entrance with mud. Nuthatches climb downwards as well as upwards!

Woodpeckers have special feet that helps them climb on tree trunks. Their long, sharp bill also help to make nests by digging holes in tree trunks.

Flicker

Chisel-like bill helps to hammer holes in dead wood. Then with their long barbed tongues, they pick up the grubs. These bills are also equipped with a special shock absorber that prevents injury to the brain.

Sipping

Hummingbirds are small colourful, birds. But they have a very long, slender bill, which is perfectly suited to sip nectar from flowers.

Sunbird

With its long, probing beak and tongue, the sunbird sips nectar from flowers. It resembles a hummingbird. But it is found in Africa and Asia.

White eyes are found in southern Asia and feed on nectar, fruits and insects.

The hummingbird uses its thin bill as a straw to suck up nectar.

While visiting a flower, a hummingbird also helps pollinate the flower.

Strainer

Waterbirds like ducks, geese and swans have long, flat bills that help to strain small plants and animals from water.

Spoonbills are named after their flattened, spoon-shaped bills. They hunt in muddy water. They swish their bills from side to side through the water to disturb the animals. Although they cannot see their prey, their sensitive bills help them feel it. And snap! They down the prey.

Flamingoes are large pink or pinkish white birds.They live near lakes, marshes and seas in enormous colonies. Flamingoes have strange beaks that they use as a strainer.

The edges of a mallard duck's bill are fringed to strain plants, seeds and small animals from mud and water.

With its strange beak upside down, the flamingo sweeps it from side to side and takes in the water along with small shrimps. The tongue helps to squirt out the water. Hair-like fringes on the beak strain out the food.

The beak of a spoonbill is long and flat, broadening out into a flattened spoonshape at the end.

Shredder

Carnivorous birds like eagles, hawks, ospreys, falcons, owls and vultures have strong, hooked beaks for tearing flesh. They are birds of prey and hunt small animals. With their strong hooked bills, they tear their prey into bite-sized pieces.

The peregrine falcon is the fastest bird. It is a great acrobat. It can catch other birds in mid-flight.

Although shrikes are perching birds, they behave like miniature birds of prey. They have sharp, hooked bill and strong legs with sharp claws that allow them to catch large insects, small birds and mammals.

With its powerful beak, a bird of prey can tear apart meat almost like a shredder.

The bald eagle feeds on fish, rabbits, waterbirds and even young deer!

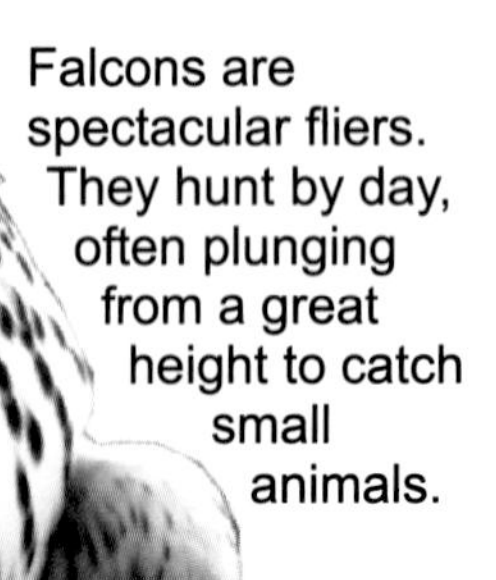

Falcons are spectacular fliers. They hunt by day, often plunging from a great height to catch small animals.

FEET

ADAPTATIONS

Bird feet

The size, shape and characteristics of a bird's feet is determined by how it uses its feet and on its environment. The feet are adapted to help a bird get its food and to allow it to move around when not in flight.

We walk on our feet, but birds walk on their toes. What seems to us as the knee is in fact the bird's ankle heel or joint. The knee is hidden under its feathers.

Our foot has five toes, but birds only have four toes. Our little toe is their missing fifth toe, or digit.

A bird's leg close-up

Knee

Ankle

Birds have claws

Toes

A human's leg close-up

Knee

We have nails

Ankle

Toes

An ostrich has a two-toed foot.

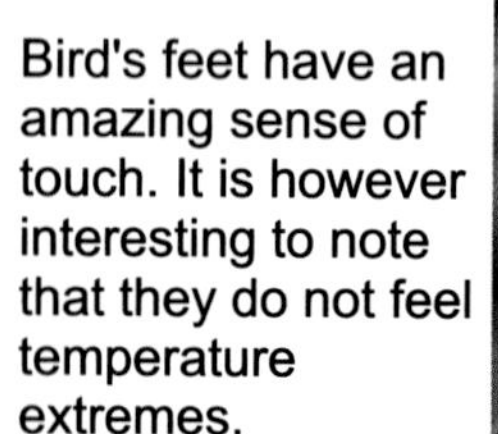

Bird's feet have an amazing sense of touch. It is however interesting to note that they do not feel temperature extremes.

Arctic owl in snow

Ospreys have an outer toe apart from its four toes to help it hold fish.

A bird's feet is covered with scales. The colour of the feet vary from grey, white, black, brown, tan and even pink to help them blend in their environment.

Perching feet

Perching birds usually spend their time hopping on branches of trees in search of food. Their small, lightbodies are supported by four-toed feet. Three of their toes point forwards, and one points backwards. This backward toe is as long as the forward middle toe. This arrangement of toes helps perching birds to get a better grip when it lands on branches.
When the bird lands on a perch, a tendon in the backward toe tightens, so the toes lock. When the bird wishes to move, it straightens its legs, and the tendon is unlocked.

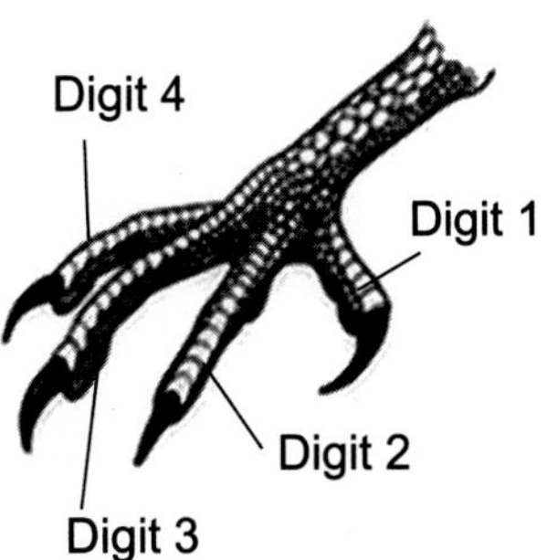

This is the typical foot of a perching bird. It is called the anisodactyl foot. The backward toe is the bird's first digit. The second digit is the inner toe, the third digit is the middle toe and the fourth digit is the outer toe.

When a perching bird perches on a branch, the muscles in its legs make its toes curl. This helps it to get a grip on the branch.

The feet of the robin are meant for perching. They help it to do almost anything – from hopping to walking and also nimbly holding on to any object.

Tree clinging

Woodpeckers, toucans, barbets, owls some parrots, jacamars and honeyguides have zygodactyl foot. This type of foot is excellent for clinging to the trunk of trees. The zygodactyl foot is the second most common toe arrangement.

The first and the fourth digits of a zygodactyl foot are backwards and the second and third digits face forwards. The toes in the back give the bird more support.

Owls also have this type of toe arrangement, but they can rotate their fourth digit to the front. This helps it to perch, grab its prey and hold it as it flies.

The tridactyl foot of a woodpecker help it to cling to the tree while pounding on a tree — tap, tap, tap — in search of insects and grubs under wood.

Parrots use their feet much as we use our hands. They hold the food in their food and raise it up to their beak.

Zygodactyl foot

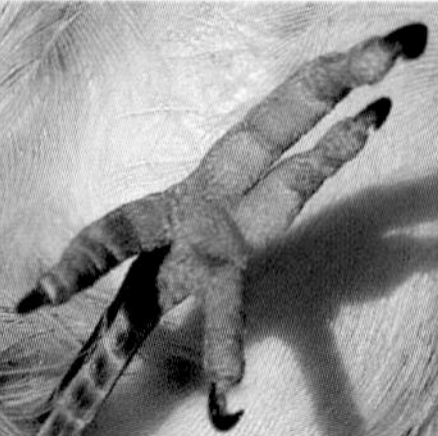

Webbed feet

Waterfowl like ducks, geese and swans are excellent swimmers. They use their big, webbed feet as paddles to float on water. The toes have webbing between them. The webbing connects the toes to make a large paddle of a foot.

Pelicans, boobies, cormorants, frigate birds and anhingas have all their toes webbed. The four toes are joined by webbing making them strong swimmers.

The large, webbed feet of pelicans are used for both propulsion and steering.

On land, waterfowl, especially ducks walk awkwardly because their legs are set far on their body for better swimming.

The webbed feet of waterfowl help them to propel themselves through water. Only the front three toes are webbed, the smaller toe being raised.

Birds like coots and grebes do not have real webbing, but have wide-lobed toes.

Talons

It is easy to identify a bird of prey. With a sharp, hooked beak, curved claws called talons and an air of majesty, birds of prey have become a symbol of power.

Thick, scaly skin

Sharp, curved talon

Long, backward pointing talon

The talons are sharp enough to puncture vital organs and break slender bones. Three of the 4 toes point forwards and one points backwards.

The common kestrel's diet consists mainly of small mammals (including voles and mice), insects and amphibians. The sharp talons help to catch the prey.

Having spotted a fish while flying high in the air over the water, an osprey darts often many feet below the surface — fastens its long talons into the fish's back, drags it up and flies away with it.

Wading feet

Wading birds like herons and egrets have long, featherless legs for wading. They have three long forward-pointing toes and one long backward-pointing toe. The toes are much longer than toes of perching birds and some have webbing between them to keep them from sinking into the marshy and muddy rivers and ponds.

Jacanas or lily-trotters have toes as long as our fingers! They spend much of their time walking across leaves of water lilies and other floating plants.

Long toes help in distributing their weight and preventing them from sinking

Cranes and some waterbirds lose heat through their legs because there are no feathers on them. To save as much heat as they can, they stand on only one leg while tucking the other up against their body. They also go to sleep while standing!

HOW ARE

BIRDS IMPORTANT?

Role

We probably see more birds than any other kind of animal. In large cities, towns, villages, schools; gardens, on trees, in bushes, in the air, in winter, in summer — in short everywhere and at all times. One reason why birds are seen everywhere is that the world in which they live — air — has not been conquered by any other animal.

Each animal has its own special place in the world and it has special features or talents that help it survive. Birds come in all shapes and sizes. They have different shaped beaks to eat different things, different colours – some for blending in while some to look pretty for their mates and different feet to survive in different environments.

Bald eagle is the national bird of the USA.

Dove is the symbol of peace.

Peacock is the national bird of India.

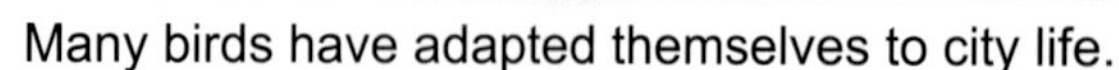

Many birds have adapted themselves to city life.

Small carnivores

Had it not been birds, like woodpeckers, warblers and thrushes, the Earth would have been infected with insects and worms, some very harmful for plants and trees and some for other animals and human beings.

Pied wagtail

The pied wagtails and barn swallows often live near stables and farms where they can feed on flies and other insects.

A woodpecker drills through rotting wood and eats grubs and insects.

During summer, there is an increase in grubs, caterpillars, flies and other insects. So they breed during this time to ensure that their chicks have abundant supplies.

Barn swallows

Thin, curved bill perfectly suited to pick up insects.

Treecreepers spend most of their time climbing up a tree trunk from the back in a spiral in search of insects in the bark.

Flycatchers suddenly emerge from a perch to catch flying insects in their bills, hence their name.

These oxpeckers hitch a ride on the buffaloes. But they rid the buffaloes' hide off parasites.

Large carnivores

Birds of prey, like owls, eagles, kingfishers, hawks, cuckoos, peacocks, falcons and condors, help to control rat, vole, mice, lizard, rabbit and frog population. Had it not been them, our crops and farms would have been in peril. Waterbirds also help to keep down the populations of frogs, toads and amphibians.

Not all kingfishers hunt fish. Some even eat small reptiles and rodents.

Birds of prey have all the gadgets to make them powerful hunters — a strong beak, large wings and sharp claws.

Eagle

Hawks are smaller then eagles. Some stay among vegetation and ambush small birds.
They have short, rounded wings and a small tail.

Bustards are large birds, almost the size of turkeys, that live in Africa, Asia and Australia. They feed on seeds, fruits, insects and other small animals.

Scavengers

When an animal dies, scavengers clean up the carcass and keep our forests, cities and rivers clean. Birds like condors, vultures and crows feed on carrion (dead bodies). Other birds of prey may also feed on carrion if it is available.

The biggest bird of prey is the vulture. But it is not actually a predator. It is a scavenger. Vultures have weak bills and so they can eat flesh that is soft and rotten.

The bearded vulture or lammergeier carries large bones from the carcass high into the air and then drops them onto rocks below. The bones smash and the bird lands to feed on the marrow inside.

Crows have a multi-purpose bill that helps them to eat fruit, seeds, insects, fish and even carrion. It uses its beak like a Swiss army knife !

White-backed vulture have a poor sense of smell, but extremely good eyesight. This enables them to spot a carcass from high in the air.

The California condor is one of the biggest flying birds. Sadly it is on the verge of extinction.

The neck and the head do not have feathers. So vultures can poke their heads inside carcasses without the fear of getting their feathers clogged with blood.

HOMING

Courting

Like all living things, birds too reproduce. When birds become mature enough to start a family, they try to attract a mate. The different gestures that they adopt to attract a suitable mate is called courtship behavior. It is usually the male bird that courts the female. The birds of paradise are the most spectacular of all birds. There are 42 species of birds of paradise and they are found in the rainforests of northern Australia, New Guinea and nearby islands. The males of the species have colourful plumage that they use to court females.

Greter bird of paradise

About 12-20 male greater birds of paradise gather in a tree to dance during courtship. The dominant male stays at the centre.

The male blue bird of paradise hangs upside down from a branch, opens his wings and spreads his tail. Then he shakes his feathers and gives out a loud cry to the female nearby.

The elaborate bower of the male spotted bowerbird made out of grass and twigs is ready for inspection by the female. He has decorated it with fruits, flowers and other objects.

Master builders

Birds are great engineers. They can craft elaborate nest in different shapes and sizes without any instructions or practice. They use mud, clay, grass, leaves, feathers, cotton, saliva, etc. to make their nests. In some species, it is the male that builds the nest. In some species, the responsibility is shared by both the male and the female. But in most species, it is the female that builds the nest.

Village weaverbird

The male weaverbird uses thread stripped from large leaves and blades of grass to make his nest.

Birds use all sorts of materials to make their nests. Often they gather rubbish such as bits of net and string. They make their nests in the oddest of places.

Tailorbird

Male tailorbird builds a nest of leaves. He pecks a series of holes down the sides of the leaves, stitching the leaf edges together with blades of grass.

These swallows have made nests in holes pecked and dug out of cliffs and riverbanks.

Why birds make nests?

Spring is a busy time for birds. They build their nests and lay their eggs. Birds build nests to protect their eggs and young ones from predators. Nests provide security, warmth and comfort to their young ones. During the breeding season, certain hormones trigger the urge to build nests.

One of the most unusual phenomenon in the bird world is the brood parasite. They do not build nests or take care of their young ones. They are cunning and have found a way to get other birds to take care of their young ones. The cuckoo is a typical example of a brood parasite.

The cuckoo waits near a reed warbler's nest.

When the warbler flies off, the cuckoo eats one of the warbler's eggs and replaces it with its own.

Mother hornbill seals herself inside her nest. She incubates her eggs and when they hatch, it is the duty of the father hornbill to provide food for his family. The mother will come out only when her young ones are ready to fly.

When the baby cuckoo hatches out, it shoves off all the warbler's eggs

The baby cuckoo now gets all the attention. Soon it grows larger than its foster parents.

Eggs

Eggs have to be saved from predators. The quail has laid its eggs on the ground. But they blend with the stones and pebbles and escape from being noticed.

All birds lay eggs. The eggs are quickly formed inside the female bird's body and laid. The eggs are then incubated outside the body. Since birds have to fly, the offspring cannot grow inside its body. And the large size of an egg makes it difficult for the female to retain more than one egg in its body. Flying with eggs inside its body would require more energy.

Although bird eggs appear fragile, they are tough. The convex surface can withstand considerable pressure without breaking. This is to ensure that when parents sit on the eggs to incubate, they do not break.

Eggs come in four basic shapes.

Egg-shaped eggs are the most common form of egg.

Cliff-nesting seabirds lay long, thin eggs that roll around in a circle instead of over the ledge.

Owls lay round eggs.

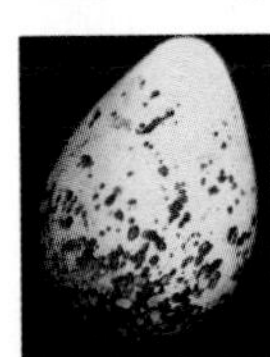

Plovers lay top-shaped eggs — one end rounded and other quite pointed. Such eggs remain at the centre of the nest.

This is how a typical egg will look like when viewed from above.

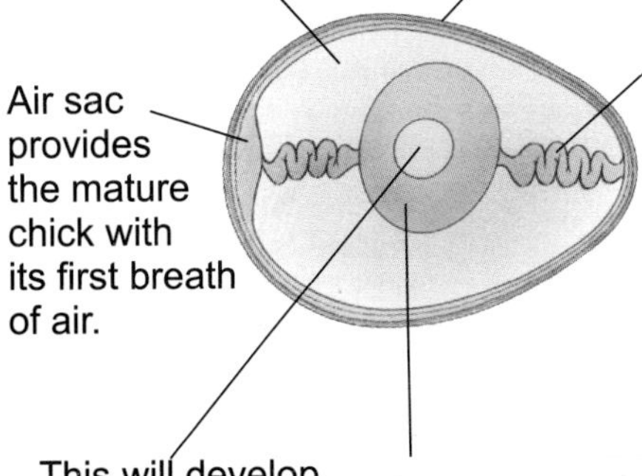

Albumen is the embryo's water supply. It also protects the embryo from shock and sudden temperature differences.

Eggshell made up of three membranes. The shell is porous. Thus allowing oxygen in and carbon dioxide out.

Air sac provides the mature chick with its first breath of air.

Chalaza is a twisted string-like structure that suspends the developing embryo in the albumen and also ensures that it remains above the yolk.

This will develop into embryo.

Yolk is a fatty food store for the developing embryo.

From egg to chicken

Eggs hatch only when they receive the right temperature. So parents, sometimes only the females, take turns to keep their eggs warm. This process is called incubation.

Some birds have short incubation periods and the hatchlings are born blind, naked and helpless. Hatchlings born to birds with long incubation periods are born fully feathered and are able to fend for themselves.

The male Emperor penguin incubates the egg on his feet, through the Antarctic winter. When the egg hatches, the female will return and take care of the chick.

After the air in the air sac is used up, the chick needs another oxygen source. So it pokes a tiny hole in the eggshell and breathes through it.

When the embryo is fully developed, it sometimes makes cheeping noises which help the parents know that it is about to hatch.

When the chick is ready to emerge, it pecks in the blunt end of the egg in the form of a ring.

Young chicks learn to recognize their mother by sight.

The chick uses its egg-tooth, a hard tip on the upper mandible. Lying on its back, the chick will continuously raise its head and push the egg tooth against the eggshell. As the chick straightens, the eggshell is pushed apart into half.

Newborn chicks are covered with wet downy feathers. They will lose the egg-tooth after a few days.

Parenting

Most birds take care of their young for the first days or weeks of their lives. Because the chicks are born helpless, the parents protect and feed their offspring, until the young have learned to look after themselves.

Starling with chicks

Spoonbill feeding its large chicks

Parenting is full time work. The chicks are ever-hungry. So they have to be feed all through the day.

Grebes carry their young ones on their backs.

The sandgrouse lives in dry deserts. Sometimes the male sandgrouse has to fly many kilometers to find water. Once he finds it, he soaks his breast feathers with water and flies back to his nest so that his chicks can drink the water.

Female birds have dull feathers so that they may not be noticed by predators.

CHAPTER FOUR

INVENTORS AND INVENTIONS

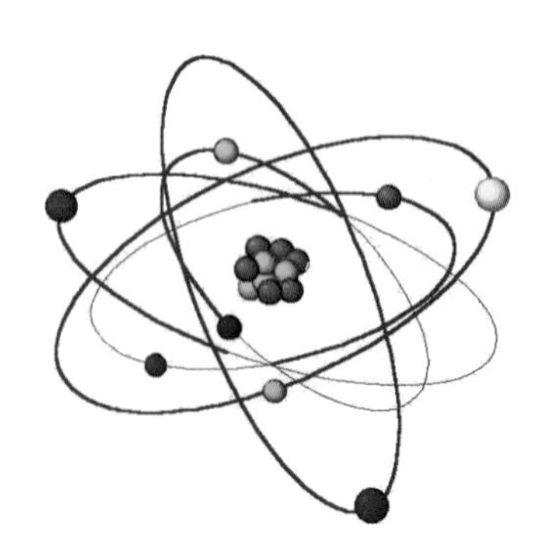

MEDICAL INVENTIONS

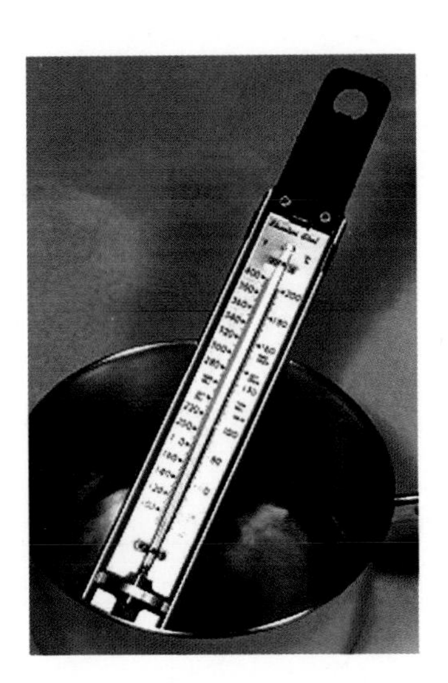

MATHEMATICS

MODERN INVENTIONS

TIMELINE

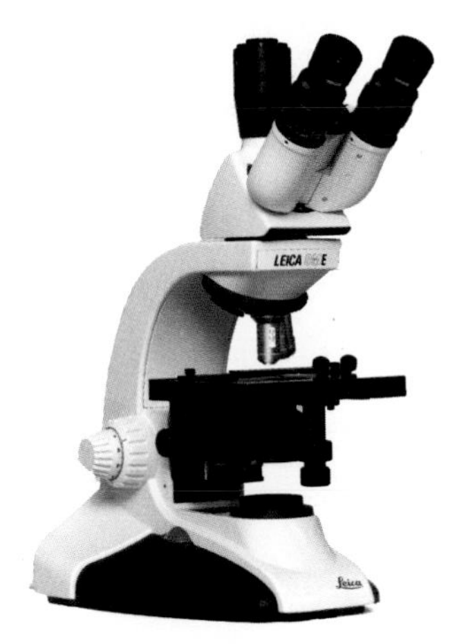

EARLIEST

INVENTIONS

Fire

Through the centuries, there has been an intimate relation between fire and man. Man perhaps knew about fire when lightning struck trees. They perhaps noticed that fire could keep them warm and also kept wild animals away.

So they added more dry wood and kept the fire burning. Later they learnt to make fire.

Fire also helped them to discover the art of baking clay objects and vessels. Baking helped clay objects to last longer than sun-baked ones.

Earlier man learnt to initiate fire by rubbing two stones together.

Man later also discovered the art of cooking raw meat. Cooked meat tasted better and could be digested faster. The early fires formed the nuclues for human grouping, and became tribal or communal fires, from which the individual family fires began.

Invention of fire improved the lifestyle of early man to a great extent.

Writing

Ancient Mesopotamians are credited with the invention of writing. Clay tablets from around 3200 BC show that they had developed a system of writing called cuneiform.

Writing emerged in many different cultures and in numerous locations throughout the ancient world. It was not the creation of any one man.

The Sumerians of ancient Mesopotamia are credited with the invention of writing. They evolved the cuneiform.

However, the Sumerians of ancient Mesopotamia are credited with inventing the earliest form of writing which appeared on the clay tablets dated 3500 BC. These writings were in the form of simple pictures, or pictograms that represented an object or an idea.

When people of ancient civilisations traded in goods, they felt the need to keep a record of their sales and purchases. Clay tablets dating back to 3200 BC were discovered in Mesopotamia which suggests that they kept records by making tiny pictures.

About two centuries later, they discovered a form of writing called cuneiform. Instead of pictures, they made wedge-shaped patterns with a chopped-off reed on wet clay tablets. Then the tablets were left to dry in the sun.

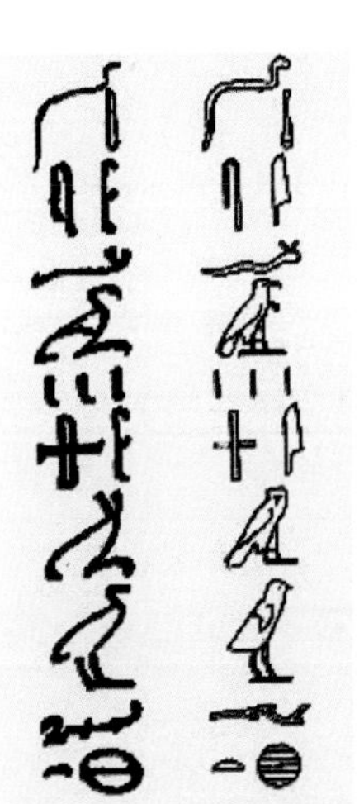

Sometime around the same time Egyptians invented the hieroglyphics script.

Each hieroglyph represents a common object in ancient Egypt.

Hieroglyphs could represent the sound of the object or they could represent an idea associated with the object.

Wheel

The credit of the invention of the wheel goes to the ancient Mesopotamians. According to archaeologists, the wheel was probably invented in around 8000 BC. The oldest wheel known however, was discovered in Mesopotamia and probably dates back to 3500 BC.

Before the invention of the wheel, early men placed rollers beneath heavy objects so that they could be moved easily.

Later they began to place runners under a heavy load, which they discovered would make it easier for the load to drag. This was the invention of the sledge.

The rollers were changed into wheels. In the process of doing so, wood between the grooves of the roller were cut away to form an axle and wooden pegs were fastened to the runners on each side of the axle. When the wheels turn, the axle turned too in the space between the pegs. The first wooden cart was thus made.

The wheel was further improved on later by the Egyptians. They made wheels with spokes, which could be found on Egyptian chariots of around 2000 BC. Over in Ancient India, chariots with spoked wheels dating back to around 1500 BC were also discovered.

Today, wheel has indeed undergone a drastic transformation from a simple one made of wood to the pneumatic rubber tyres that we see on vehicles today. A veterinarian, John Boyd Dunlop (1841–1921), succeeded in making what was probably the most crucial advance in the development and marketing of the inflatable tyre.

This agate cylinder seal is engraved with a scene showing the Persian king standing in a chariot fitted with wheels with spokes.

Money

No one knows when some form of money was first used as a medium of exchange. In the early civilizations, people directly bartered or exchanged good and services. But the problem with barter system was to determine the exact value of the goods. Using money made this process much easier.

As societies and economies developed, money was used more and more for ordinary trade. In ancient Europe, valuable items such as iron arrowheads were exchanged for goods.

Earlier, transactions were made through barter system in which one good or service was exchanged for the other.

In Africa and Oceania rare shells or feathers were used. In Egypt, around 1500 BC, gold ingots were weighed and stamped to show their maximum exchange value.

Babylon had a highly developed monetary system with banks and credit, as did ancient Greece and Rome.

Coinage was probably invented in ancient China and reinvented in what is now Turkey. Paper currency was invented in China around the 9th century.

Coins and notes emerged much later in the 9th century

Paper

Paper is manufactured from interlaced fibers, usually from plants, but sometimes from cloth rags and other materials. It is formed by pulping the fibers and pressing them flat to form a solid surface. The invention of paper is generally credited to Is' ai Lun, a Chinese court official, in about AD 105.

The Chinese had probably made paper from hemp fibers but it was thick and uneven and was probably used for packing rather than writing on.

The oldest known piece of paper used for writing dates from AD 110, Is' ai Lun was the first to succeed in making paper from vegetable fibers, using mulberry tree bar, rags and old fishing nets, all of which were soaked, crushed and pressed.

The art of paper making was kept secret for 500 years but it eventually spread throughout the world.

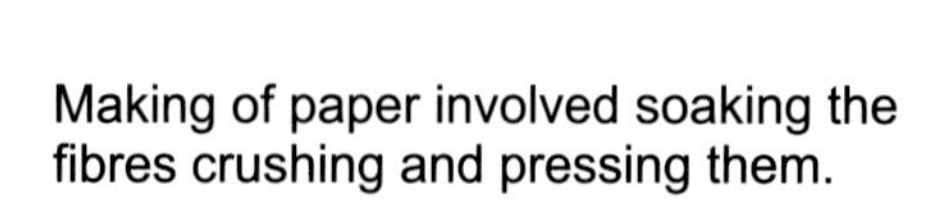

Making of paper involved soaking the fibres crushing and pressing them.

Tools

Tool making marks an important juncture in evolution. The Oldowan stone tools from Hadar, Ethiopia, are among the oldest known, dating back 2.3 million years. The discovery of the tools has raised the still-unanswered question of who these tool-makers were.

At first, single tools, such as chipped pebbles or flaked stone implements, were used for all purposes.

The ability to make tools indicated the evolution of large brains. It also marked the transition from a tree-based locomotion style to the upright-walking stance that freed the hands. It took place at least 4 million years ago and possibly as far back as 6 million years ago. It took considerable change in the hands and fingers to create the deft manipulative abilities of the *Homo* species.

Major changes show up in the fossil record of the species known as *Homo habilis*, or "handy man". They had a mobile thumb joint, powerful muscles to bend the fingers, and large fingertips — all adaptations that may have made possible the making and use of stone tools. The human brain was expanding and undergoing reorganization.

Over time, a variety of tools were made for specific purposes. By about 100,000 years ago, Neanderthal cultures had several types of tools and were using bone implements.

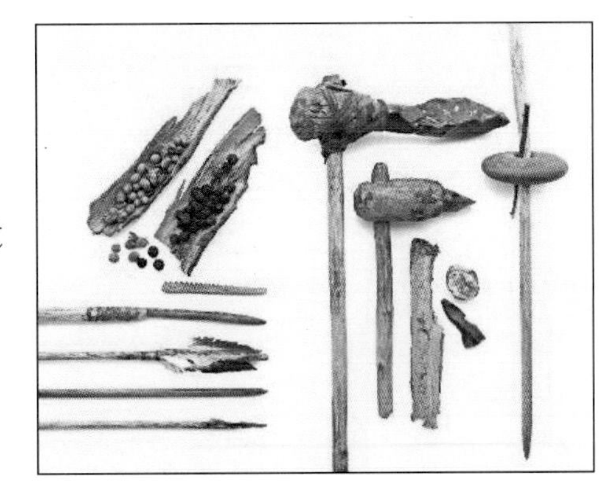

By 8000 BC, stone tools became highly polished and varied.

Metals

Metallurgy is one of the oldest applied sciences. Metals were discovered sometime in 6000 BC. Today, there are 86 known metals. In the 19th century, only 24 of these metals had been discovered and, of these 24 metals, 12 were discovered in the 18th century. Four of these metals arsenic, antimony, zinc and bismuth were discovered in the 13th and 14th centuries, while platinum was discovered in the 16th century. The other seven metals, known as the Metals of Antiquity, were the metals upon which civilisation was based. These seven metals were gold 6000 BC, copper 4200 BC, silver 4000 BC, lead 3500 BC, tin 1750 BC, iron 1500 BC and mercury 750 BC.

Stone Age man learned to make gold into jewelry and ornaments, because he found out that it could be formed into sheets and wires easily. The discovery of copper was of more significance than gold as the first tools, implements and weapons were made from copper. By 3600 BC, the first copper smelted artifacts were found in the Nile Valley and copper rings, bracelets, chisels were found. By 3000 BC, weapons, tools etc. were widely found.

By 2500 BC, Sumerians had recognized that if different ores were blended together in the smelting process, a different type of copper, which flowed more easily, was stronger after forming and was easy to cast, could be made.

Iron making did not become an everyday process until 1200 BC. Iron weapons revolutionized warfare and iron implements did the same for farming. Iron and steel was the building block for civilization. Interestingly, an iron pillar dating to 400 AD remains standing today in Delhi, India. Corrosion to the pillar has been minimal a skill lost to current ironworkers.

Iron Pillar at Qutab Minar, Delhi.

Printing press

Printing is the process of making many copies of a document using movable characters or letters. The process was developed independently in China and Europe. Before the invention of printing, copies of a manuscript were made by hand which took a lot of time and labour.

Johannes Gutenberg

The printing press made the mass publication and circulation of literature possible. Derived from the presses farmers used to make olive oil, the first printing press used a heavy screw to force a printing block against the paper below.

The Gutenberg press with its wooden and later metal movable type printing brought down the price of printed materials and made such materials available for the masses.

Johannes Gutenberg was a German goldsmith and inventor best known for the Gutenberg press, an innovative printing machine that used movable type. On September 30, 1452, Johannes Gutenberg's Bible was published becoming the first book to be published in volume.

The invention of the printing press helped usher in an era of enlightenment. This great cultural rebirth was inspired by widespread access to and appreciation for classical art and literature, and these translated into a renewed passion for artistic expression. Without the development of the printing press, the Renaissance may never have happened.

What civilization gained from Gutenberg's invention is incalculable. Gutenberg was born between 1394 and 1400 and died in 1468.

Canon

SCIENCE AND

TECHNOLOGY

Theory of Relativity

Albert Einstein

The theory of relativity was propounded by German physicist, Albert Einstein. About 1912, Einstein began a new phase of his gravitational research, with the help of his mathematician friend Mariel Grossmann, by phrasing his work in terms of the calculus.

Einstein was most famous for developing the Theory of Relativity, out of which came the famous equation $E = mc^2$. After a number of false starts, he published the definitive form of the general theory in 1915.

In it the gravitational field equations were covariant, that is similar to Maxwell's equations, the field equations took the same form in all equivalent frames of reference.

In 1905, he suggested that light is absorbed in the form of packets of energy, now called photons. For this he also received the Nobel Prize for Physics in 1921.

Also in 1905, he developed the special Theory of Relativity. These theories are the basis for all our ideas about the history and structure of the universe.

Einstein believed that there could be more universes.

Electric bulb

The credit of the invention of electric bulb goes to Thomas Alva Edison. In 1880 Edison discovered that electricity would flow from the bulb's glowing filament onto a metal plate inside the bulb. This discovery is known as the "Edison Effect".

Thomas Alva Edison

It is the basis for the entire field of electronics. Edison has over 1000 inventions to his credit. He was born in Milan, Ohio, in the United States of America.

In the 1860s, he worked as a telegraph operator in the United States and Canada.

In 1877, inspired by the work he had done on improving Bell's telephone, Edison invented the phonograph.

Then he invented a practical light bulb, that glowed for 1,589 hours. Later he established the Edison Electric Light Company for distributing electricity to wide area.

The inventions of radio tube is also credited to this luminary scientist.

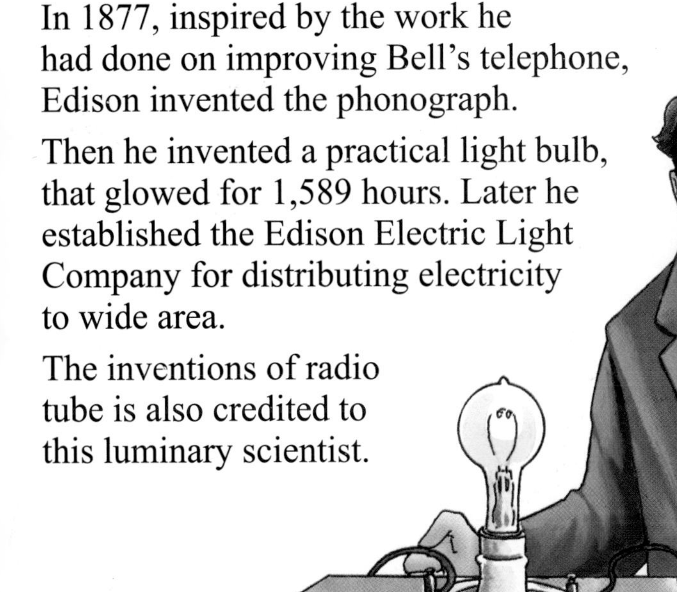

Telescope

There still is some uncertainty about who actually was the first to invent the telescope, as there have been stories of a "magical" telescopic device dating as early as the sixteenth century. Moreover, some historians believe that Giambattista della Porta of Naples discovered the telescopic properties of lenses in 1589 and even Galileo Galilei has been credited with inventing the telescope. At least two other Dutch spectacle makers, Hans and Zacharias Janssen, made similar devices about the same time as Lippershey.

Hans Lippershey (1570-1619), spectacle maker from the United Netherlands is traditionally credited with inventing the telescope (1608). On Oct. 2, 1608, he formally offered his invention, which he called a kijker ("looker"), to the Estates of Holland for use in warfare. The Estates granted him 900 florins for the instrument but required its modification into a binocular device. His telescopes were made available to Henry IV of France and others before the end of 1608.

Hans Lippershey (1570-1619)

One story relating to the development of the telescope involves Lippershey noticing two children playing with lenses in his shop. The children observed that when they looked through two lenses, a weather vane on a nearby church appeared to be larger and clearer. According to the story, Lippershey tried it himself and realized the amazing possibilities. He then placed a tube between the lenses to make a telescope. Lippershey called his invention a "kijker", meaning "looker" in Dutch and in 1608, applied for a patent with the Belgian government. Even though he was paid very well for his invention, a patent was not granted because it was felt that the simple device could not be kept a secret.

Laws of gravity

Gravity is the force which pulls everything around us and us down towards the ground. Object feel heavy because of the force of gravity on them.

Sir Issac Newton

The law of gravity was discovered by Sir Isaac Newton. He realized that gravity is what held everything around us, and also the planets and stars in place.

Newton was born in Woolstherpe, Lincolnshire. He went to study in Cambridge in 1661 but had to return home in 1665 because of the plague.

It seems to have been then that he discovered the laws of mechanics and the law of gravity, as well as the beginnings of mathematical calculus.

He had also published a book in 1686, in which his theories explained the movements of the planets and the Moon in orbits. We lost this great scientist in 1727.

The fall of apple towards the ground inspired Newton to propound the Law of Gravity.

Law of buoyancy

Buoyancy is the name given to the upward forces exerted on an object when it is in a liquid or gas.

These forces appear because the pressure in a fluid increases with depth, so that the upward pressure exerted on the bottom of the object is greater than the downward pressure exerted on the top.

Archimedes

The Law of Buoyancy was given by Archimedes. He was a Greek mathematician and inventor who lived in Syracuse, Sicily.

His work led him to make same important basic scientific discoveries.

He also worked out the laws of levers and pulleys. One well-known story about him, says that one day he got into a bath tub and it overflowed.

He jumped out and ran through the town shouting 'Eureka !' (Greek for 'I have found it').

He had suddenly realized how to measure the volume of gold in the king's crown.

If he put it into a vessel full upto the brim with water, the water that overflowed would be the same volume as the crown.

Archimedes invented a water-screw and worked out the laws of levers and pulleys.

Steam engine

An engine is a machine used to convert energy into mechanical work. The energy is supplied by a fuel.

Energy stored in the fuel is released by burning, or combustion. There are two types of engine — the internal combustion engine and the external combustion engine.

James Watt

The steam engine is an example of an external combustion engine. In this type of engine the fuel is burned outside the engine.

James Watt was a British engineer and inventor whose improvements to the steam engine made it into a useful source of power.

In 1764 he invented an outside condenser (which turned waste steam back into water).

He then designed engines in which the steam acted on both sides of the piston.

The watt (unit of power) was named after him.

James Watt invented steam engine that revolutionized the world of transport.

Telephone

A telephone is a device designed to transmit speech in the form of electric movements or radio waves. It enables people to talk to each other over long distances.

Alexander Graham Bell

The inventor of this marvellous device was Alexander Graham Bell (1847–1922).

Bell was born and in Edinburgh and educated in Edinburgh and London universities, but lived for most of his life in the United States of America. He taught deaf children and was therefore interested in finding ways of sending out sounds.

In 1873, he moved to the US as a professor at Boston University. In 1876, he invented the world's first workable telephone. It had certain disadvantages, it had to be moved quickly from mouth to ear and the sound was very faint even when the speaker shouted. American inventor Thomas Alva Edison soon produced a much powerful and successful telephone.

Bell's telephone worked by changing sound produced by the human voice into electric current. This current could then be transmitted along a wire and changed back into sound at the other end.

Television

Television is a system used to broadcast moving pictures and sound by radio waves or by cable, over a distance.

John Logie Baird

Pictures are converted into electrical signals by cameras. John Logie Baird (1886–1946), a Scottish engineer and entrepreneur, became the first person ever to transmit a television picture by radio waves.

In 1884, Paul Nipkow, a German scientist, invented a disc with a spiral of lenses that split an image into lines as it rotated. Baird used a Nipkow disc in his television.

In 1926, Baird held the first public demonstration of his mechanical television at the London departmental store 'Self Ridges' on Oxford street in London. Electronic television was developed in the 1920s and 1930s.

The BBC used Baird's system to broadcast news and shows from 1929.

• IT'S FACT •

• A television on standby uses one-third as much electrical power as a television that is switched on.

Radio

In 1888, German physicist Heinrich Hertz demonstrated the existence of radio waves. This discovery was used by Guglielmo Marconi to build his radio system in 1895.

Radio is a form of broadcasting that uses radio waves to transmit and receive information.

Guglielmo Marconi

Radio waves with very short wavelengths pass through the atmosphere into space and are used to communicate with spacecraft.

Radio waves can be sent around the world by bouncing them off one of the layers of atmosphere known as ionosphere.

He began experimenting with transmitting radio waves in 1894. He became successful the following year.

By inventing the antenna and improving his receivers, he succeeded in sending radio waves over about 2.5 km.

He increased the range of his transmissions to 15 km and set up a land station in Italy to communicate with warships (20 km) at sea.

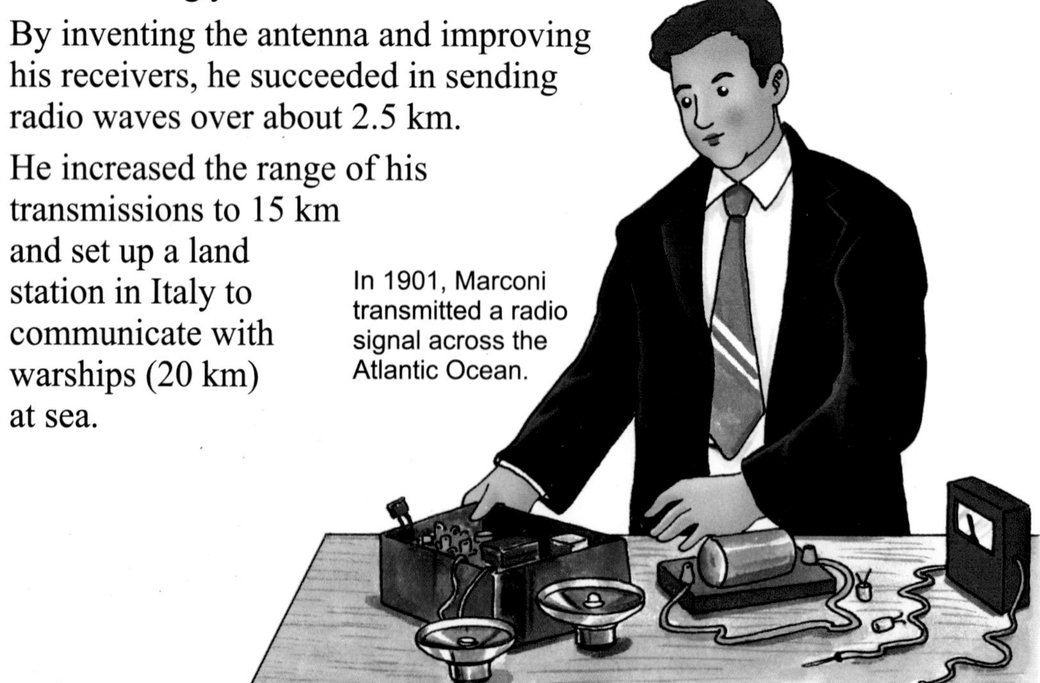

In 1901, Marconi transmitted a radio signal across the Atlantic Ocean.

Electric motor

An electric motor is a machine that converts electrical energy into mechanical energy. It relies on the fact that a wire carrying an electric current moves in a magnetic field.

Michael Faraday

There are electric motors in refrigerators, hair-dryers, food processors, clocks and many other appliances that we use every day at our homes.

Michael Faraday (1791–1867) was a British physicist and chemist. His experiments are the basis for our understanding of the laws of electricity and magnetism.

In 1831, he found that when he moved a magnet through a coil of wire, an electric current was produced in the wire.

This enabled him to make the first electrical generator or dynamo. In 1825, Faraday discovered benzene and was the founder of electrochemistry. He also discovered elements by using electrolysis.

• IT'S FACT •

- A generator is an electric motor in reverse. Turning the coil inside the magnet's field produces an electric current.

Electricity

As early as 600 BC, the Greeks were aware of the peculiar properties of amber, a yellow- colored resin that oozed out of certain trees and hardened. When rubbed with a piece of fur, amber attracted small pieces of material such as feathers.

Benjamin Franklin was a printer, statesman, prolific writer and inventor.

Two thousand years later, in the 16th century, William Gilbert, court physician to Queen Elizabeth I, proved that many other substances are also electric. Intrigued by Gilbert's ideas, Otto von Guericke in Germany made a device in 1665 that could generate sparks of what came to be known as static electricity.

In 1747, Benjamin Franklin (1706–1790) in America concluded that all materials possess an electrical fluid and that the action of rubbing transferred electric fluid from one body to another, electrifying both. Franklin defined the presence of electric fluid as 'positive' and the lack of fluid as 'negative.' Today we know that the phenomenon of electricity involves the movement of tiny subatomic particles, called electrons, named after the Greek for amber.

• IT'S FACT •

- In 1752 Benjamin Franklin proved that lightning is electric by flying a kite in a thunderstorm. Attached to the string was a metal key. As lighting struck the kite, a spark flashed as electricity passed down the string from the key.
- The body's nerves carry electric currents to and from the brain at speeds of up to 400 km per hour.

Franklin performed the famous kite-flying experiment and proved that lightning was a farm of electricity.

Raman effect

C. V. Raman

A rainbow often appears and delights us. We see in it shades of red, orange, yellow, green, blue, indigo and violet. The white ray of the sun includes all these colours. When a beam of sunlight is passed through a glass prism, a patch of these colour bands are seen. This is called the spectrum. Spectral lines in it are characteristic of the light passing through a prism. A beam of light that causes a single spectral line is said to be monochromatic.

Raman spent a long time in the study of the scattered light. On February 28, 1928, he observed two low intensity spectral lines corresponding to the incident monochromatic light. Years of his labour had borne fruit. It was clear that though the incident light was monochromatic, the scattered light was not monochromatic.

Thus Raman's experiment discovered a phenomenon which was lying hidden in nature. The phenomenon attracted the attention of research workers all over the world. It became famous as the 'Raman Effect'. The spectral lines in the scattered light were known as 'Raman lines'.

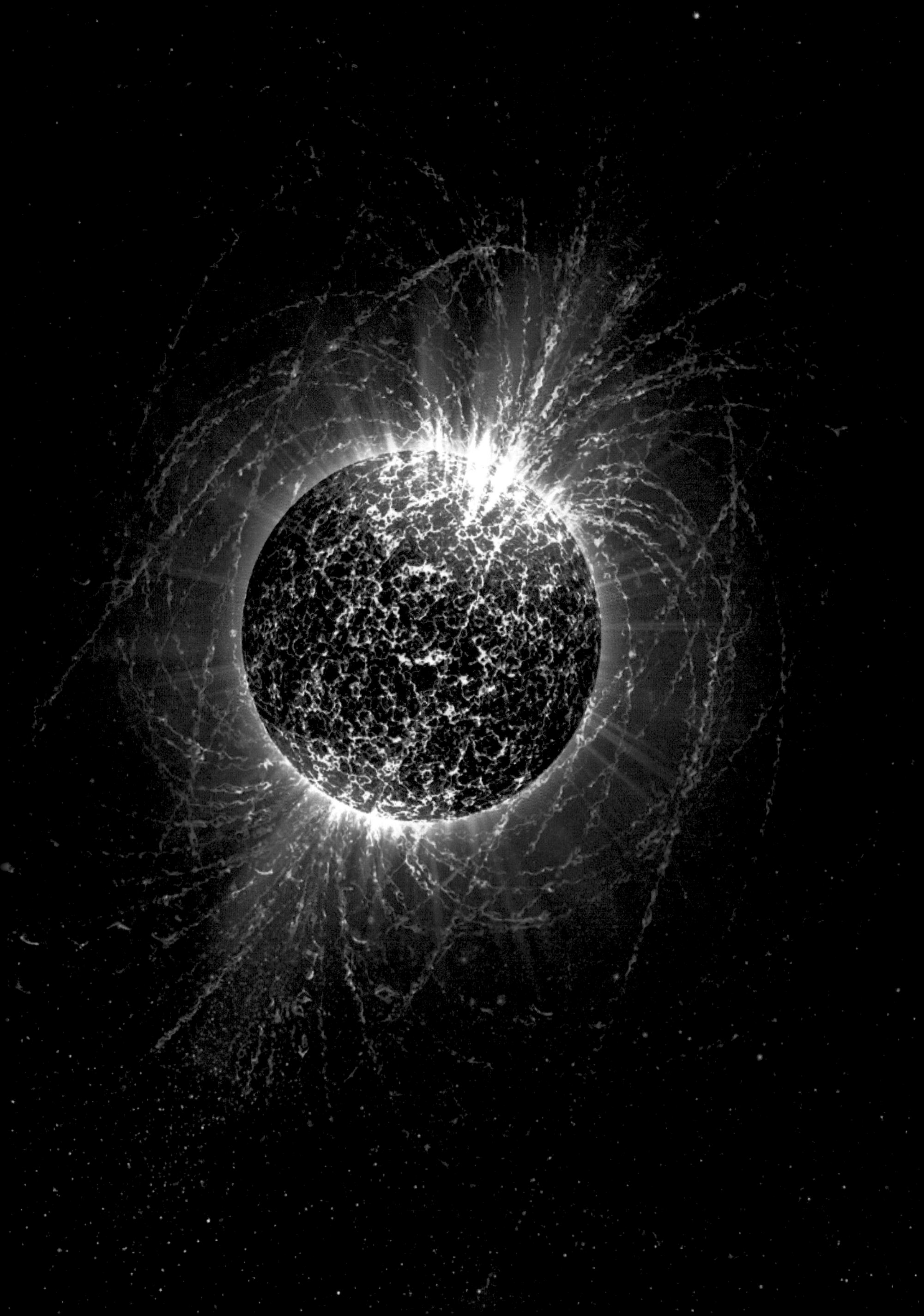

CHEMICAL

INVENTIONS

Law of conservation of matter

Antonie Lavoisier (1743–1794), a French chemist, played a major role in formulating the law of conservation of matter.

Antonie Lavoisier

According to this law, a quantity is said to be conserved if, no matter how complicated the system, it does not change.

For example, in chemical reactions the total number of atoms of every element is conserved. When hydrogen is burned in oxygen to form water, there are just as many hydrogen and oxygen atoms in the water at the end as there were in the beginning.

It was believed that since all substances are made up of atoms, the total amount of mass present would also be conserved.

However, the theory of relativity tells us that mass is a form of energy and that it can be converted into other forms, for example, heat. It is the total energy, not just mass, which is conserved.

This effect is too small to be measured in chemical reactions, but is important to nuclear energy.

Energy is neither created nor destroyed. It is transformed from one form to another.

Radium

Radium is a chemical clement. It is a whitish metal found in uranium ore. It also occurs in the water from some mineral springs and in sea water.

Marie and Pierre Curie in the laboratory.

Radium is radioactive. It gives out harmful rays. These rays can actually be tapped for the benefit of mankind. It is used to treat cancer patients. Fruits and vegetables can be preserved for longer periods if they are subjected to radiation.

Radium was discovered in 1898 by the Polish-born scientist Marie Curie and her husband Pierre. Along with Henri Becquerel, they were awarded the 1903 Nobel Prize in physics for their work in discovering radioactivity.

Marie isolated two new elements — radium and polonium and discovered plutonium. She received the 1911 Nobel Prize in chemistry for her work.

Marie Curie was the first woman to win a Nobel Prize.

• IT'S FACT •

- The name radium comes from the Latin word radius, meaning 'say'. The Curies named polonium after Poland, Marie Curie's homeland.
- Metallic radium has high chemical reactivity. It is attacked by water with vigorous evolution of hydrogen and by air with the formation of the nitride.

Periodic table

The periodic table is an arrangement that contains all the known elements in order of increasing atomic number.

Dmitri Mendeleev

Elements with atoms of similar structures have similar properties and so are positioned close to each other.

Elements can be divided into metals and non-metals but these groupings are very large. Therefore, the metals are divided up into the three groups : alkali metals such as magnesium, the transition metals such

Alkali metals

Inner transition series

Transition metals

Non-metals

1 Hydrogen H								
1	2							
3 Lithium Li	4 Beryllium Be							
11 Sodium Na	12 Magnesium Mg							
19 Potassium K	20 Calcium Ca	21 Scandium Sc	22 Titanium Ti	23 Vanadium V	24 Chromium Cr	25 Manganese Mn	26 Iron Fe	27 Cobalt Co
37 Rubidium Rb	38 Strontium Sr	39 Yttrium Y	40 Zirconium Zr	41 Niobium Nb	42 Molybdenum Mo	43 Technetium Tc	44 Ruthenium Ru	45 Rhodium Rh
55 Caesium Cs	56 Barium Ba	57-71 Lanthanide series	72 Hafnium Hf	73 Tantalum Ta	74 Tungsten W	75 Rhenium Re	76 Osmium Os	77 Iridium Ir
87 Francium Fr	88 Radium Ra	89-103 Actinide series	104 Element 104	105 Element 105	106 Element 106	107 Element 107	108 Element 108	109 Element 109

57 Lanthanum La	58 Cerium Ce	59 Praseodymium Pr	60 Neodymium Nd	61 Prometheum Pm	62 Samarium Sm	63 Europium eu	64 Gadolinium Gd	65 Terbium Tb
89 Actinium Ac	90 Thorium Th	91 Protactinium Pa	92 Uranium U	93 Neptunium Np	94 Plutonium Pu	95 Americium Am	96 Curium Cm	97 Berkelium Bk

as iron, and the inner transition series such as uranium.

Dmitri Mendeleev was a Russian chemist who drew up the first periodic table. From gaps in the table, he was able to predict the existence of elements that were yet to be discovered.

Periodic Table

			3	4	5	6	7	8
								2 Helium He
			5 Boron B	6 Carbon C	7 Nitrogen N	8 Oxygen O	9 Fluorine F	10 Neon Ne
			13 Aluminium Al	14 Silicon Si	15 Phosphorus P	16 Sulphur S	17 Chlorine Cl	18 Argon Ar
28 Nickel Ni	29 Copper Cu	30 Zinc Zn	31 Gallium Ga	32 Germanium Ge	33 Arsenic As	34 Selenium Se	35 Bromine Br	36 Krypton Kr
46 Palladium Pd	47 Silver Ag	48 Cadmium Cd	49 Indium In	50 Tin Sn	51 Antimony Sb	52 Tellurium Te	53 Iodine I	54 Xenon Xe
78 Platinum Pt	79 Gold Au	80 Mercury Hg	81 Thallium Tl	82 Lead Pb	83 Bismuth Bi	84 Polonium Po	85 Astatine At	86 Radon Rn

66 Dysprosium Dy	67 Holmium Ho	68 Erbium Er	69 Thulium Tm	70 Ytterbium Yb	71 Lutetium Lu
98 Californium Cf	99 Einsteinium Es	100 Fermium Fm	101 Mendelevium Md	102 Nobelium No	103 Lawrencium Lr

Atoms

Atom is a Greek word that means that 'which cannot be divided further'. The popular belief was that all matter on the Earth was made up of these tiny bits known as atoms.

John Dalton

This belief did not carry a scientific evidence. The first atomic theory was put forward in the year 1803 by an English scientist named John Dalton (1766–1844).

He observed by weighing equal volumes of gases that their weights were different and concluded that all matter in any state consisted of very small particles called atoms.

He also noted that atoms of different elements had different properties and weights. So he proposed that molecules are made from atoms combined in simple ratios.

In 1808, Dalton published the first table of comparative atomic weights.

• IT'S FACT •

- The sizes of atoms of elements vary regularly throughout the periodic system.

Neutrons

In 1911, New Zealand-born physicist Ernest Rutherford (1871–1837) discovered the atomic nucleus. In 1919, he became the first person to split an atom.

James Chadwick

Every atom has a nucleus, which contains protons and, except hydrogen, neutrons, with electrons spinning around it.

The neutron is very similar in mass to the proton, but carries no electric charge. This makes it harder to detect since it does not react to or produce electric forces.

Atoms with different numbers of neutrons but the same number of protons in their nucleus are known as isotopes.

They behave in the same way chemically although their nuclei have different masses. The neutron was discovered in 1932 by James Chadwick.

Using the radiation from radioactive isotopes to bombard other atoms resulted in the emission of neutrons. Neutrons are important in nuclear energy, since they can be absorbed by the nuclei of some atoms causing the nucleic to split into two.

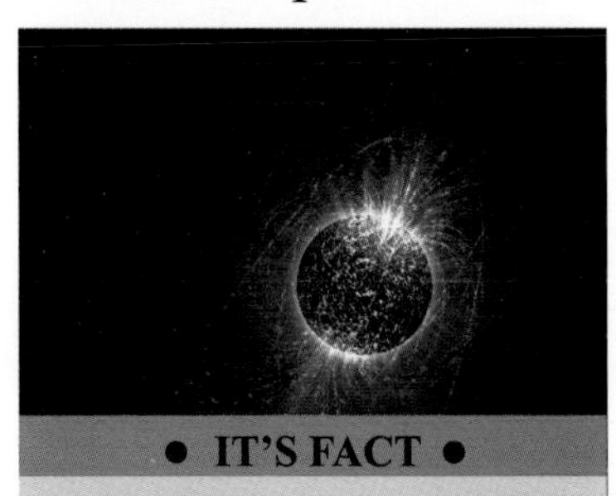

• IT'S FACT •

- Fast neutron detectors are most commonly based on the elastic scattering of neutrons from nuclei.

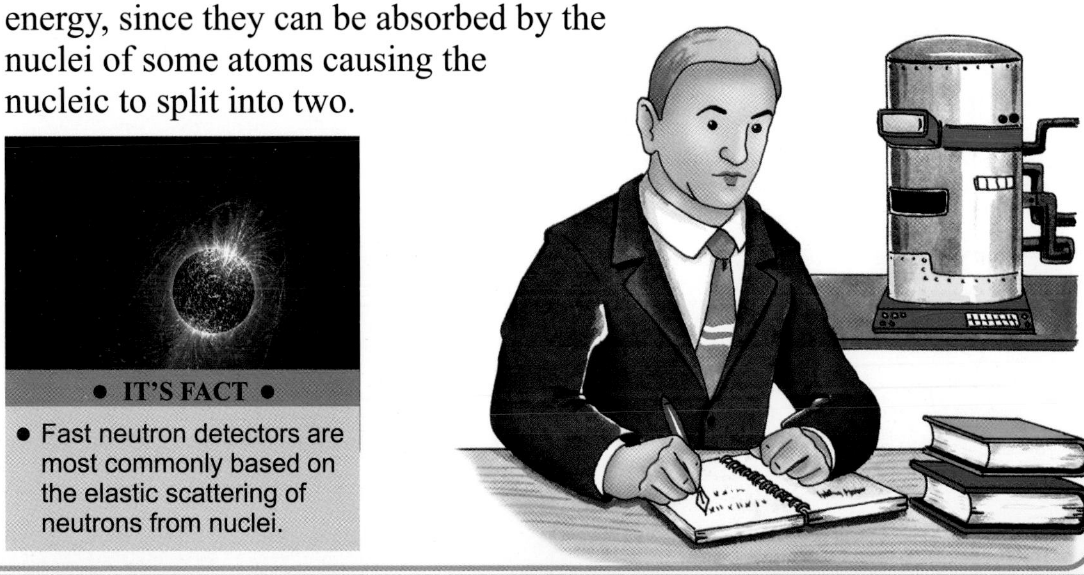

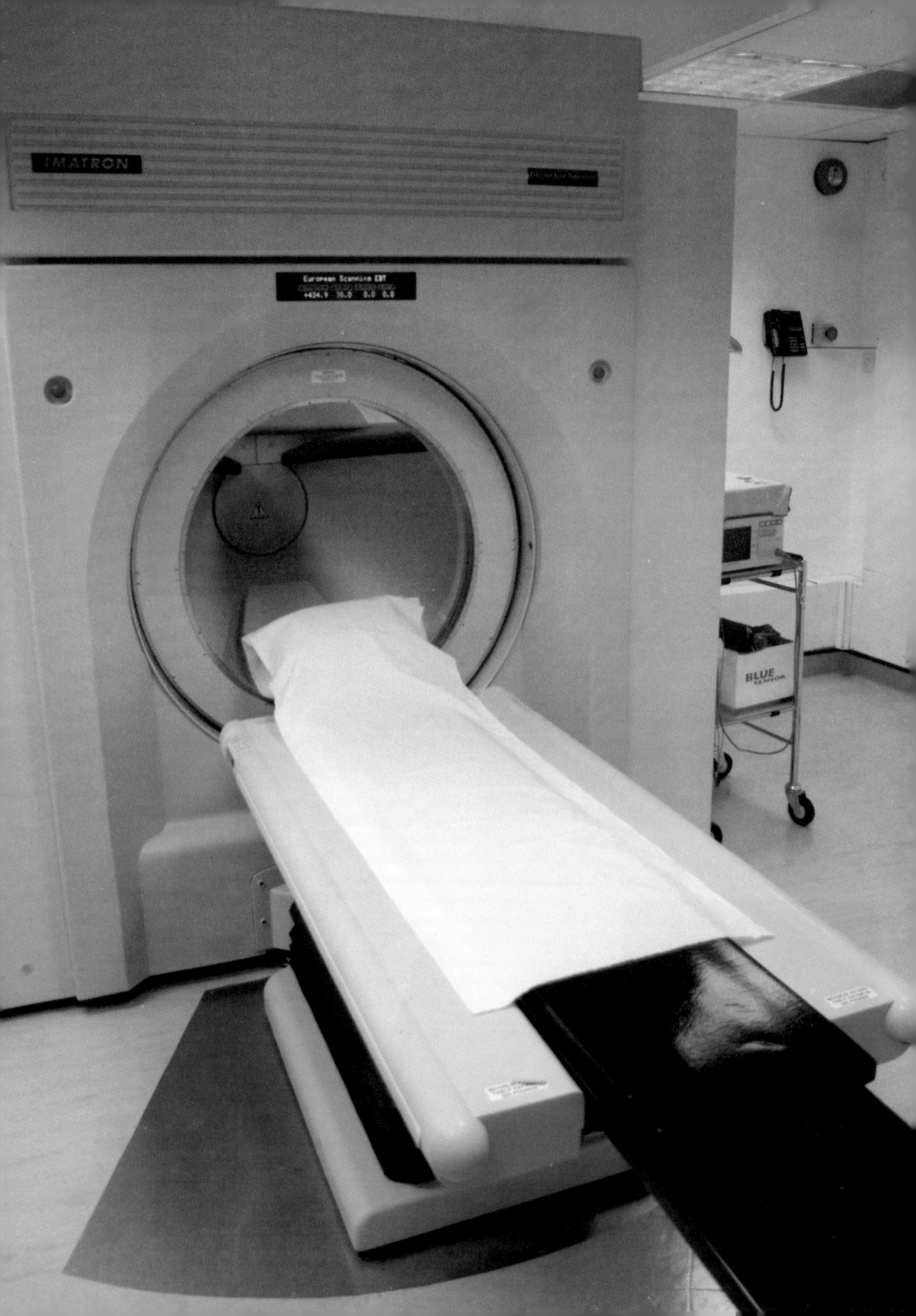
IMATRON
BLUE SENSOR

MEDICAL

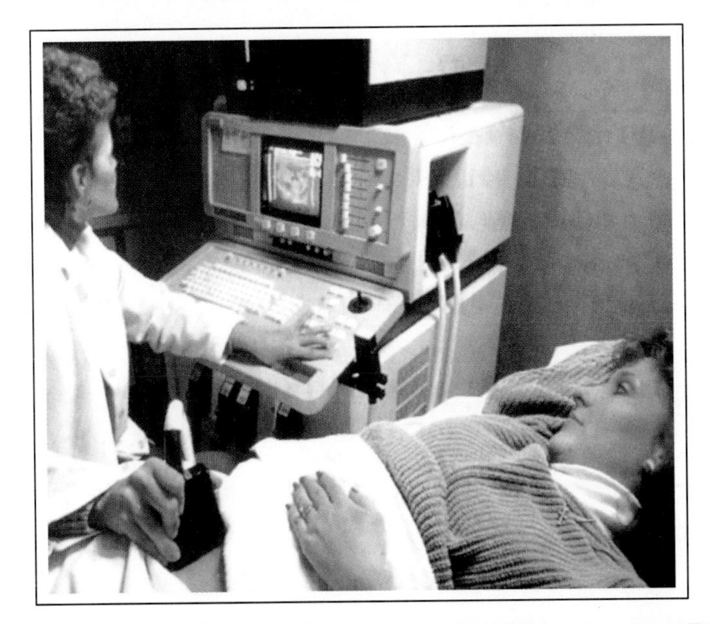

INVENTIONS

Medicines

Hippocrates was a Greek physician born in 460 BC on the island of Cos, Greece. He became known as the founder of medicine and was considered as the greatest physician of his time. He based his medical practice on observations and on the study of the human body.

Hippocrates

He held the belief that the body must be treated as a whole and not just a series or parts. He rejected the superstitious views of his time that considered illness to be caused by possession of evil spirits and disfavors of the Gods.

He accurately described disease symptoms and was the first physician to accurately describe the symptoms of pneumonia as well as epilepsy in children. He believed in the natural healing process of rest, a good diet, fresh air and cleanliness.

Hippocrates traveled throughout Greece practicing his medicine. He founded a medical school on the island of Cos, Greece and began teaching ideas.

He soon developed an oath of Medical Ethics for physicians to follow. This oath is taken by physicians today as they begin their medical practice. It is known as Hippocrates' Oath. He died in 377 BC. Today Hippocrates is known as the "Father of Medicine".

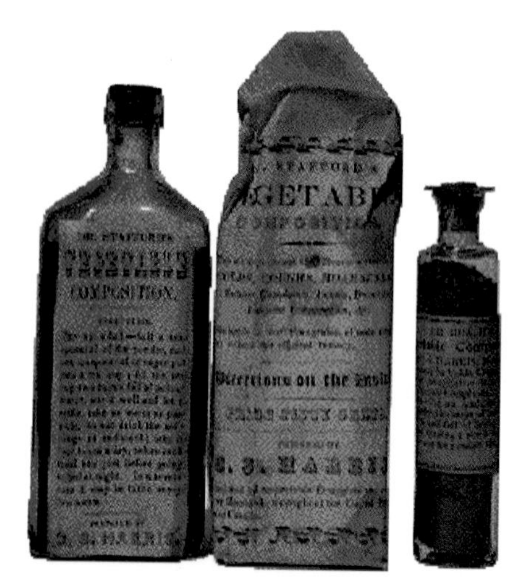

Thermometer

A thermometer is a device for measuring temperature. Most thermometers are based on the principle that certain substances expand when heated.

In about 1603, the great Italian scientist Galileo Galilei invented an instrument known as a thermoscope that comprised a small glass flask the size of a hen's egg with a slender neck around 36 cm (16 in) long.

The open end of the neck was placed in a little water which rose and fell in the neck according to the temperature of the air in the flask.

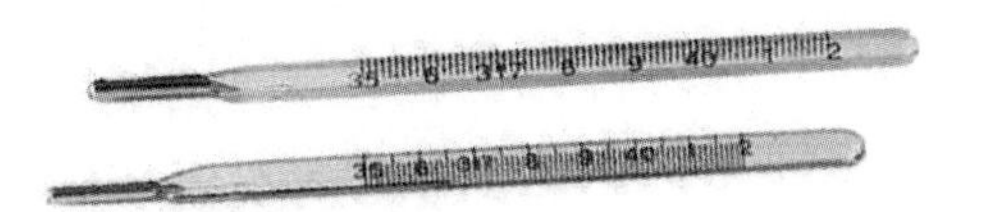

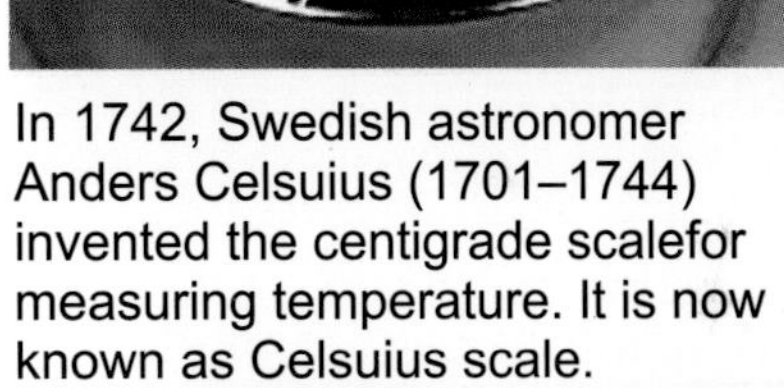

In 1742, Swedish astronomer Anders Celsuius (1701–1744) invented the centigrade scalefor measuring temperature. It is now known as Celsuius scale.

The mercury thermometer was invented by Gabriel Daniel Fahrenheit in 1714. A mercury thermometer contains mercury inside a thin glass tube. As the mercury heats, it rises up the tube.

He also invented the temperature scale that bears his name — Fahrenheit scale.

0° was the point at which a mixture of ice, salt and water froze and at 32°, water froze. The boiling point of water was 212°.

Gabriel Fahrenheit

X-rays

Wilhelm Roentgen

X-rays are one kind of electromagnetic radiation. X-rays are made when powerful beams of electrons hit a metal target. They can pass through some materials such as our skin and flesh. X-rays allows doctors to see inside a human body.

In November 1895, German physicist, Wilhelm Conrad Roentgen was working with a cathode-ray tube and a fluorescent screen. He noticed that some form of radiation was lighting up a screen that was shielded from the cathode rays. He called the radiation 'x-ray'.

He gave their name so because the letter X is often used to stand for something. A month later, he took the first x-ray photograph. It showed the bones in his wife's hand. For this exemplary work, he received the Nobel Prize for physics in 1901. He was the first prize winner.

Modern medical X-ray photographs, using carefully controlled doses of X-rays, can reveal the structure of soft tissues as well as hard structures such as bone.

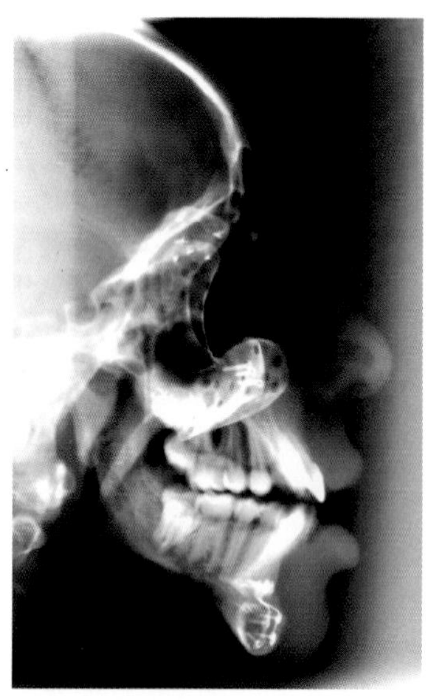
The X-ray of a person's face showing the facial bones and teeth.

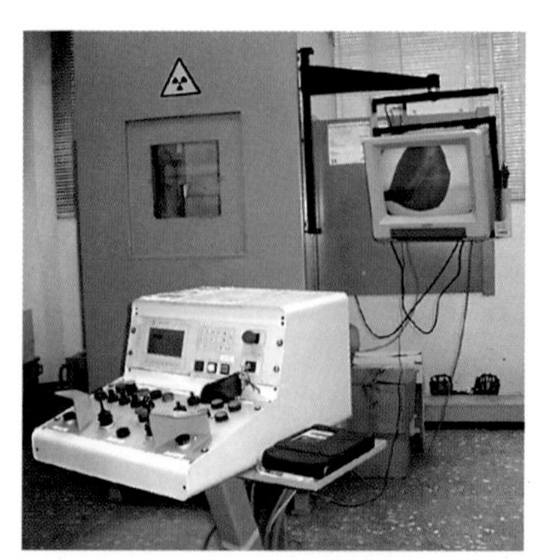
Modern X-ray machine

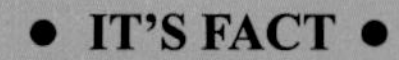
• IT'S FACT •

- The Sun was the first celestial object determined to give off X-rays with proved to be intrinsically weak X-ray source.

Ultrasound machine

Medical diagnostic ultrasound system use high-frequency sound waves to produce images of soft tissues and internal body organs.

First introduced to the medical world in the 1950s, it is a widely used diagnostic imaging machinery today.

Ultrasound examinations are non-invasive and generally considered safe at the power levels used for diagnostic examinations.

Ultrasound is used in obstetrical, abdominal neurological, vascular and cardiac applications.

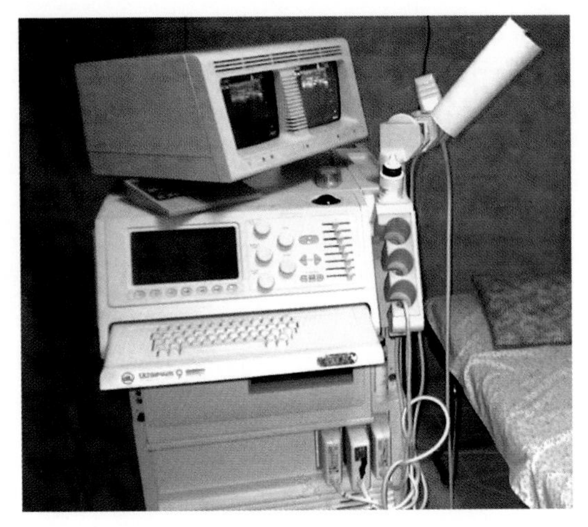

Modern Ultrasound Machine

During the early 1970s, the technology advanced to grey scale ultra sound systems that produce static images of internal organs easily recognizable to physicians.

Later in the 1970s, the development of real-time ultra sound imaging enable physicians to see continuous live-action images of the area under investigations.

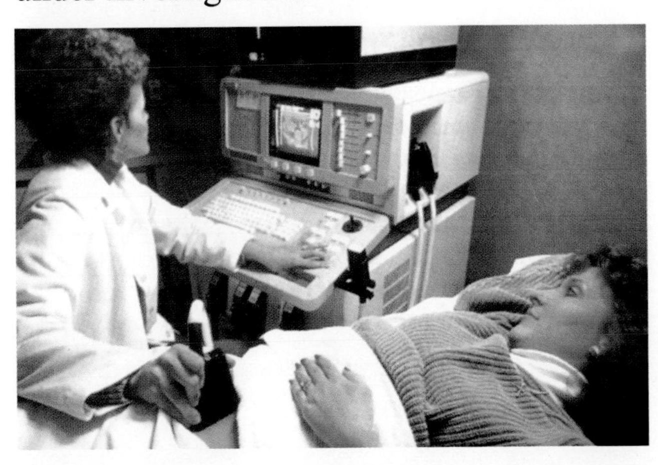

Here the doctor uses ultrasound to find out the well-being of the baby growing inside its mother.

Stethoscope

Stethoscope is a medical instrument used in listening to sounds produced within the body, chiefly in the heart or lungs.

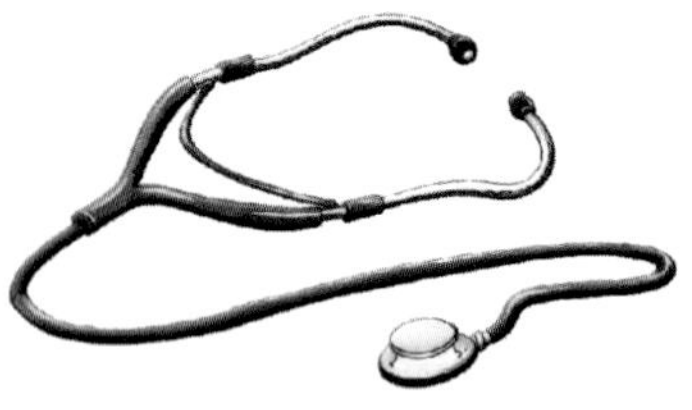

Stethoscope allows us to listen to sounds produced within the body.

It was invented by the French physician R.T.H. Laennec, who in 1819 described the use of a perforated wooden cylinder to transmit sounds from the patient's chest to the physician's ear.

This monaural stethoscope was modified to more convenient forms, but it has been largely supplanted by the binanral type with two flexible rubber tubes attaching the chest piece to spring-connected metal tubes with earpieces.

R. T. H. Laennec

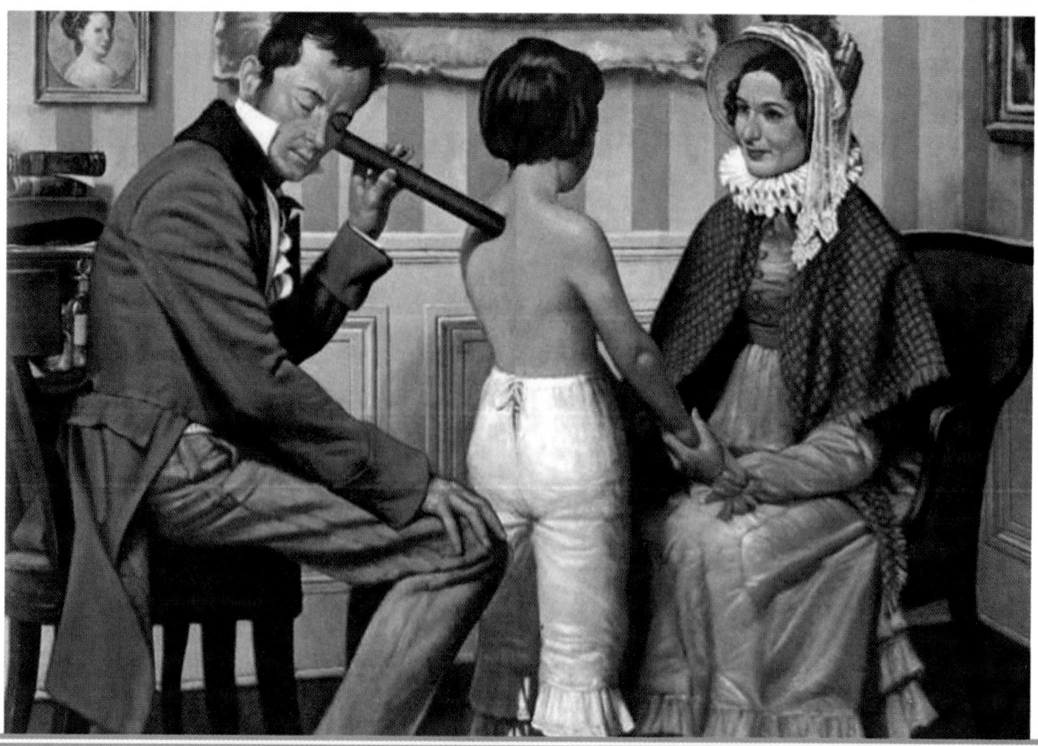

Antibiotics

Antibiotics are chemical substances produced by a living organism, generally a microorganism, that is harmful to other microorganism.

Sir Alexander Fleming

Although antibiotics are released naturally into the soil by bacteria and fungi, they did not come into worldwide prominence until the introduction of penicillin in 1942.

In 1928, Alexander Fleming (1881–1955) noticed that colonies of bacteria growing on a germ culture medium had been unfavorably affected by mould, Penicillium notatum.

In 1945, Fleming won Nobel Prize for medicine with Ernst Chain and Howard Florey who purified and showed that penicillin was highly effective against many serious bacterial infections.

The principle governing the use of antibiotics is to ensure that the patient receives one to which the target bacterium is sensitive, at a high enough concentration to be effective and for a sufficient length of time to ensure that the infection is totally eradicated.

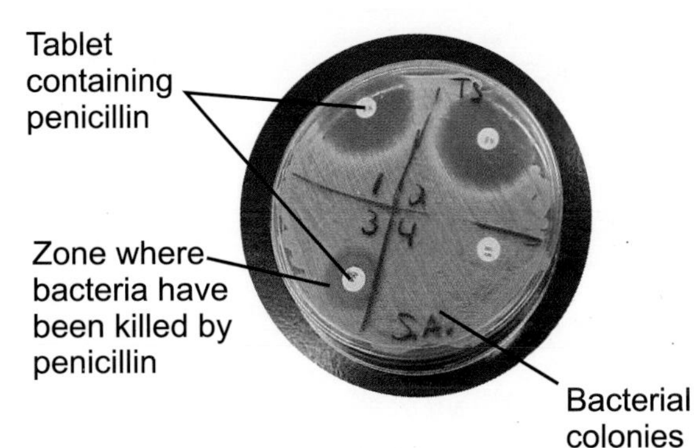

• IT'S FACT •

• An antibiotic may kill virtually all the bacteria causing a disease in a patient, but a few bacteria that are genetically less vulnerable to the effects of the drug may survive.

MATHEMATICS

Zero

Zero is the mathematically defined numerical function of nothingness that is used not for an evasion but for an apprehension of reality. The 'nothing' has been the exclusive territory of mystics and neocheaters.

They thrive on 'nothing' in non reality, and create their mystical edifice of power and dominance upon nothing.

The discovery of zero and the development of the place value numeration had to wait for a more intellectual climate – a flourishing business and commercial atmosphere.

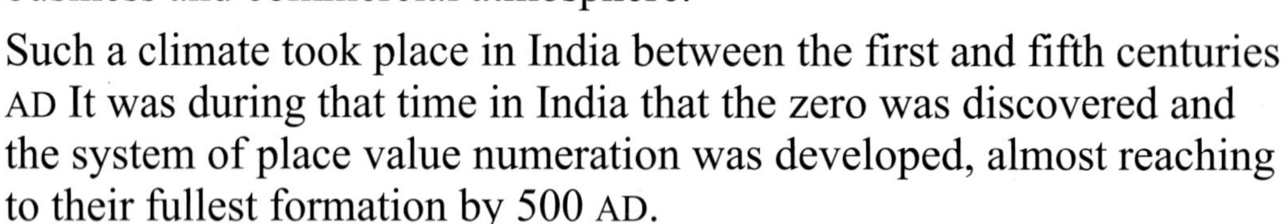

Such a climate took place in India between the first and fifth centuries AD It was during that time in India that the zero was discovered and the system of place value numeration was developed, almost reaching to their fullest formation by 500 AD.

Increased commercial activities during the first three centuries in India called for further developments in navigational technology and astronomical science, and for an evolution of a written computational methodology for recording the process of calculations that were employed in navigation, astronomy and business. To accomplish these ends, zero was discovered.

• IT'S FACT •

- Early Chinese did not have a symbol for zero, the invention and use of their abacus suggests that they had an implied appreciation for positional base notation and zero as a number.

Pythagorean Theorem

Pythagorus was the great Greek philosopher and mathematician who formulated principles that influenced the thought of Plato and Aristotle and contributed to the development of mathematics and Western rational philosophy.

Pythagorus

Pythagorus is generally credited with the theory of the functional significance of numbers in the objective world and in music. Other discoveries attributed to him include the Pythagorean theorem for right angles.

According to the Pythagorean theorem, in a right-angled triangle, the sum of square of base and square of perpendicular (Height) is equal to the square of hypotenuse.

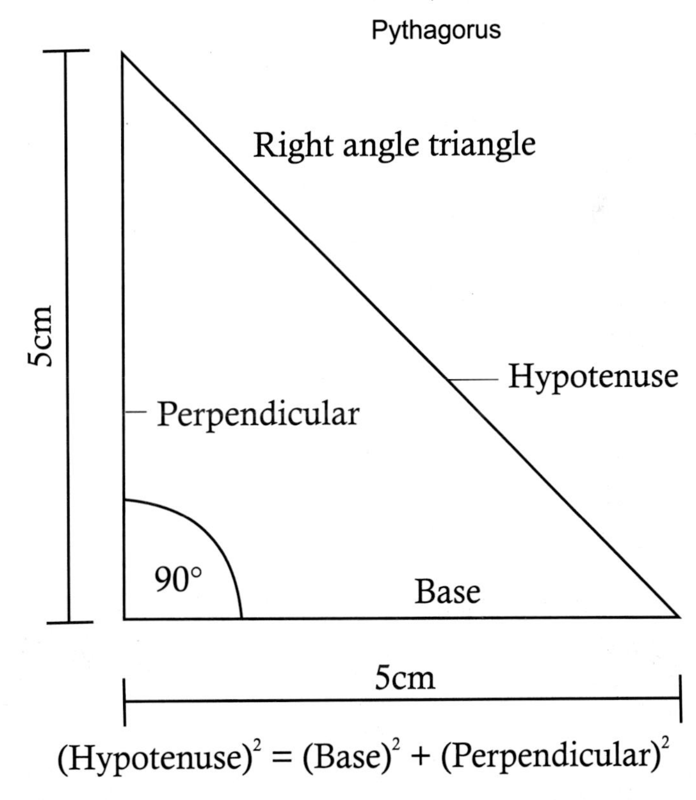

$$(\text{Hypotenuse})^2 = (\text{Base})^2 + (\text{Perpendicular})^2$$

Geometry

Geometry is the study of points, lines, angles, surfaces and solids. One of the outstanding achievements of the ancient Greeks was the construction of a deductive system of geometry which beginning with principles that they regarded as obviously true and derived from experience, culminated in quite deep theorems, some of which are still an important part of mathematics.

Euclid

The elementary part of the deductive system of geometry was set forth in Euclid's Elements. It was the first textbook in geometry.

The book was a compilation of knowledge that became the centre of mathematical teaching for 2000 years.

Probably no results in Elements were first proved by Euclid but the organization of the material and its exposition are certainly due to him.

The long lasting nature of *Elements* must make Euclid the leading mathematics teacher of all time.

• IT'S FACT •

- Towards the end of the 19th century, the keenest thinkers in the field of geometry became increasingly concerned about the lack of true rigour in Euclid's presentation.

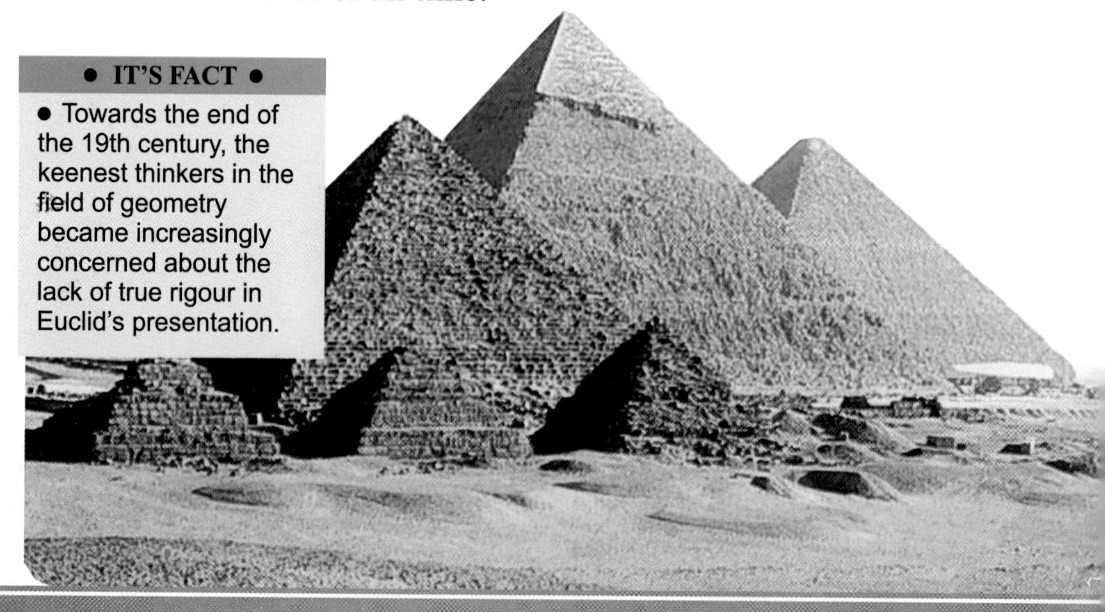

Abacus

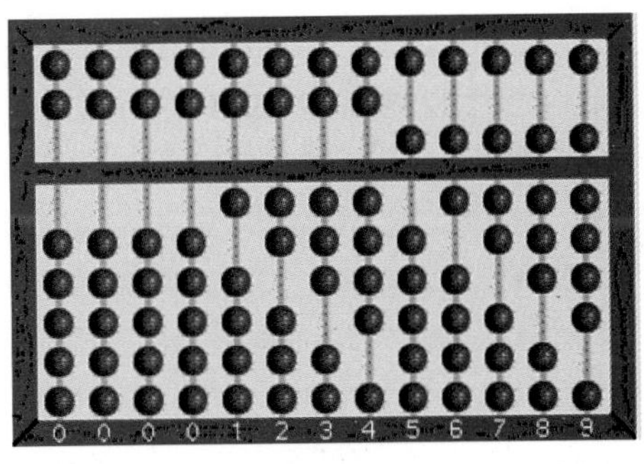

Abacus

Abacus was a calculating device, probably of Babylonian origin, that was long important in commerce. It is the predecessor of the modern calculating machine and computer.

The earliest abacus was a board or slab on which a Babylonian spread sand so that he could trace letters for general writing purposes.

As the abacus came to be used solely for counting and computing, its form was changed and improved.

In the Roman abacus, the board was given grooves to facilitate moving the counters in the proper files. Another form, common today, had the counters strung on wires.

The abacus, generally in the form of a large calculating board, was in universal use in Europe in the Middle Ages, as well as in the Arab world and in Asia.

It reached Japan in the 16th century. The introduction of the Hindu-Arabic notation, with its place value and zero, gradually replaced the abacus, though it was still widely used in Europe as late as the 17th century and survives even today in China, Japan and the Middle East.

The Japanese still use the abacus for counting.

Calculator

Calculator is a machine for automatically performing arithmetical operation and certain mathematical functions.

Modern calculators are the successors of a digital arithmetic machine devised by Blaise Pascal (1623–1662) in 1647.

Apart from inventing the calculating machine, Pascal also invented the barometer, the hydraulic press and the syringe.

Later in the 17th century, Gottfried Wilhelm Leibniz created a more advanced machine and especially in the late 19th century, inventors produced calculating machines that were smaller and less laborious to use.

In the early decades of the 20th century, desktop adding machines and other calculating devices were developed.

Some were key-driven, others required a rotating drum to enter sums punched into a keyboard, and later the drum was spun by electric motor.

The modern calculator is installed with an integrated circuit that can perform calculations much more quickly than a person. It can be programmed to solve mathematical problems.

• IT'S FACT •

- Frank Stephen Baldioin was an inventer best known for his development of the Monroe calculator. His first calculator, the arithmometer, could add, subtract, multiply and divide.

MODERN

INVENTIONS

Car

When the French army was interested in finding a way to move cannons on land, Nicolas-Joseph Cugnot (1804–1925) came to the rescue. He made two vehicles, which were the first steam-powered vehicles to run on roads.

Nicolas–Joseph Cugnor was a pioneer of steam-driver engines

In 1876, German engineer Nikolaus Otto invented a gas engine and in 1885, Gottlieb Daimler adapted Otto's engine to make a petrol engine.

In 1885, Carl Friedrich Benz (1844–1929) invented a three-wheeled motor car. Benz used an internal combustion engine that he had invented himself. It cooled with water. The car drove at the speed of 24 km per hour.

Benz later, produced a four-wheeled car in 1893.

By the end of the 19th century several hundred people had bought motor cars.

In 1908, Henry Ford opened the first modern car assembly line and began to produce his Model T car in great numbers.

Aeroplane

An aeroplane is a fixed wing aircraft that is heavier than air. It uses a jet engine as a source of energy to fly.

Man has been always fascinated with the idea of flying. Centuries ago, Leonardo da Vinci drew sketches of aircraft and rockets.

Howeve, it was not until the 19th century that flying was actually possible for man.

In 1808, British inventor George Cayley built the first heavier-than-air craft called glider. In 1877, Otto Lilienttal, a German glider builder invented an arched-wing glider.

On December 17, 1903, Wright brothers were successful in making the first controlled powered flight in a heavier-than-air machine that they built. The maiden flight carried the passenger to a distance of 30 m in 12 seconds!

Wright brothers, Orville and Wilbur.

By original scientific research, the Wright brothers discovered the principles of human flight. As inventors, builders and flyers, they further developed the aeroplane, taught man to fly, and opened the era of aviation.

• IT'S FACT •

- The Boeing 747 (Jumbo Jet) is the largest and most powerful plane. It can carry up to 500 passengers. It stands as high as a 6-storey office block and weighs over 370 tonnes. It has a maximum speed of 969 km/h (602 mph) and a wing-span of over 70 m (232 ft).

Rocket

As early as 200 BC, Archimedes, the Greek scientist, had drawn sketches of a rocket. And by about 1150, the Chinese were using rockets powered by gunpowder.

In 1883, Konstantin Isiolkovsky, a Russian school teacher produced notebooks containing sketches of spaceships fueled with liquid oxygen and liquid hydrogen.

Goddard's work remained unrecognized during his lifetime.

The occupants were shown in a pressurized cabin with double wall protection against meteoroids.

In 1921, Robert Goddard (1882–1945) in the USA began experiments with liquid fuels and on March 16, 1926, at Auburn, Massachusetts, he became the first person to launch a liquid propellant rocket, fueled by gasoline and liquid oxygen.

In 1927, German rocket enthusiasts founded the society for space travel. They approached the German army and demonstrated their repulsor rockets.

In 1933, a special section of the Army Weapons Department was established, Werner von Braun of the society for space travel was placed in charge of rocket development.

In April 1937, a major rocket research station was completed near the village Peenemunde on the Baltic coast.

The large A-4 rocket (called the V2 by the German High Command) was developed here.

Hot-air balloon

A **balloon is a kind of aircraft.** It is lighter than air and cannot be steered. Balloons are made from a large, round bag and attached by ropes to a basket.

It is believed that a small hot-air balloon was used in Portugal in 1709.

In 1782, the Montgolfier brothers, Joseph Michel and Jacques Etienne, observed that smoke from a fire made a silk bag rise up into the air.

On June 5, 1783, they gave a public demonstration of their discovery in the town of Annonay. Their balloon stayed in the air for about 10 minutes, travelling more than 1.6 km at an altitude of about 1830 m.

In September that year, the brothers put a sheep, duck and rooster aboard the balloon to see what effect altitude might have on living creatures.

Montgolfier brothers

The same year in October, Francois Pilatre de Rozier became the first human to fly in a balloon. On that occasion the balloon was kept tethered, but in November, Rozier and Marquis d' Arlanded made the first balloon, trip traveling across the city of Paris.

Hydrogen, and later helium, was found to be superior to hot air for filling balloon because it is inherently lighter than air and does not need to be heated to produce the lift.

Atom bomb

In 1938, German Scientist Otto Hahn succeeded in splitting the uranium atom, leading to the possibility of an atomic chain reaction.

Otto Hahn

Fearing that Nazi Germany might build an atom bomb, scientists convinced President Roosevelt to begin the American effort.

The Manhattan Project, as it was called, was spread over 37 sites and employed 43,000 people, physicist J. Robert Oppenheimer was appointed director of the weapons laboratory at Los Alamos, New-Mexico.

After much difficulty, in 1945, a supply of uranium – 235 pure enough to be used in the bomb arrived at Los Alamos, where it was fashioned into a weapon.

This bomb was first detonated over the Japanese city of Hiroshina on 6 August 1945. A Second type of bomb used plutonium. This bomb was tested at Alamogordo, New Mexico.

• IT'S FACT •

- The first atomic bomb to be used in warfare used uranium. It was dropped by the United States on Hiroshima, Japan, on August 6, 1945.

Artificial satellite

Any artificial object that orbits an astronomical object in space is called an artificial satellite.

The Space Age began on 4 October 1957, when the first artificial satellite, Sputnik I, was placed in orbit by the Soviet Union.

The first American satellite, Explorer, was launched on 31 January 1958.

Today, hundreds of artificial satellites circle the Earth, providing communication links, weather observations, navigational aids, military information gathering and other functions.

Most satellites are lifted into orbit by rockets, but the United States has also placed satellites in orbit from the space shuttle.

Satellites are usually powered by solar cells with batteries to provide back-up when the satellite is in shadow.

• IT'S FACT •

- The first artificial satellite to be placed in orbit was Sputnik 1, launched on October 4, 1957, by the Soviet Union.3

Personal computer

A computer is an electronic device that converts data into information. A personal computer is a type of micro computer i.e., a small digital computer that uses only one microprocessor.

A microprocessor is a semiconductor chip that contains all the arithmetic, logic, and control circuitry needed to perform the functions of a computer's central processing unit.

Computer

Personal computers generally are low-cost machines that can perform most of the functions of larger computers but use software oriented toward easy, single-user applications.

A typical personal computer assemblage consists of a central processing unit ; primary, or internal, memory, consisting of hard magnetic disks and a disk drive; various input / output devices, including a display screen, keyboard and mouse, modem, and printer; and secondary, or external, memory, usually in the form of floppy disks or CD-ROMs.

Computers small and inexpensive enough to be purchased by individuals for using in their homes first became feasible in the 1970s, when large scale integration made it possible to construct a sufficiently powerful microprocessor on a single semiconductor chip. The use of personal computers continued to multiply as the machines became more powerful and their application software proliferated. By 1997 about 40 percent of all households in the United States owned a personal computer.

Genetics

On Feb. 28, 1953, Francis Crick and James Watson announced "we had found the secret of life." That morning, Watson and Crick had figured out the structure of deoxyribonucleic acid, DNA. And that structure a "double helix" that can "unzip" to make copies of itself confirmed suspicions that DNA carries life's hereditary information.

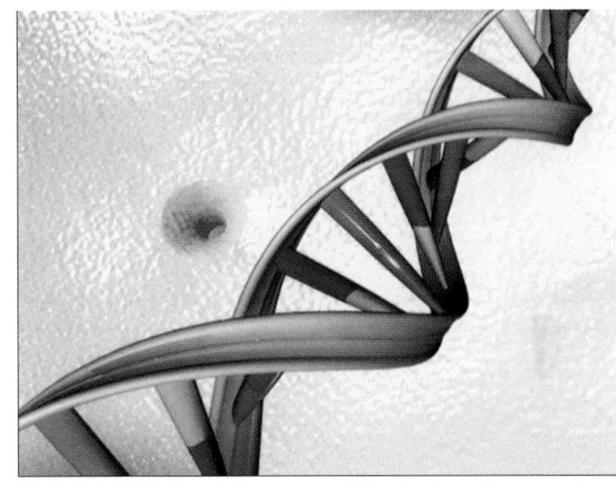

The double helix in DNA consists of two right-handed chains that are coiled about the same axis.

Crick and Watson used the results from previous studies and X-ray diffraction data from Maurice Wilkins and Rosalind Franklin to help them determine DNA's molecular structure. By 1953 they had built a model which incorporated all known features of DNA, and proposed the double helix structure which is commonly referred to as the Watson-Crick model of DNA. A new understanding of heredity and hereditary disease was possible once the structure of DNA was determined.

Modern biotechnology also has its basis in the structural knowledge of DNA in this case the scientist's ability to modify the DNA of host cells that will then produce a desired product, for example, insulin.

In 1962, James Watson (1928), Francis Crick (1916–2004), and Maurice Wilkins (1916–2004) jointly received the Nobel Prize in medicine or physiology for their determination in 1953 of the structure of deoxyribonucleic acid (DNA). Because the Nobel Prize can be awarded only to the living, Wilkins's colleague Rosalind Franklin (1920–1958), who died from cancer at the age of thirty-seven, could not be honored.

Motion picture

Auguste and Louis Lumière are credited with the world's first public film screening on December 28, 1895. The showing of approximately ten short films lasting only twenty minutes in total was held in the basement lounge of the Grand Cafe on the Boulevard des Capucines in Paris and was the very first public demonstration of their device they called the cinematograph which effectively functioned as camera, projector and printer all in one.

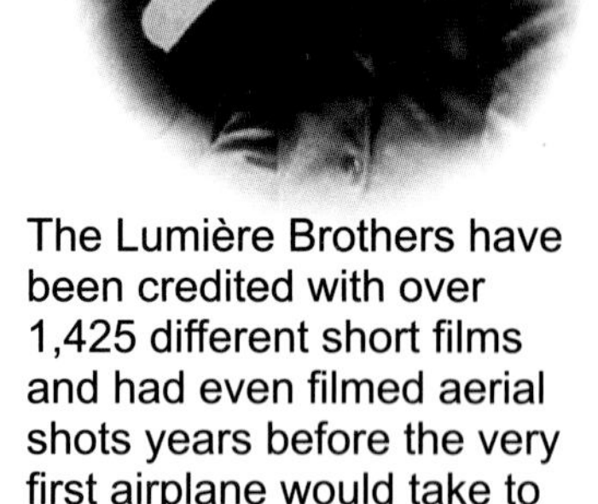

The Lumière Brothers have been credited with over 1,425 different short films and had even filmed aerial shots years before the very first airplane would take to the skies.

Antoine Lumière (the father of Auguste and Louis) considered the potential of motion pictures when he watched a demonstration of Edison's Kinetoscope in Paris. He was very impressed. So he returned home and described what he saw to his sons, but he also added, "You can do better. Try to get that image out of the box."

Following their father's advice, Auguste and Louis began work on creating their own camera. Within a matter of months, the Lumières had patented their own device, then nameless, for "obtaining and viewing chronophotographic prints."

Their film sequence of a train pulling into the station reportedly had audiences screaming and ducking for cover as they believed that the train itself was about to plow into the theater.

The Lumières soon opened a theater for exhibiting their films. Audiences were enthralled. Soon the Lumières trained additional cameramen and sent them on missions around the world.

Microscope

Microscope is an instrument that produces enlarged images of small objects, allowing them to be viewed at a scale convenient for examination and analysis.

The image may be formed by optical, acoustic, or electronic means, and it is received by direct imaging, electronic processing, or a combination of these methods. The microscope may be static, in which the object is viewed directly, or dynamic in which the image is built up by successive scans of the object.

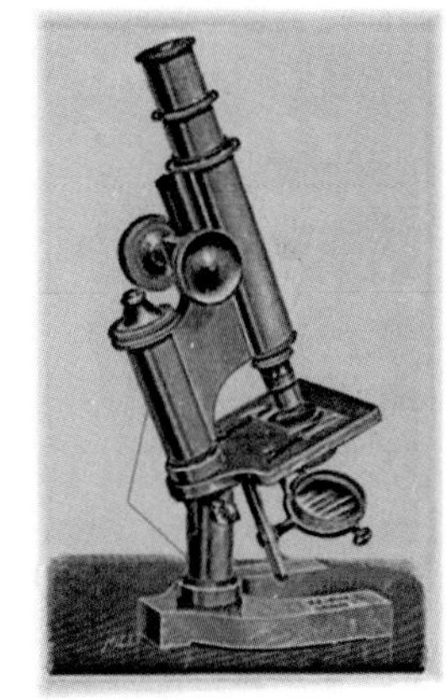

Microscope

The magnifying power of a microscope is an expression of the number of times the object being examined appears to be enlarged.

Magnifying power is a dimensionless ratio. The resolution of a microscope is a measure of the size of the smallest detail on the object that can be observed. Resolution is expressed in linear units, usually millimetres.

The most familiar type of microscope is the optical, or light, microscope, in which lenses are used to form the image. Optical microscopes can be simple, consisting of a single lens, or compound, consisting of several optical components in tandem.

Special microscopes, such as acoustic microscopes or scanning tunneling microscopes, use other physical effects, further extending the range of objects that can be viewed. Indeed, with a scanning tunneling microscope, even individual molecules and atoms can be seen.

Heart transplant

Heart transplatation is a medical procedure involving the removal of a diseased heart from a patient with heart muscles damaged beyond surgical repair and its replacement with a sound heart, usually from a person who has just died.

The first heart transplant was carried out by Dr. Christian Barnard.

He was born in South Africa in 1922. He worked as a surgeon at a hospital in Cape Town. After further training in America, he became a leading heart surgeon.

In December 1967, he transplanted the heart of a 59 year old man. This was the first operation of its kind and made Barnard a household name worldwide.

Barnard had demonstrated that heart transplants were possible. Even though many of his patients died soon after their operation, he had taken the first steps into a new form of surgery which is now routined in medical practice. In 1974, Christian Barnard carried out the first double heart transplant.

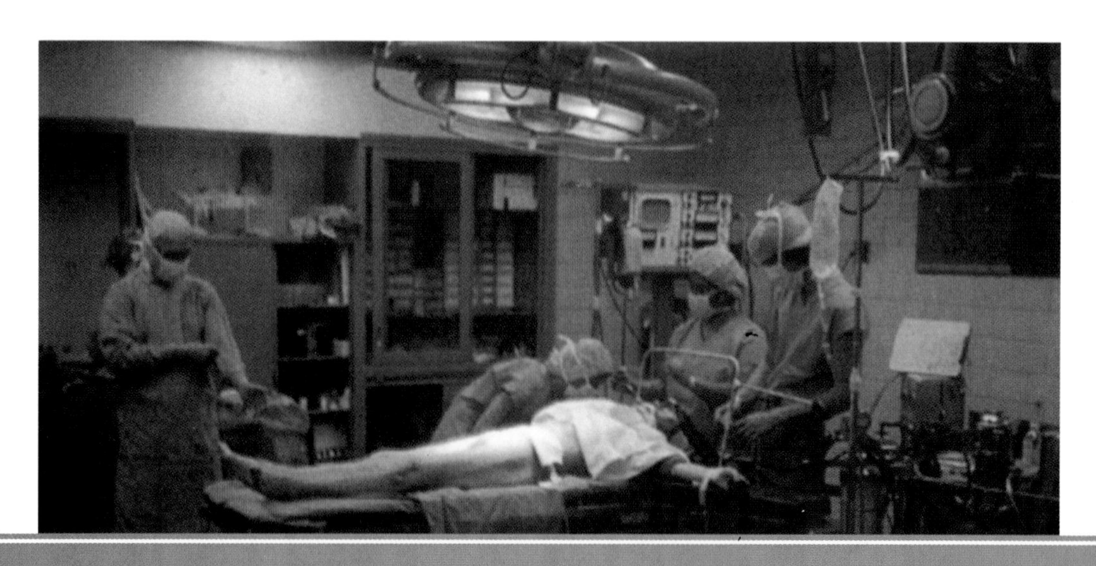

TIMELINE

Timeline

2, 500, 000 years ago the first tools are used.
1,000, 000 years ago people learn to use fire.
200, 000 years ago stone hand axes are used.

5000 BC : First forms of writing appear.
4000 BC : Wheel is invented.
1400 BC : Glass is made in Egypt and Mesopotamia.
430 BC : An optical telegraph is used in greece.
140 BC : Paper is made in China and used as a packing material.
AD 105 : Lun invents paper that can be used for writing.
AD 880 : Paper money is used in China.
1150 : Chinese make the first rockets.
1280 : Spectacles (glasses).
1443 : Guttenberg invents the printing press and prints the Bible
1450 : Johann Gutenberg invents printing with movable type.
1509 : First watch invented in Germany.
1540 : Artificial limbs.
1590 : Zacharias Janssen invents the compound microscope.
1608 : Hans Lippershey invents the telescope.
1654 : The grand Duke of Tuscany invents the sealed liquid thermometer.
1714 : The mercury thermometer
1742 : Anders Celsius invents the centigrade scale of temperature.
1760 : Benjamin Franklin invents the lighting rod.
1765 : James Watt redesigns Newcomen's steam engine making it six times as effective.

1783 : The first hot-air balloon invented by the Montgolfier brothers.

1784 : Benjamin Franklin invents bifocal lenses.

1792 : Claude Chappe invents the optical telegraph.

1792 : The ambulance Invented.

1796 : Vaccination Invented.

1808 : Humphrey Davy develops the first electric powered lamp light.

1819 : R.T.H. Laennec invents the stethoscope.

1821 : Michael Faraday invents the electric motor.

1822 : Charles Babbage develops his Differential Engine.

1822 : Joseph Nicephare Niepce produces the first Photograph.

1832 : Charles Babbage invents the first computer, his Analytical Engine.

1835 : Telegraph system invented in USA

1837 : Samuel Morse patents his telegraph using a dot/dash code.

1846 : Anaesthesia Invented.

1853 : The syringe Invented.

1865 : Antiseptic Treatments Invented.

1867 : Typewriter Invented.

1868 : George Leclanche invents the dry cell battery.

1876 : Alexander Graham Bell invents the telephone.

1876 : Karl Paul Gottfried von Linde builds the first practical refrigerator.

1879 : Joseph Swan and Thomas Alva Edison roduce the first practical electric light bulbs.

1885	:	Karl Benz invents the petrol-driven car.
1885	:	Anti-rabies vaccination Invented.
1887	:	Contact lenses Invented.
1890	:	Telephone wires are put up in New York.
1895	:	Guglielmo Marconi invents Radio.
1895	:	Auguste and Louis Lumiere invent the cinematograph.
1895	:	X-rays Invented by Wilhelm Conrad.
1895	:	First human glider flown by Otto Lilienthal.
1899	:	The first successful airship, the Zeppelin, invented by Ferdinand von Zeppelin.
1903	:	The first airplane flown by the wright brothers (first powered flight).
1908	:	Model T ford car first made.
1913	:	Portable record player invented.
1915	:	Paul Lawgiver invents sonar.
1922	:	The BBC (British Broadcasting Corporation) is formed.
1925	:	Vladimir Zworykin patents a colour television system.
1926	:	The Jazz Singer, the first talking motion picture is released.
1926	:	John Logie Baird produces television images.
1927	:	'The Jazz Singer' is the first film with sound.
1928	:	Antibiotics Invented.
1930	:	Frank Whittle patents the jet engine.
1936	:	The BBC starts the world's first regular television service
1938	:	Lazlo Biro invents the ballpoint pen.
1940	:	Modern helicopters invented by Igor Sirkorsky.

1942 : First nuclear reactor build.
1943 : Alan Turing develops colossus, the first electronic calculating machine.
1945 : The first atom bomb is detonated.
1945 : Microwave oven invented
1947 : First supersonic (faster than the speed of sound) flight.
1948 : Edison invents a camera and film that develops pictures inside the camera.
1948 : William Shockley invents the transistor.
1950 : Ultrasound Machine Invented.
1956 : Video recorder invented.
1957 : Sputnik I, the first artificial satellite, is launched.
1962 : Telstar satellite sends an image across the earth.
1965 : Vietnam War is shown on television.
1967 : The first heart transplant was carried out by Dr. Christian Barnard.
1967 : First successful supersonic passenger jet (Concorde).
1969 : First manned mission to the Moon (Apollo 11)
1970 : Early version of the Internet is developed.
1971 : Computer microprocessor is pioneered.
1972 : Pocket Calculator invented.
1981 : Laptop computer invented.
1981 : Space shuttle launched.
1982 : Compact Disk players are introduced.
1983 : Early mobile phones.
1983 : The computer mouse is introduced.
1995 : Introduction of Windows 95 makes computers and internet popular.

CHAPTER FIVE

HISTORY

LONG LONG AGO

ANCIENT WORLD

THE MIDDLE AGES

LONG LONG

AGO

History and Archaeology

The word history has many meanings. It is an account of past events in sequence of time. It is the study of events, their causes and results, and it is all that is preserved or remembered about the past.

Archaeology is the study of people of the past by the scientific analysis of the things that have been left behind by these people. People who study history are called historians and archaeologists.

These people study objects (artefacts), features (buildings) and scofacts (seeds or animal bones). They gather information by digging the soils and excavate the possessions and the dead remains of our forefathers. Study of past helps us to understand the future of our civilization.

The famous idol of king Tutankhamun.

Anexcavation site

The body of a Danish woman buried in AD 95. Her body was preserved from decay by being in a peat bog.

Cave paintings found by archaeologists.

Our forefathers

We all know that human beings emerged from the apes some five million years ago. The early humans were more ape-like than humans. They lived in groups and obtained their food by wandering in the forests, slowly and gradually, they started walking in an upright posture.

Earlier, they used crude stone tools but gradually they shifted to the finer tools. They discovered fire and started living in caves or thatched huts. With the passing of time, they devised farming and began to settle down in communities. That was the beginning of the first civilization.

Living in caves made early man protected. They soon learned about fire and its benefits.

The development of humans from ape-like creature.

Basic needs

The first people lived by gathering fruits, berries, roots and hunting wild animals. They lived in caves and in huts made from branches and mammoth bones. Earlier, they used to eat raw food. But the discovery of fire brought cooking in their lives.

The early humans were no less creative than us. They used to make little clay models of women and of animals. They also painted pictures of animals deep inside the caves. Cave art: Early artists painted pictures of their animals and the scenes they used to see around them. As towns and cities grew, temples and important buildings were decorated with carvings and paintings.

Village life

Slowly and gradually, the humans started domesticating wild animals and kept them in herds. Animals provided them with meat, milk and wool. Taming of animals simplified their lives to a great extent. They were no longer required to wander in search of food. They started settling in villages.

Their lives changed with the development of agriculture. People discovered that certain plants could be grown or cultivated to provide crops. Farming and civilizations grew up in several parts of the world, including China, Africa and Central America. The earliest farmers settled around 10,000 years ago, in what is often called the fertile crescent. This was an area of land which was watered by the Tigris, Euphrates and the Nile rivers.

An artist's impression of a scene from an early human settlement in a fertile crescent.

ANCIENT

WORLD

Sumerians and Babylonians

Sumerians were the first people to settle in Mesopotamia more than 7000 years ago. Their civilization consisted of a number of cities that existed as independent nations. The Sumerians devised the first known writing system. They used to write on clay tablets. Sumerians were skilled craftsmen. Their public buildings and royal graves were finely built.

After the end of Sumerian domination, Babylonians came into being. They began to dominate southern Mesopotamia under their sixth ruler, Hammurabi. He was a very efficient ruler and had well-trained armies. Babylonians were great mathematicians. They devised a system of counting based on number 60.

Some of the wedge-shaped ('cuneiform') characters in the Sumerian writing system looked like objects, others were symbols.

Ishtar was the goddess of war to the Assyrians, but a mother-goddess to the Babylonians.

A reconstruction of the Ziggurat at Ur. On the top was the temple, where the king (who was also the high priest) performed religious rites and sacrifices. The Ziggurat was built of sun-baked clay bricks.

The new year festival was celebrated by passing through the northern entrance to Babylon. The gate was decorated with blue glazed tiles, decorated with yellow and white figures of bulls and dragons.

Ancient Egypt

The fertile Nile valley was an ideal place for the emergence of Egyptian civilization. Every year, the flood in the river Nile used to leave behind fertile sediments on the lands. So, the Egyptians decided to farm the land by storing the flood waters. This marked the beginning of agriculture in Egypt. Their main crops included wheat, barley and flax. They also used to make business transactions by a system called bartering. Normally, they exchanged gold, grains and papyrus sheets for silver, iron, horses, cedar wood and ivory.

Egyptians were famous for their art and architecture. They believed in life after death. They used to put the mummified bodies of their rulers in large pyramids. These pyramids are centres of tourist attraction even today.

The dead bodies of Pharaohs and nobles were embalmed so that they would 'live' forever by a process called mummification. The body was put inside a coffin like this one with a portrait painted on the outside.

The Great Sphinx is a mysterious rock sculpture, with a human head on the body of a lion.

Tutankhamun became the king of Egypt at the age of 9 and died when he was about 18. His tomb is one of the most attractive tombs around the Valley. More than 60 royal tombs are spread around the valley of the kings. Its four rooms contained more than 5,000 objects- from ostrich feathers and model ships to a throne and a gold death mask.

Cleopatra, the last queen of Egypt, was well-known for her beauty and intelligence. Two famous Romans, Julius Caesar and Mark Antony, fell in love with her.

The Hebrews

The tribe living in the area between Egypt and Mesopotamia comprised of Hebrews. They were wanderers and frequently moved from one place to another with their possessions. Finally, they settled to form the kingdom of Israel. Around 1020BC, the Israelites prospered under three great kings-Saul, David and Solomon. David united the tribes of Israel. Solomon was one of the wisest kings in history. His rule brought order and peace. Under his rule, Jerusalem became one of the richest cities of that time. After his death the kingdom split up as Israel and Judah both of which were captured by the Assyrians. From then on, the hebrews were called Jews.

The copy of an Egyptian wall-painting shows a group of Hebrews asking permission to enter Egypt.

Moses, the leader of the Hebrew people, received the two tablets from God. The stone tablets bear the Ten Commandments, as described in the Old Testament. They became the basis for Jewish law.

King Solomon

Solomon was the son of David, the greatest Israelite king who ruled from 1010 to 970 BC. David defeated the Philistines and enlarged the kingdom, making Jerusalem his capital city. Solomon saw to the building of the Temple in Jerusalem, the most sacred centre of the Jewish religion. After Solomon's death Israel split into two separate kingdoms.

Ancient India

Around 3000 BC a great civilization flourished around the river Indus, known as Indus valley civilization. Mohenjodaro and Harrappa were the two unique and largest cities of this civilization. This mighty civilization came to an end around 3100 years ago for unknown reason.

Archaeologists have found hundreds of artefacts during the excavation of MohenjoDaro. Many, such as this bronze figure of a dancing girl.

The Indian subcontinent was invaded by a group of people from Central Asia known as Aryans. Aryans lived in tribes but later they started settling down and became farmers. Aryans brought Sanskrit language with them. The ancient Vedas were also written in Sanskrit.

The Aryans introduced the caste system in India. Society was divided into four castes- Brahmins, Kshatriyas, Vaisyas and Shudras. Brahmins were the educated priests and scholars. Kshatriyas were the soldiers. Vaisyas were farmers and merchants. Shudras were the servants who were ranked below these three castes.

Prince Siddhartha who lived about 2500 years ago became known as the Enlightened One or Buddha. Buddhism is now one of the world's principal faiths.

Aryans Caste System

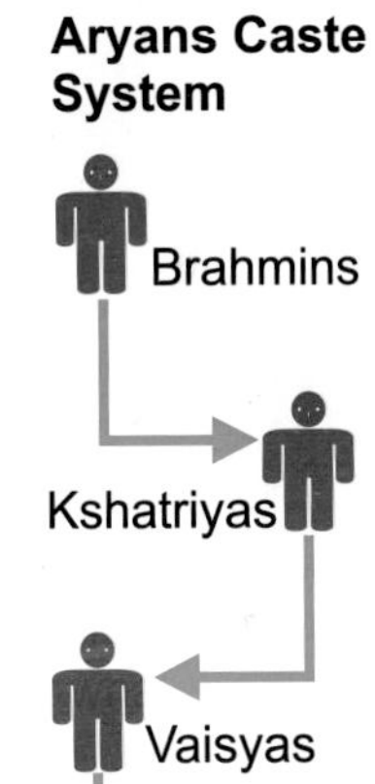

The artist's impression of the daily life in the city of mohenjodaro.

Seals and Writing

More than 1200 seals like this have been found in Mohenjodaro. They were used by merchants to stamp, bales of goods. No one has yet worked out what the writing on them means.

Ancient Greece

Greece is the land of mountains. It is famous for its beautiful coastlines. The inmates of ancient Greece were great sailors and scholars. Two of the world's greatest philosophers, Socrates and his pupil Plato, came from Athens the richest Greek city. Most of the rules of geometry and arithmetic were invented by Greek mathematicians, such as Euclid and Pythagora.

Alexander

The Greeks held competitions in sports, music and drama in honour of their gods. The most famous were the Olympic games held every four years at the sanctury of Zeus at Olympia.

Sculpted head of a Greek goddess. Some of the finest creations by Greek artists were the statues of gods and goddesses which were displayed inside temples.

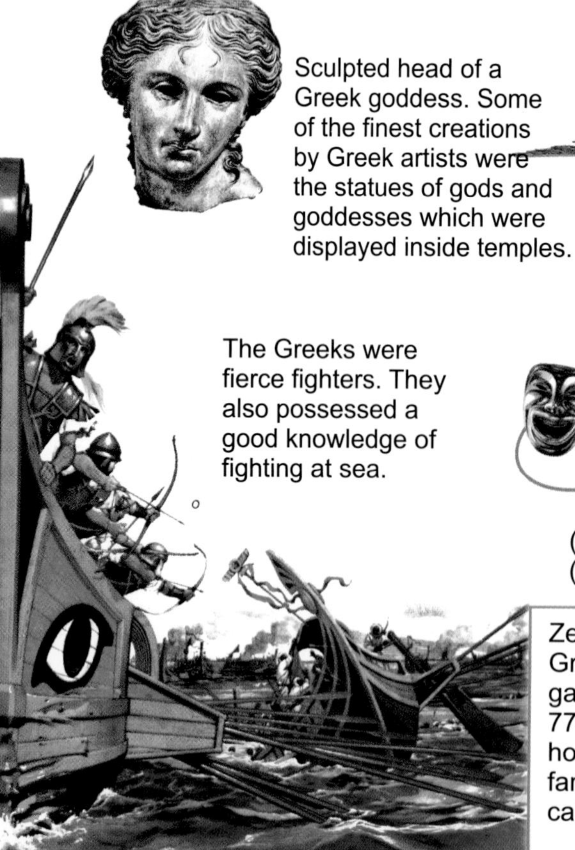

The Greeks were fierce fighters. They also possessed a good knowledge of fighting at sea.

Greek actors wore masks to show what kind of character (comic or tragic) they played. The finest play-writers were the Athenian dramatists Aeschylus, Sophocles, Euripides (who wrote tragedies) and Aristophanes (who wrote comedies.)

Zeus was the king of the Greek gods. The first Olympic games, which took place in 776 BC, were held in his honour. Zeus was head of a family of gods and goddesses called the Olympians.

Roman Empire

The city of Rome was founded in 753BC. According to the legends, Rome was founded by the twin grandsons of king Numitors, Romulus and Remus. The early Rome was ruled by Etruscan kings, of whom Homulus was the first.

Etruscans were greatly influenced by the Greeks. They adopted their alphabets, wore garments like the Greeks did and believed in Greek gods. Romans were great warriors. Their emperors had efficient armies. Soldiers were equipped with spears, shields, swords, body armours, helmets and leg guards.

A armed Roman Soldier

Dress of a wealthy Roman couple. The man wears a toga, or cloak, over a long shirt. The woman has a high waisted dress. They both wear leather sandals.

According to legend, Rome was founded by two brothers, Romulus and Remus. They were the twin grandsons of King Numitor. The king's wicked brother Amulius put the babies in a basket to float down the River Tiber to their deaths. The basket came to land, and the babies were suckled by a she-wolf who had heard the babies' cries. They were reared by a shepherd until one day they were reunited with their grandfather. They founded Rome, but quarreled and Remus was killed leaving Romulus to become the first king.

Julius Caesar was the most efficient Roman aristocrat. His year of birth is debated as he was claimed to be a descendant of God. He wanted to conquer vast territories to expand the Roman empire. His unmatched military power and capability of crushing the enemies soon made him the sole ruler of Rome for life. In 58 BC, he conquered part of northern Italy, Gaul, Germany and Britain. His popularity fetched him jealous rivals too. He was murdered by two Roman senators, Brutus and Cassius, in 44 BC.

Ancient China

The Chinese civilization emerged on the banks of three rivers- the Huang Ho (yellow river), the Chang Jiang (Yangtze) and the Xi Jiang (west river). According to the legends, Hsia was the first dynasty of China which came to power more than 4000 years ago.

Confucius –The Great Chinese teacher.

Emperor Wu Di (martial emperor) returns on a horse back to western Han capital.

Great wall of China was constructed during Qin dynasty.

Ancient Africa

The earliest human remains have been found in Africa, but still the continent's history is not much known. The first great African civilization apart from ancient Egypt, emerged in Nubia around 2000 BC. It was the kingdom of Kush. In 3BC, the capital of Kush shifted to Meroe which became an important centre of iron-working.

This wall paintings from an Egyptian tomb.

To smelt iron, the iron ore was put into an earthen furnace. Bellows were then used to raise its temperature so that the ore was turned into metal.

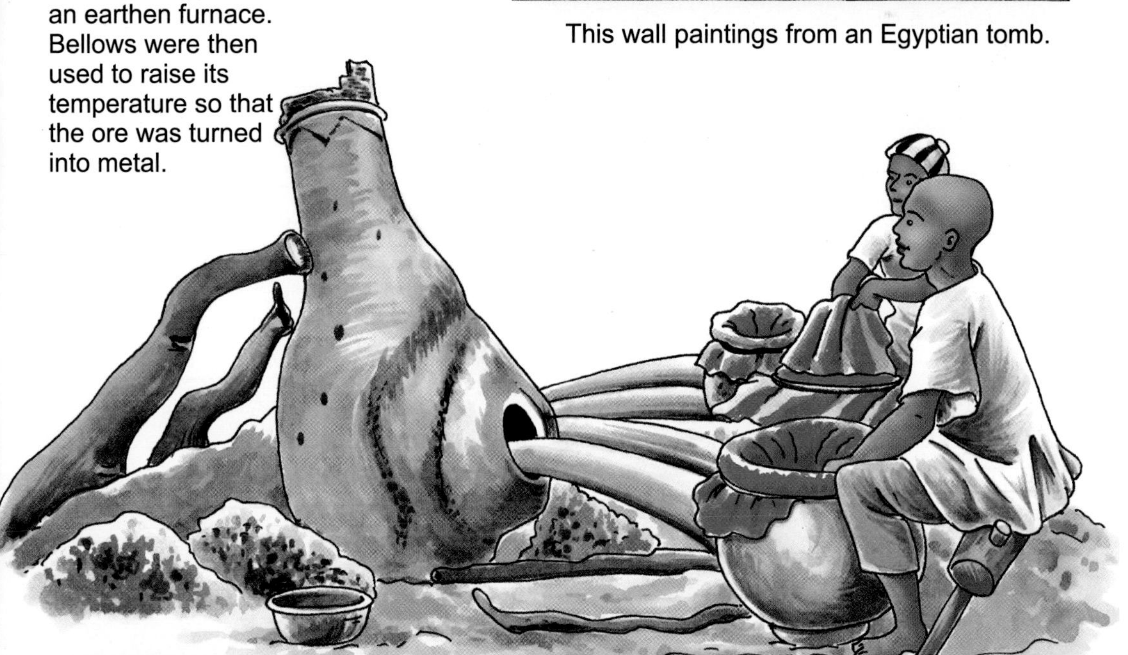

Beginning of trade

After the people started settling down in villages and communities, trade came into existence. Earlier, people used to make business transaction through barter system. In this system goods were exchanged for something of equal value. Goods traded included gold, wine, silk, pottery, grains, woollen clothes and furs. For centuries all these goods were bartered, but slowly tokens came into use.

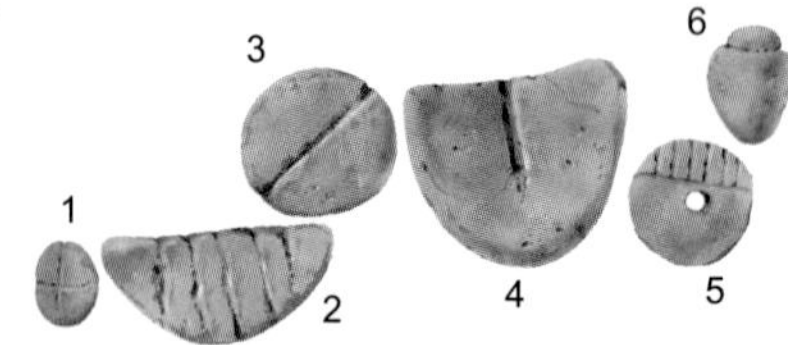

The Sumerians used clay tokens for trading as shown in this scene. It is thought that there was a different token for each commodity being traded. Of the tokens shown here 1 represents one sheep, 2 one metal ingot, 3 and 4 are unknown, 5 represents one ewe and 6 a jar of oil.

Archaeological studies have shown that, merchants used to keep records of what they traded by marking symbols on the clay tablets. Historians believe that these clay tablets mark the beginning of writing.

Owl coin
A silver four drachma 'owl' piece was the best-known coin in the ancient Greek world. Issued in Athens, it symbolized the owl eyed goddess, Athena.

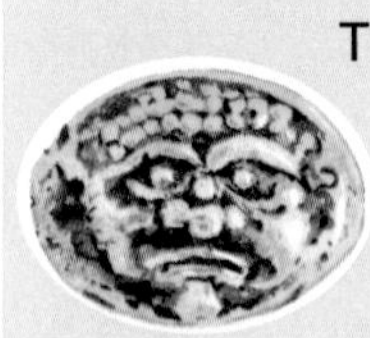

The first coins were made in Anatolia, Turkey, from electrum, a mixture of gold and silver. The face stamp guaranteed its weight.

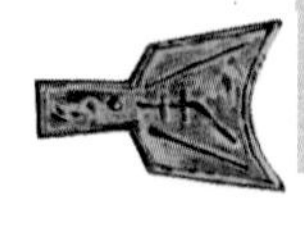

Early Chinese money was shaped like a spade.

It is believed that silk was discovered in about 2690 BC by the Empress Hsi-Ling Shi, the wife of the legendary 'yellow Emperor', Huang Ti. The empress found that the silkworms ate the leaves of mulberry trees so she had groves of mulberries planted to feed the insects. Because the empress cultivated silkworms, the ladies of her court did so too. Silk was so valuable that for centuries, it was used as a form of money. It remained a closely kept secret by the Chinese for about 3000 years.

The Chinese particularly valued jade and carved a lot of jewellery from it, like this open ring.

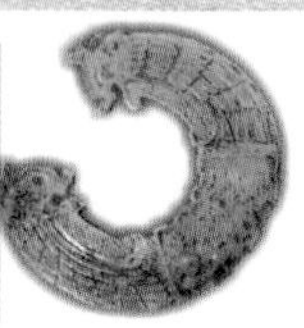

Communication of trade

Trade gave birth to communication. Initially, people used to keep the records of their trade by writing down the information. The earliest writings were found in Mesopotamia where Sumerians drew tiny pictures on clay tablets. Slowly, these pictures were replaced by wedge-shaped patterns.

After that, the Egyptians invented a writing system of their own, called nieroglyphics. They wrote on sheets of papyrus, made from the papyrus reeds.

Chinese devised a system of writing which included over 2000 different characters. They used to write on oracle bones.

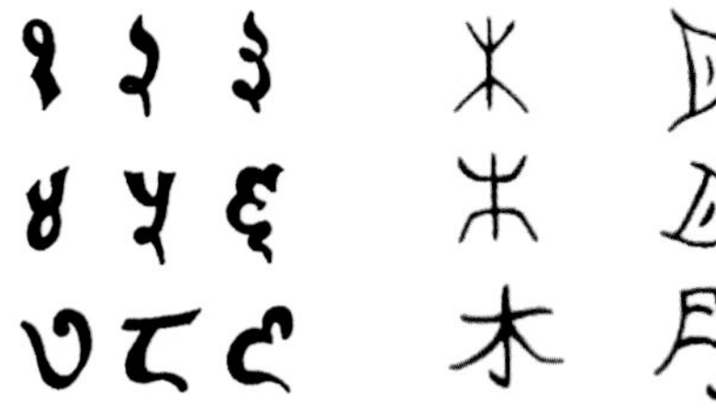

around 1500 BC

before 216 BC

after AD 200

Arab numerals tree moon bird

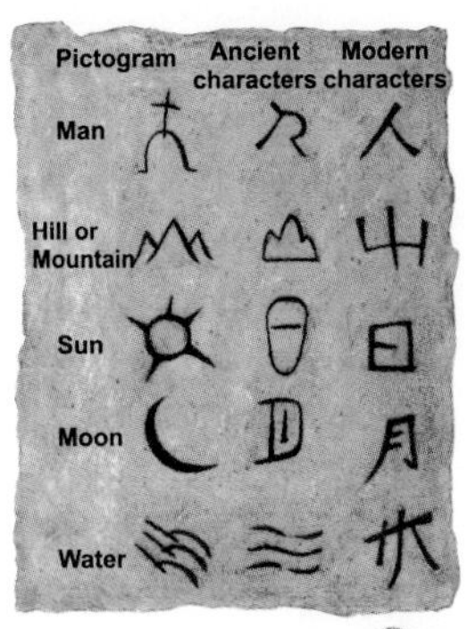

There was more than one Chinese language, but everyone who could read could understand Chinese writing. This was because each symbol stood for an object, not a sound.

The Shang kings were superstitious. They consulted 'oracle bones' before making any important decision. A soothsayer would read the signs in animal bones cracked by heat and advise the king accordingly.

Scribe schools

In Ancient Egypt, only educated scribes could read and write. Boys who were trained to be scribes, laboriously wrote and copied each day. At first they wrote on useless objects such as broken pottery; when their work improved they were allowed to write on papyrus, a precious kind of paper. Girls wree educated at home, learning domestic skills from their mothers.

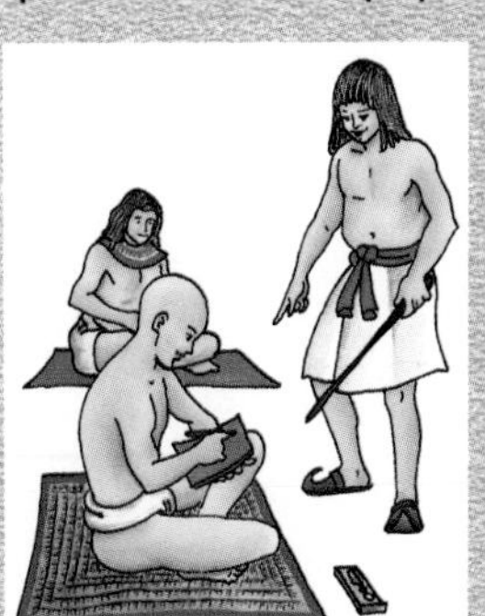

Religions

The first religions came into existence as an attempt by people to come to terms with things they could not explain. These things included birth, death, diseases etc. The first farmers worshipped nature gods, such as the Sun and the Moon, so that they could get good harvests. Sumerians worshipped nature gods.

Egyptians, believed in life after death. They buried mummified bodies of their Pharaohs along with boats, food, jewellery, clothes which they believed could help them in their journey to the other world.

Greeks worshipped many gods. They considered Zeus to be the mightiest god. Apart from Zeus, they also worshipped Appolo, Sarpedon, Poseidon etc.

Many Romans had a shrine of their gods inside their houses. This one is from a house in Heculaneum.

Sumerian legends contain many well known stories. The Great Flood was sent to punish men who had made the god angry. They warned one good man, Ut-napishtim, to build a boat. The flood destroyed everything on Earth except the boat. Ut-napishtim sent out birds to find land. Finally one bird did not return and Ut-napishtim and his family were saved.

People and culture

The settlement of people in towns and cities gave birth to big and mighty empires. By the 1st century, four great empires ruled the world. The Roman empire which covered Europe and North Africa was the most powerful one. China was under the Han dynasty. In the middle East, Sassanians held power. On the other hand, India was under the great Gupta empire.

All these empires had strong and wealthy governments. Traders acted as the catalysts between the empires and helped in the spread of ideas and knowledge. The empires were constantly threatened by the barbarians. They had to spend a lot on the maintenance of the armies. By 450 AD, these empires collapsed.

The Phoenicians were famous for the red-purple colour of their textiles. They used a dye extracted from molluscs. The name 'Phoenician' comes from a Greek word meaning red-purple.

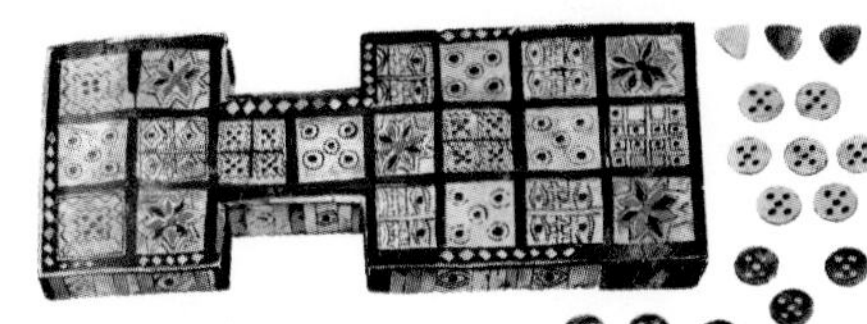

Game board

A gaming board, counters and dice dating from between 3000 and 2000 BC. Sadly the rules of the game have not survived.

The early Chinese people wore warlike clothes. These two are Shang warriors.

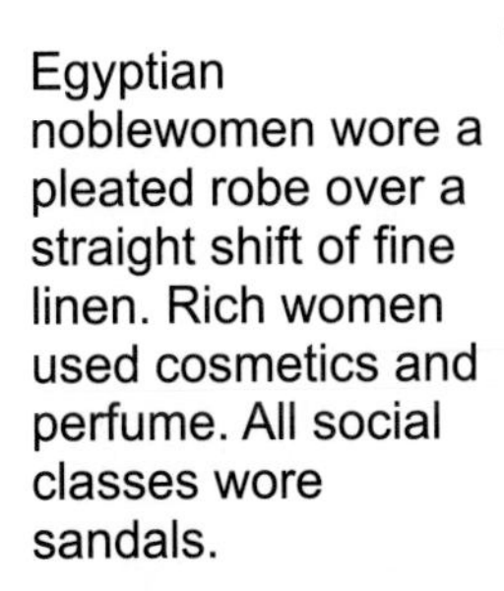

Egyptian noblewomen wore a pleated robe over a straight shift of fine linen. Rich women used cosmetics and perfume. All social classes wore sandals.

Much of our knowledge about the ancient Greeks comes from vases and vessels. They were decorated with scenes from daily life showing what the Greeks wore, how they lived and so on.

THE MIDDLE

AGES

Byzantine Empire

The Byzantine empire was a centre of learning, where the knowledge of ancient Greeks was merged with the novel teachings of the Christian church. At first, this empire controlled only a small part of land around the Aegean sea. Then under the emperor Justinian's reign, the empire was expanded to the eastern coast of the mediterraneans. The empire produced gold, grain, olives, silk and wine, and these were traded for goods like spices, precious stones, furs and ivory, from the far east and from Africa.

A 19th century print of the emperor Justinian and his influential wife Theodora. Through war and diplomacy, Justinian made Byzatium the greatest power in the eastern Mediterranean.

Byzantine traders used gold coins called bezants. These coins have been found across Asia as far as China and as far west as the British Isles.

This Byzantine mosaic is inside the church of San Vitale in Ravenna, Italy. Ravenna was briefly the Capital of the Byzantine empire. It shows Theodora, wife of the Emperor Justinian presenting a gift for the church to two bishops.

St Sophia, or the Church of Holy Wisdom, was built in Constantinople for Justinian between 532 and 537. It took over 10,000 people to construct it.

Chariots raced around the track in the Hippodrome. Entrance was free (the emperors knew that the races kept the mob amused). As well as thrilling and often dangerous races, there were animal fights, dancing girls and circus acts to entertain the huge crowds.

The Vikings

Vikings were the people who ventured from their homelands of Norway, Denmark and Sweden in search of treasure and better farmland. They were skilled metalworkers. They also made excellent wooden ships which could easily sail up rivers and rough seas. Vikings used to attack and plunder coastal towns.

But all viking were not raiders. Some of them were wandering farmers, who always looked for new lands. Many of them settled in parts of Britain, France, Iceland, Greenland and North America.

Swords were highly valued by the Vikings. They often decorated them with gold and silver.

Viking soldiers often carried a spear in battle. It was made of ash wood and had an iron head.

A Viking man and woman in everyday clothes. These were practical, rather than fashionable. Their silver jewellery was sometimes cut up and used as money.

Odin was the chief of the Viking gods. Legend says that he lost his eye to gain knowledge in payment for a drink at the well of knowledge. Tales also say he opened two ravens, Thought and Memory. He sent them out daily to report on happening in the World.

Viking warriors sailed in longships which often had a dragon's head at the front. Although the Vikings usually fought in small groups they were fearless fighters both at sea and on land.

The Franks and Charlemagne

Charlemagne was a very powerful ruler of Western Europe. He was a frank. The franks were people who invaded the Roman Empire when it collapsed in the 5th century and then settled in Northern France. Charlemagne was a great warrior. His aim was to convert the inhabitants to Christianity. To achieve this goal, Charlemagne tortured those who opposed him. He was a ruthless ruler. He invaded and conquered northern Italy. He fought with the people of Hungary and the Saxons in Germany. He also invaded Spain. At the time of his death, he was the most powerful ruler in Europe.

Under Charlemagne, the Frankish empire expanded greatly, taking in neighbouring Bavaria and Lombardy. The Franks finally conquered Saxony after around 30 years of bitter fighting.

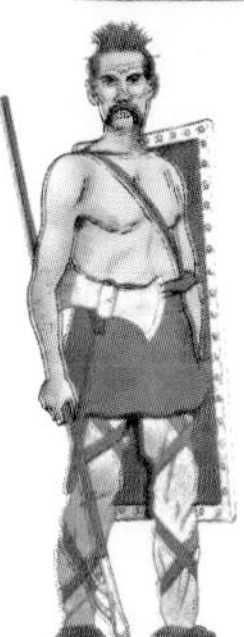

A 6th century Frankish warrior carried a number of weapons into battle. These included a battle-axe and an angon, a barbed spear used for throwing or stabbing.

Charlemagne was a great military leader and his kingdom became the most powerful in Europe. He also tried to improve the conditions of his subjects.

The horn of Roland, a Frankish hero killed at the battle of Roncesvalles in AD 778.

The Franks were farmers. Frankish peasants ploughed the field on estates, called manors, which belonged to nobles or lords. They did this with the help of wheeled ploughs.

Knights

The Knights were the soldiers who served the lords in the wartime. But knighthood was not just about fighting. A knight was expected to be just and honourable as well as brave, to help the weak and protect the poor. They protected the peasants who lived and worked in the farms, in return they got service charges and a fixed share of harvest. They were given continuous training. Sometimes tournaments were organised to test their skills. In such tournaments, they used to compete with each other.

The knights were given proper training ever since their childhood. They were taught to ride and shoot at the age of 6. They excelled in fighting by the age of 14 and at 16, they used to become proper knights.

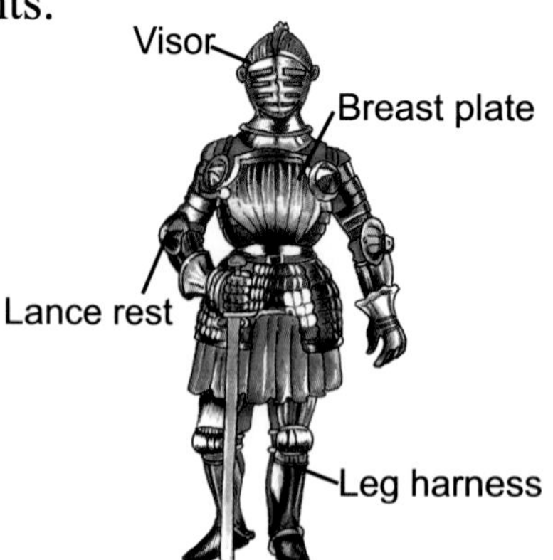

Similar dress code often made it difficult for the knights to recognize each other. They were not supposed to kill the men on their own side. To make this easier they painted their shields with simple patterns. Soon all the men in the same army used the same pattern.

Two orders of knights active during the Crusades were the Knights Templar(left) and the Knights of St John (right), also known as Hospitallers because they set up a hospital for pilgrims in Jerusalem. Their long robes, or surcoats, kept the hot sun off their armour.

The troubadour tradition of poetry and music first started in the 11th century in southern France. These minstrels sang songs of love, chivalry and religion.

American civilization

In the northern and southern parts of America, a number of civilizations emerged. The most powerful civilization was the Maya which lasted over 700 years. The Mayans lived in well organized cities with their own rulers. The Maya cities were huge and magnificent. They had spectacular stone pyramid temples. All the cities had a sacred centre. The largest city was Tikal.

The Mayans wrote in hieroglyphs (picture writing). This type of writing was found on huge stone monuments and in books they made from bark paper.

The figures found in Mayan ruins often show richly dressed people such as this priest wearing an ornate headdress.

A Mayan priest wore an elaborate feathered headdress. The Maya worshipped many gods. Priests led ceremonies in the pyramid-temples. Sacrificial offerings were made to please the gods, who included the Jaguar.

The fine stone bowl carved in the form of an animal was the work of a Chavin sculptor.

The Mayans played a ball game which had religious importance for them. In vast courts, they bounced a solid ball backwards and forwards using hips, thighs and elbows, aiming for a hoop in the side wall.

Rise of Islam

In 610, an Arab merchant founded a new religion called Islam. Its followers were called Muslims. They believed that God has sent many prophets or teachers, including Moses and Jesus Christ, but Muhammad was the greatest of all.

Muslims believe in one God, Allah. Wherever they went, they spread their religion.

Muslims were great scientists, artists and astronomers. Hence, the cities governed by the Muslims used to be extremely magnificent. Today, Islam covers the largest part of the world after Christianity.

The old mosque at Mecca. Muhammad used to pray in the courtyard of his home. As a result, Islamic mosques have an open space where people gather five times a day to pray.

The crescent moon and star became important symbols in Islam, and were often incorporated into architecture and other designs. The Islamic year calendar is based on the cycles of the Moon.

The stories for The Thousand and One Nights came from many different countries, including India, Syria and Egypt.

Arab traders carried cargo and passengers across the Indian Ocean in ships called dhows. They also spread Islamic culture and ideas.

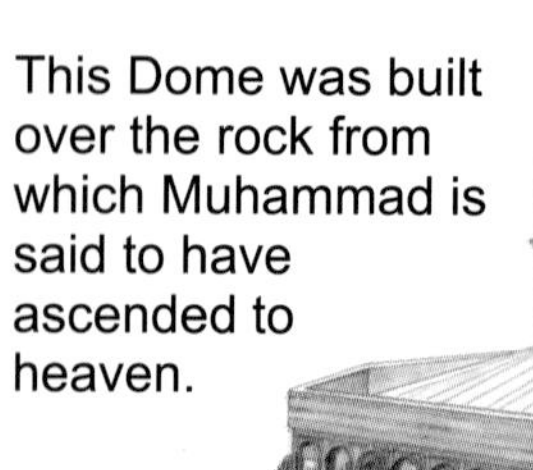

This Dome was built over the rock from which Muhammad is said to have ascended to heaven.

Mughals of India

India was governed by Mughal empire around five centuries ago. Babur founded the Mughal empire when he invaded northern India from Afghanistan in 1526. After the death of Babur, Humayun ascended the throne who could not hold it. In 1540, he was chased out of India to Persia. However in 1555, he returned, regained his empire but before he could achieve his goal, he died in an accident.

After this, his son, Akbar became emperor and ruled until his death in 1605. Akbar was the greatest Mughal emperor. He had a group of nine gems in his court which comprised of persons excelling in various different fields. Though he was a Muslim, he had a soft corner for the Hindus. He had allowed the Hindus to worship their gods. He himself married a Hindu princess to set an example.

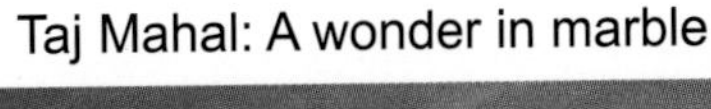

Taj Mahal: A wonder in marble

China then

Apart from Europe, other empires also were developing. The ancient Chinese emperors built a great empire in China for a long time. At that time, China was the world's most sophisticated, technologically advanced country.

A paper maker at work.

Kublai Khan, the new Mongol emperor shifted his capital to Beijing. Chinese silks, porcelain and other luxuries surprised the traders all over the world.

China will always be remembered for its invention of fine postal system and its paper currency. Chinese discovered various technologies such as paper-making. Other inventions include magnetic compass and gunpowder rockets.

A canon from the 14th century. It is made of strips of iron, held together with hoops. The arrival of gunpowder from China in the 13th century completely changed warfare and weapons.

The Chinese silk industries employed thousands of workers, especially women, to weave silk on looms.

The Mongol Empire

The Mongols were the nomads who lived on the plains of central Asia. The greatest Mongolian king was chief Temijin who brought all the tribes under his rule. He was also called Genghis Khan which meant lord of all.

Mongolians were great warriors. They continued their attacks and invasions even after the death of Genghis Khan. Enemies feared their speed and ferocity. After victory, they slaughtered people and plundered treasure.

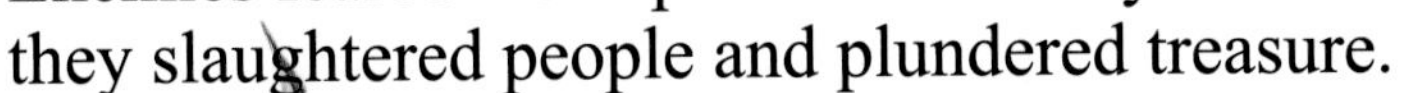

In battles, the Mongolian warriors wore helmets made of iron or hard leather. Their armour was made of iron plates linked together by strong leather things.

Genghis Khan was a ruthless warrior. He was known for destroying entire cities and their populations during his conquests. Yet he succeeded in keeping the peace across his vast empire.

The ancient Persian game of polo, played there since the 6th century BC, was adopted by the Mongolians because it helped to give their warriors the excellent skills in horsemanship necessary for fighting battles.

The Mongolians lived on the flat, grassy steppes of Asia, wandering with their herds of sheep, goats and cattle. They carried their tent like homes, called yurts, around with them.

Shoguns and Samurais

Shoguns ruled Japan as hereditary-military dictators from 1192 to 1868. Shoguns were members of a warrior class, called Samurai. Samurais were always prepared to fight to the death for their daimyos (overlords), to whom they swore undying loyalty.

Like the medieval knights in Europe, Samurai believed in the values of truth and honors. They committed suicide in the case of losing their honour.

A Samurai's chief weapons were a bow of boxwood or bamboo and a single edged sword. Samurai were trained from childhood and followed a strict code called Bushido. Battles were almost ceremonial, with a series of individual duels accompanied by flag signals, drums and gongs.

A Samurai's chief weapons were a bow of boxwood or bamboo and a single edged sword. Samurai were trained from childhood and followed a strict code called Bushido (warrior's way).

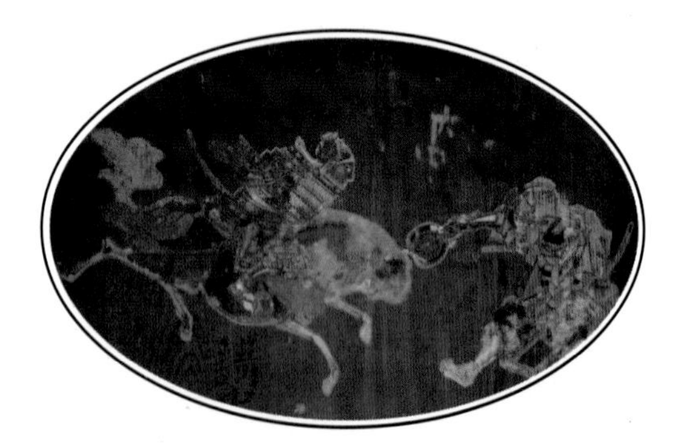

A japanese Samurai warrior on horseback was a frightening sight. Samurai armour was made of enamelled metal links or very thick strips of leather, which made it flexible. They fought with bows and arrows and with long curved swords. A Samurai's sword was his most treasured possession. It had a razor sharp edge for cutting but a soft iron core enabling it to withstand many blows.

African Kingdoms

During the 17th century, Africa was a patchwork of different people, kingdoms and empires. In west African coast, the new kingdom of Dahomey was set up by king Akaba in 1625. In 1689, Osei Tutu founded the powerful Asante empire and built its Capital at Kumasi. It grew wealthy from trade, especially cola nuts and gold and by selling slaves.

Africa provided slaves needed to work for the rapidly growing industries in the Americas. Millions were shipped across the Atlantic.

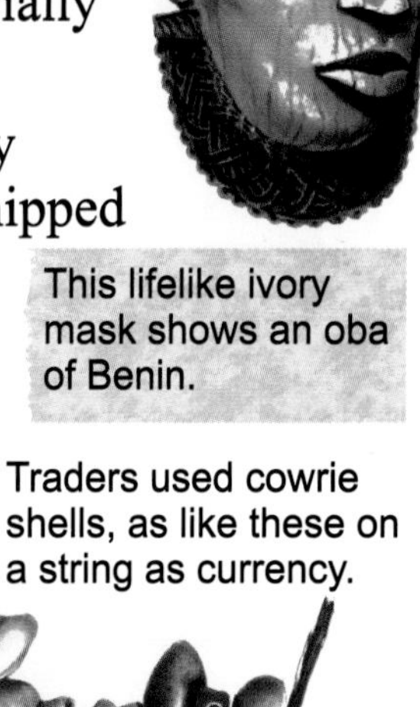

This lifelike ivory mask shows an oba of Benin.

Traders used cowrie shells, as like these on a string as currency.

The craftsmen of Africa were skilled in metalworking.

Great Zimbabwe

One of the greatest African mysteries was the walled city of Great Zimbabwe, after which modern Zimbabwe is. named. The.. massive stone. ruins were built of granite blocks from the 11th to the 14th centuries, but.. nobody knows why or by whom. Great Zimbabwe appeared to have been a centre for religion and the gold trade.

Wars and weapons

Viking Warrior

Wars and conquests were the primary factors responsible for the creation of the great empires. In order to maintain themselves in power, the kings and emperors maintained well-equipped armies. Cavalry and elephants were widely used. In the Greek empires, the pike was the main weapon. During the Roman times, sword was considered to be the most efficient weapon.

There used to be two types of battles-land and naval. Land warfare had two main forms. In open warfare, the two sides faced each other and in siege warfare, the enemy town was surrounded until the walls were breached. In naval battles, the ships first tried to subdue each other and then pulled alongside.

Mongol warriors fought on horseback. They controlled their horses with their feet, leaving their hands free to shoot arrows and hurl spears.

Viking warriors sailed in long ships which often had a dragon's head at the front. Althought the Vikings usually fought in small groups, they were fearless fighters both at sea and on land.

Soldiers fought with a long bow, primitive canon, and crossbow.

Buildings and art

Art and architecture reached its zenith during this time. The art was used for religious purposes. Byzantine churches were decorated with mosaics and with holy pictures called icons. Muslims concentrated on calligraphy, while the Germanic people showed their skills in making gold and silver jewellery.

The Chinese made pottery and porcelain. Just like art, architecture too flourished throughout the world. Europeans liked to build fine castles of wood and stone. The Roman houses had a solid timber frame and their walls were made of wattle and daub. Muslims built their mosques and buildings as light and airy as possible.

A sanctuary knocker on an abbey door was so called, because criminals could find temporary refuge there.

This statue of Buddha was found at Helgo in Sweden.

Most of the Slav states followed the Eastern Orthodox religion. Churches and homes were decorated with religious paintings, called icons.

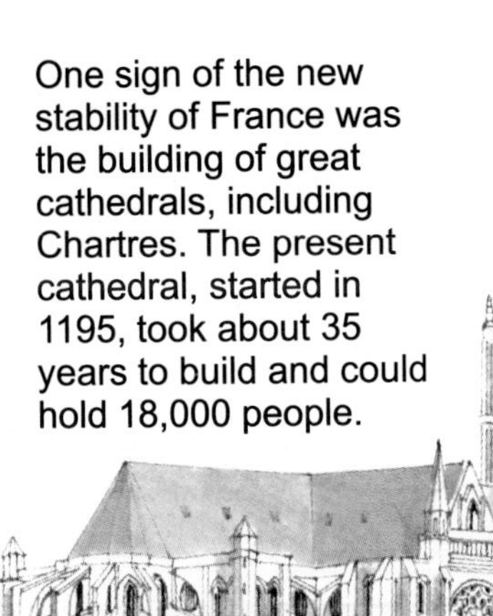

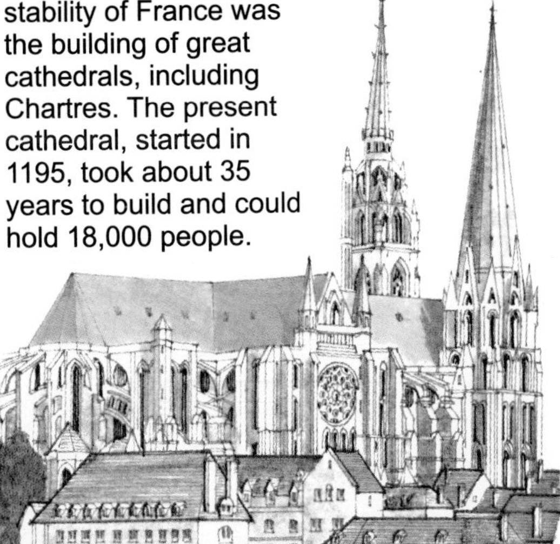

One sign of the new stability of France was the building of great cathedrals, including Chartres. The present cathedral, started in 1195, took about 35 years to build and could hold 18,000 people.

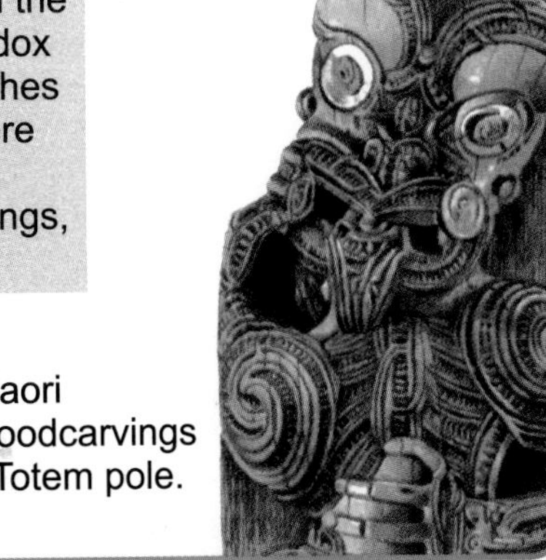

Maori woodcarvings - Totem pole.

People then

During the middle ages, a system called 'Feudalism' existed in Europe. In this system, the king gave grants of property to his most powerful noblemen. The nobles granted some part of their land to the knights, who in turn rented them to peasants.

The peasants or the small farmers paid the rent by tilling landlord's lands and by giving him a fixed share of the produce. The lives of the peasants were very hard. They had to work everyday, tending the animals and crops properly. Usually, the markets were very far away. In case of scanty produce, the peasants starved to death. Also, there were continuous dangers of diseases and violence.

Early medieval society was strictly divided and everyone knew his or her place. At the top was the king who granted land to barons and to the church. The barons built castles for defense and lived in large manor houses. In return for military service they granted land to knights. By the side of the manor house were farm buildings and the house of the bailiff who managed the estate. The farm work was done by villeins and brodars who, to protect their lord's privacy, lived in the village.

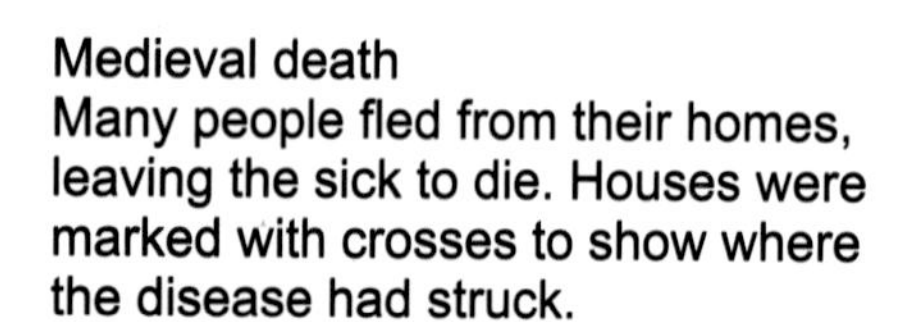

Medieval death
Many people fled from their homes, leaving the sick to die. Houses were marked with crosses to show where the disease had struck.

THE AGE OF

CHANGES

Renaissance

Renaissance first began in Italy in the 15th century. Renaissance literally meant 'rebirth' or 'revival'. This period is so called because it was marked by the great advances in learning and thinking. Helped by the invention of printing, the Renaissance gradually spread from Italy to the rest of Europe.

An early Printing Press.

Reniassance produced great artists like Michelangelo, Raphael and Leonardo da Vinci. It also gave birth to new way of thinking known as humanism. Scholars and thinkers challenged the authority of the church. Copernicus challenged the ideas about the solar system. Desiderius Erasmus aspired to reform the Catholic church and criticized the superstitions of the clergy.

St. Peter's Church in Rome, one of the world's largest Christian churches.

At the battle of Agincourt, Henry V commanded only about 900 men-at- arms and 3000 archers. The French had at least three times as many heavily armed troops, but they were badly led and organized.

Christopher Columbus crossed the Atlantic with three small sailing ships in 1492. The journey took 30 days to complete. His ships bore the cross of Christianity.

The great voyages

During the Renaissance period, the Europe undertook long sea voyages to explore the world. For this purpose, they built stronger ships.

The Portugese, under Prince Henry the navigator, were the first to take this initiative. They sailed along the west coast of Africa, looking for gold and ivory.

Christopher Columbus was the first 15th century explorer who crossed the Atlantic ocean and then returned back.

The sailors used crude maps and simple instruments to guide them. In 1519, Ferdinand Magellan undertook the first round-the world voyage. He sailed from Spain with five ships, out of which only one returned after completing the voyage.

At Sagres, Henry established a school which brought together the best navigators and geographers of Europe.

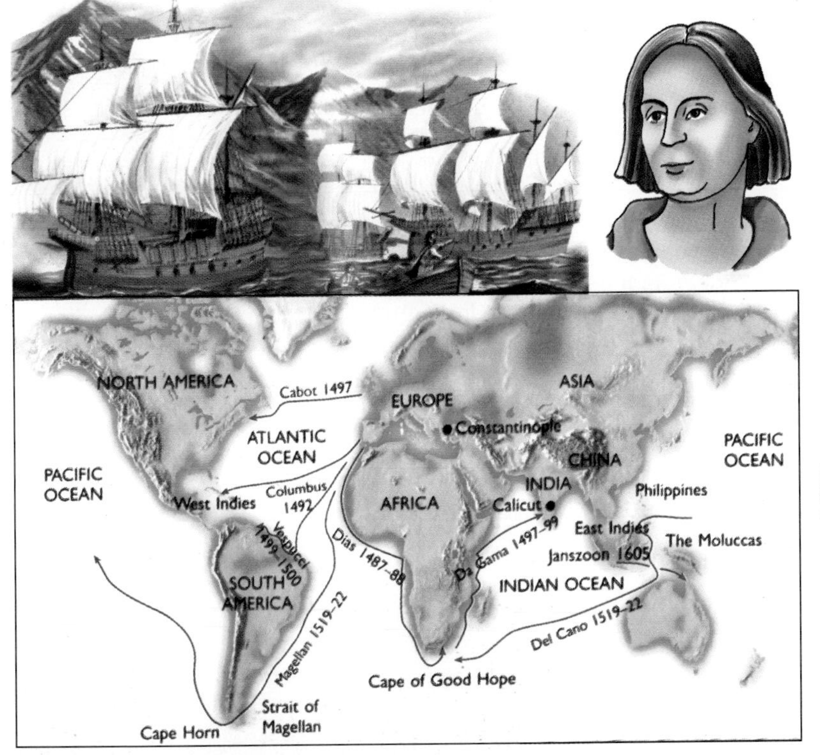

Early explorers navigated with the help of an instrument called an astrolabe.

European rulers

Queen Elizabeth was one of the most efficient rulers of England. She ascended the throne in 1558 after the death of her sister Mary. She was a protestant and passed laws which confirmed England as protestant nation. In 1572 she made an alliance with France, to give England support against her Catholic enemies.

William Shakespeare was the greatest poet and playwright of the Elizabethan age.

In the age of Elizabeth, creative arts like drama and poetry reached their zenith. During this time, William Shakespeare developed a new kind of verse drama exploring the whole range of human feelings. Poetry and painting flourished too. A poet called Edmund Spenser wrote an epic poem in praise of Elizabeth I, The Eaerie Queen. Among leading artists was Nicholas Hilliard who painted delicate miniature portraits.

At the heart of Louis XIV's reign was a glamorous court, based around his splendid palace at Versailles. Louis chose the sun as his emblem, and was known as the 'Sun King'.

Henry VIII used discontent with the Church to his advantage. To gain a divorce, he broke with the Catholic Church and became head of the Church of England.

Louis XIV of France was the most powerful European monarch in the 17th century. He became King in 1643 at the age of five.

After nearly twenty years of imprisonment, Mary was executed at Fotheringay Castle in 1587 on a charge of treason.She was said to have plotted against Elizabeth I of England many times.

Empire of the Sun

In the early sixteenth century, two civilizations namely the Aztecs in Central America and the Incas in South America reached their height.

Aztecs were fierce warriors and their empire streched across Mexico. They were efficient sculptors, poets, musicians, and engineers. They lost their empire at the hands of Spanish treasure-seekers in 1521.

The Inca empire in Peru flourished under the rule of Pachacuti and his successors. Incas built stone cities and fine roads. Just like the Aztecs, they too eventually fell to Spanish rule.

This stone shows the Aztec 20-day month. They had 18 months plus a final five unlucky days.

Aztec priest used stone-bladed knives to cut out the hearts of their victims.

The Aztecs worshiped many gods including Quetzalcoatl, feathered serpent.

The Inca ruler Pachacuti leads his army into the battle.

The Incas celebrated two festivals of the Sun. One was in June, the other in December. The emperor led the ceremonies in the great square at Cuzco. Officials from all over the empire attended.

Asia then

In this period, Asia became the centre of exploration for the European voyagers. Vasco da Gama discovered India in 1498. Later in the beginning of 16th century, where on the one hand Guru Nanak founded the Sikh religion, on the other hand Babur laid the foundation of the Mughal Empire in Delhi.

Japan was also visited by the Europeans. The first to arrive were Portuguese voyagers in 1542. Later St Francis Xavier, a Spanish missionary arrived , trying to convert the Japanese to Christianity. On the other hand, Ming dynasty in China began to lose power. China was also visited by portuguese explorers and other European traders in 1517.

The English colony of Madras was a major port for shipping cotton goods overseas. It was also the centre of a region noted for making cloth. The weavers of Madras specialized in cloth printed with brightly colored designs and scenes from Indian life.

Many Europeans in India tried to live exactly as they would have done at home.

Kabuki drama was developed in Japan in the 17th century. It combined dialogue, song, dance and music.

A Christian missionary in China during the 1500s. The main mission was led by an Italian Jesuit, Matteo Ricci, who began his work in China in 1583.

A reconstruction of Angkor Wat. The huge, elaborate temple complex is surrounded by walls and a moat that was 180 metres wide and 4 kilometres long.

Europe then

During this period, society and government saw drastic changes in Europe. In most of the areas, the feudal system had come to an end. People could then leave their lands and look for better opportunities in big towns and cities. In England, France and Spain, more powerful kings came into existence. They ruled over the entire countries and also controlled the rich noblemen much more effectively and successfully than their forefathers.

The period is also marked by a series of Europen explorations. European sailors and navigators made a number of voyages to enhance their knowledge. However, under the garb of enhancement of knowledge their main aim was just to establish contacts with the Asian spice-producing countries.

Catherine the Great (1729-1796) ruled for 34 years. Other European leaders respected Catherine for her achievements in foreign policy, but feared her power.

The Spanish Inquisition questioned people accused of heresy. This included reading books that were forbidden by the Catholic church, and having Protestant beliefs. Heretics were burned at the stake.

Town and city authorities were responsible for keeping people informed. A roll on the drum brought the citizens out to hear the town crier read the latest news.

A French officer's campaign wig of 1670. Wigs were made in all shapes and sizes, often of horse or goat hair.

Birth of USA

About 350 years ago, a group of people from England arrived in North America to settle permanently over there. They tilled the land and made business transactions with the native Americans. Though, they lived in remote areas yet they were still accountable to the king of England.

However, with the passage of time, they found it unnecessary to pay taxes to the king. As a sign of revolt, they raided three ships in Boston Harbour and threw their cargo of tea in the sea.

After six continuous years of revolt, the settlers became independent and a new country called United States of America came into existence.

Railways made the settlement of the west.

British troops attacked American defenders at the battle of Bunker Hill on 17 June 1775.

George Washington was elected as commander-in-chief of the colonists army. To many Americans at that time, he became a leading symbol of their fight for independence.

American colonists objected to paying taxes to Britain on imports. In what came to be known as the Boston Tea party, colonists disguised as Native North Americans raided British ships in Boston harbour on 16 December 1773.

French revolution

Louis XVI

Just after the new settlers of North America had acquired independence, the inmates of France too rebelled against the king, Louis XVI.

Louis XVI was a ruthless ruler. In his reign, the condition of the poor had further worsened. When in 1788, he tried to raise more money for the government, the common people revolted. The Bastille royal prison was attacked, and riots broke out all across France. The king was condemned to death and the new government passed laws to grant equal rights to everyone.

Queen Marie Antoinette, wife of Louis XVI

In 1789 a group of women marched to the palace at Versailles. They seized the royal family, and brought them back to Paris as captives.

France has a strong tradition of revolutions by the people against absolute domination by a king. In the July revolution of 1830, the people rose up against Charles X, who tried to rule with the total power of Louis XIV.

Napoleon is considered to be a great military genius.

Around 18,000 people were executed in France during the 1793 Reign of Terror. Anyone who was considered an enemy of the revolution was beheaded on the guillotine.

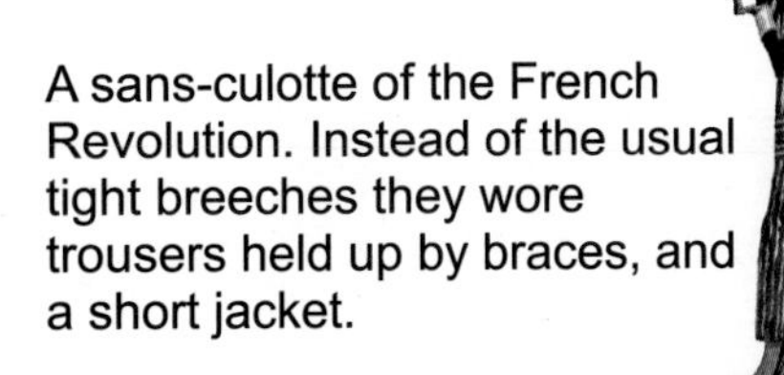

A sans-culotte of the French Revolution. Instead of the usual tight breeches they wore trousers held up by braces, and a short jacket.

Slave trade

The growing trade in Europe required a number of workers to work in the firms of cotton, tobacco, sugarcane and rice. This resulted in slave trade. The settlers imported slaves from Africa.

The black citizens of Africa were captured, chained and transferred to America. There, they were sold as slaves. Some of them died of starvation on the way. Around 15 million African slaves had already been transported to America before slavery was banned and all the slaves were freed.

Slaves working on a treadmill in a Caribbean sugar plantation in the 18th century. They were whipped if they did not work hard.

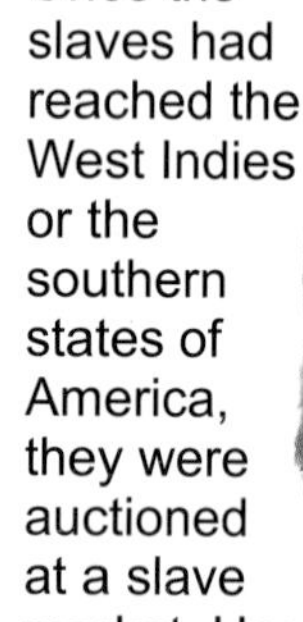

Once the slaves had reached the West Indies or the southern states of America, they were auctioned at a slave market. Here, they were treated like animals. Families were sometimes separated, and people were sold singly to plantation owners.

Some slaves escaped from plantations and set up their own village in remote mountain areas. They were always well armed to fight against anyone who tried to recapture them.

Although Toussaint's actions had impressed many Europeans, in 1802 the French sent a force to reassert their control over the Caribbean.

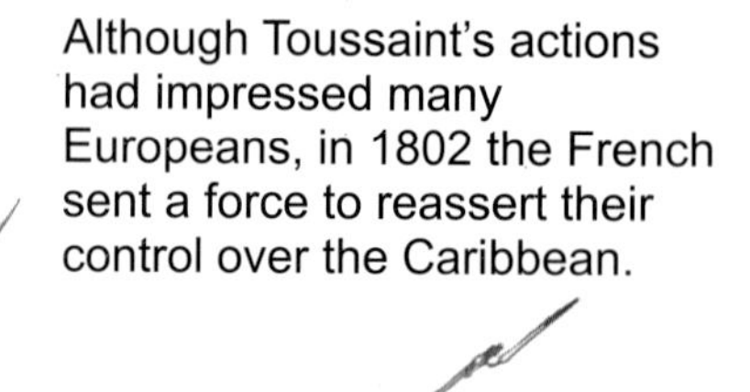

Oceania

Oceania comprised of the people living in Australia, New-Zealand and the Pacific islands. They lived by hunting, food-gathering, fishing and farming. Their cultural life included the myths of the dream time and ornate rock-painting. Around 3500 years back, the ancestors of the Polynesians reached.

Polynesian Maoris came to New-Zealand in 750 A.D. They built wooden stockades, called pas. Warriors fought from platforms on the walls. They decorated their faces and bodies with tattoos.

The Maoris were also skilled woodcarvers and decorated their houses with complicated designs. They had no metal tools and so used stone for axes to cut wood.

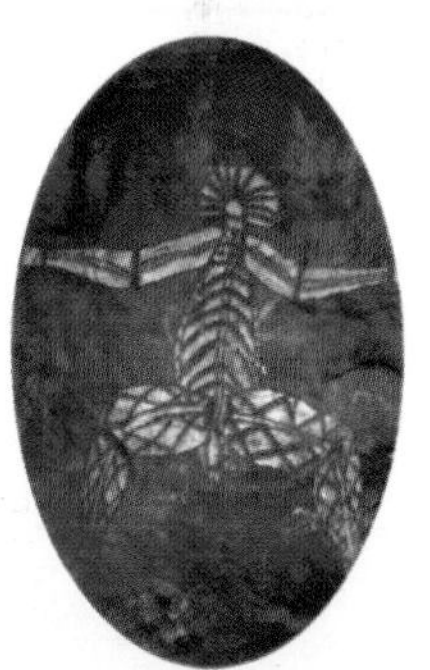

Aboriginal Art

The Maori people were skilled sailors and craftworkers who decorated their war canoes with elaborate carvings.

Captain James Cook and his crew met Maoris in New Zealand for the first time in 1769. He attempted to establish good relations with the New Zealand people.

Easter Island

The Industrial revolution

The Industrial Revolution transformed Britain completely. During this period, a number of new inventions and discoveries took place. The revolution initially began in the cotton industry. The growing demand for cheap cotton cloth transformed the spinning and weaving industry. Invention of 'flying shuttle' in 1730s doubled the speed of weaving. The 'spinning jenny' and the 'mule' produced spun thread much more quickly cheaply at cheaper rates.

Steam engines were also developed further. Abraham Darby devised a way of smelting iron by using coke. The use of steam power increased the demand for coal, and also for iron to make steam engines and other machinery. This factor expanded the coal mines and iron industry. Canals and railways were also established to transfer raw materials and finished goods from one place to another.

A seed drill made a series of even holes into which seeds fell. Before the drill was invented, seeds were scattered by hand.

The first multi-reel spinning machine, the Spinning Jenny, was invented by James Hargreaves in 1764.

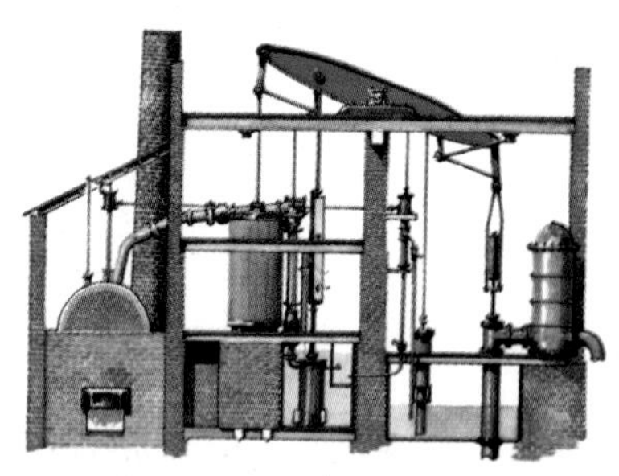

The first steam engine built by Thomas Newcomen in 1712 was used to pump water out of mines.

British Empire

The rich splendour of life for the British is reflected by this ceremonial occasion at the court of an Indian prince.

Under the rule of Queen Victoria, Britain prospered a lot. The major part of Britain's wealth came from its colonies, which provided sources of cheap raw materials and markets for British finished goods. The British set up their first trading post in India in 1612, and towards the end of the seventeenth century had bases at Madras, Bombay and Calcutta. India was the most prized colony in the empire.

The British took over Egypt to guard the route to India. However, towards the end of 19th century, some colonies started breaking away from British rule. Canada and Australia were granted home rule in 1867 and 1901 respectively. India got independence in 1947. Slowly and gradually, Britain started losing its status as a leading industrial nation. Germany and America outpaced it.

Queen victoria
Queen victoria(1819-1901)came to the throne at the age of 18 and reigned for almost 64 years. After the death of her husband, Prince Albert in 1861, she remained in deep mourning for many years.

As the demands for Indian independence increased, anti-British feeling also grew.

Robert Clive meets Mir Jafar in 1757. Mir Jafar was employed by the Mughals to fight against the British.

Calcutta was founded by the British East India Company because sea-going ships could travel up the Hooghly River and load and unload cargoes there.

THE WORLD

OF WARS

World war I

German Fokker

By the end of 19th century, Germany had emerged as a leading industrial nation posing a threat to France and Britain. Germany formed the triple Alliance with Austria-Hungary and Italy, while Britain, France and Russia formed the Triple entente. Both the groups enlarged their navies and expanded the armies. The assassination of the Austrian prince, Archduke Franz Ferdinand by a Serbian citizen triggered off the war.

Sopwith Camel

This war involved so many countries that it became popular as "The great war". Most of the war was fought from two parallel lines of trenches separated by a short strectch of 'no-man's land'. Conditions in the trenches were terrible and disease breeding.

The war came to an end on November 11 when Germany and the allies signed an arms treaty.

As a result of world war, crops were not properly attended, resulting in starvation.

Barricades were set up in the streets of Dublin in1916. On one side were the British forces, and on the other were the Republicans. Many civilians died in the Easter Rising.

World war II

Spitfire

By World War II, planes were much improved.

World war II started on September 3,1939, when Germany under the leadership of Adolf Hitler had invaded Poland. The war was fought between the Axis Powers (Germany, Italy and Japan) and the allies (Britain, France, United States, Soviet Union). It was mainly fourth in Europe; in North Africa and in South-East Asia. By this time, a lot of discoveries and inventions had taken place which were capable of mass destruction. Now, the aeroplanes were used to drop bombs over the target sections of the countries.

During this time, the nuclear bomb was invented by USA which dropped two bombs on the Japanese town of Hiroshima and Nagasaki.

These bombs completely ruined these cities. With this, World War II came to an end.

A mushroom cloud rising after the explosion of an atomic bomb.

Adolf Hitler was Known as the Leader.

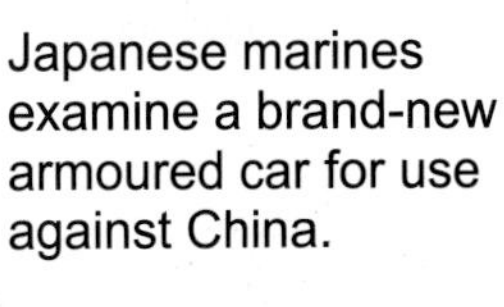

Japanese marines examine a brand-new armoured car for use against China.

From 1917 onwards, the tank was used successfully to break the stalemate of trench warfare along the Western Front.

United Nations

After the end of World War II in 1945, an organisation called United Nations (UN) was established in the hope that international disputes could be peacefully settled and friendly relation could be created among the nations. Its offices were opened in New York. Ever since, United Nations is carrying this noble responsibility of preventing the wars on its shoulders. It gives advice and money to help the poorer countries improve their conditions.

United Nations also has many other branches, called agencies, that deal with worldwide problems. Some of these agencies provide aid for people in need, such as refugees. Others are concerned with health matters, living and working conditions, and human rights.

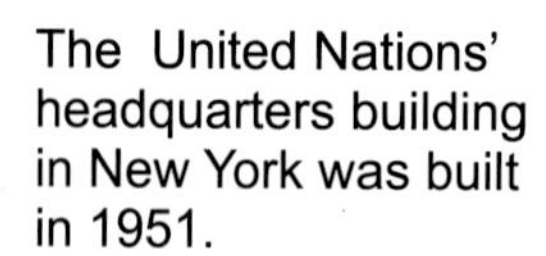

The United Nations' headquarters building in New York was built in 1951.

This is the scene of member nations participating in the General Assembly of the United Nations. This huge auditorium is large enough to allow all representatives of member nations. Each member has one vote.

UN FORCES
The United Nations symbol appears on the UN flag.

Members of the UN have to sign the UN Charter which lays out the Principles of the organization.

THE MODERN

WORLD

Exploring Space

Space has always been 'Pandora's Box' for the people. The mystery of space was partially unravelled in 1957 when the first space probe, sputnik was employed by the Russians. It was launched into space and circled around the Earth. Later in 1969, two astronauts successfully, landed on the surface of the moon for the first time.

Today there has been so much of progress, that the astronauts can even stay and work in space stations for weeks. Space probes have already been sent to Mars and Venus to collect information about them.

The international team of Martian explorers will use this kind of a planetary base.

Sputnik was the first satellite to put in orbit around the earth.

Most foods are dehydrated for the astronauts to eat. They add water to the food before eating it. Astronauts have to suck drink through straws because water floats like a ball.

Hubble's telescope
The Hubble space telescope, launched in 1990, orbits above Earth's surface and uses a mirror 2.4 m across. It is the largest telescope ever to be put into orbit. With the help of this telescope those images that are 100 times fainter shown by telescopes on earth, can be clearly seen. HST's observations are sent down to radio telescopes around the Earth.

Scientific revolution

During the mid-nineteenth and early twentieth century, the industries continued to develop with new inventions, new products and factories producing new types of goods.

By 1980, electricity and oil started being used instead of coal and steam. Oil served as fuel for the internal combustion engine which give birth to the first motor cars. Oil products also played a crucial role in the new chemical industry. They led to the development of various materials such as plastics and artificial rubber.

Computers have paced up the human life.

The invention of television brought entertainment to every household.

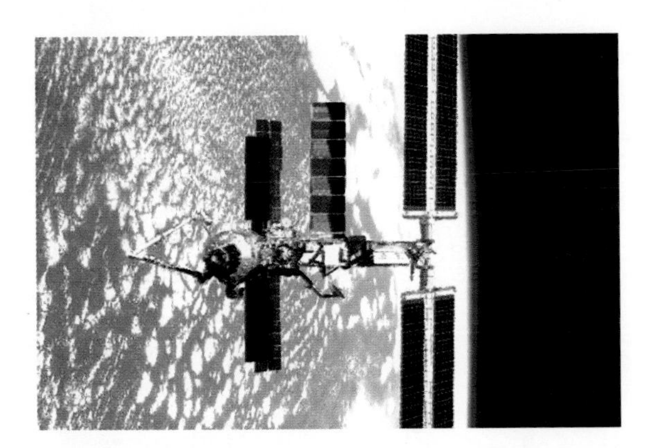

The 20th century has been a period of rapid development in the field of science and technology. This international space station will be used for research in various streams.

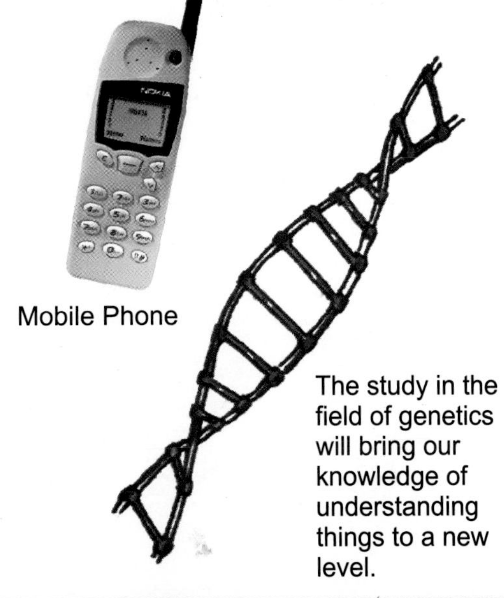

Mobile Phone

The study in the field of genetics will bring our knowledge of understanding things to a new level.

Equality

Till the mid-twentieth century, some people were treated unequally because of their race, colour, religion or caste. Black people were discriminated against in education, employment, housing, transport and health care. They did not possess the right to vote also. In 1963, Over 250000 people marched to Washington DC, to demand equal justice for everybody. The following year, the discrimination was made illegal.

Martin Luther King was an outstanding speaker.

Martin Luther King, a Baptist minister took many steps for the upliftment of black people. His efforts won him the Nobel peace prize in 1964.

Nelson Mandela votes for the first time in his life.

Global awareness

Improvement in the means of communication is one of the greatest achievements of the modern age. Revolution in communications, together with faster and more convenient ways of traveling has helped scientists to become aware of what is happening at global level. Environment is one of the major concerns of the 20th century. A number a environmental problems such as dumping of nuclear and toxic waste, extinction of wild species and destruction of rainforests are posing a threat today. Scientists are studying the causes and affects of pollution.

Many governments are now taking actions to minimize pollution and encourage people to conserve energy by recycling items.

Ozone layer

Water and air pollution

Causes and affects of acid rain

WWF is one of the organizations that help to control the extinction of wild species. WWF stands for World Wildlife Fund.

The world now

The current world is highly advanced and progressive. It may be recalled that at the dawn of the 20th century, the aeroplane was considered to be a mere dream, motor cars were rare and cinema had just started. But by the end of the 20th century, all these things were taken for granted by the vast majority of the world's population. The circles of human knowledge and curiorsity are ever widening.

Modern man is putting his knowledge to a test in various fields such as medicine, science and space technology.

The most exciting area of medicine at present is the Human Gernome project. Its aims is to discover all of the 100,000 genes in the human body. The space race which started during the cold war has still not lasted. Today, the former superpowers are working together on projects in space.

Everyone hopes that the coming generations will not see a repeat of the terrible slaughter of world war I and II.

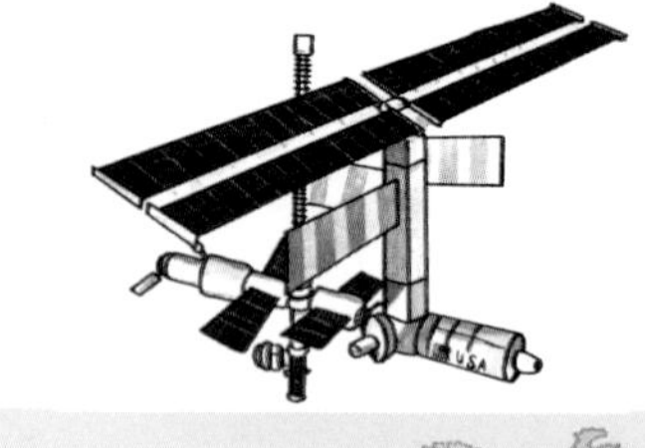

The Soviet space station Mir was launched in 1986. It was designed to stay in orbit for long period, so that complicated scientific experiments could be carried out on board.

The first man on the Moon was the American astronaut Neil Armstrong. He described walking on the Moon as one small step for a man, one giant leap for mankind.

Glossary

almonds A deciduous tree, native to Asia and northern Africa and having alternate, simple leaves, pink flowers, and leathery fruits.

anthropology is the study of humanity. It has origins in the natural sciences, the humanities, and the social sciences. The term "anthropology", pronounced is from the Greek *anthrōpos*, "human", and *-logia*, "discourse" or "study", and was first used in 1501 by German philosopher Magnus Hundt.

archaeology studies human history from the development of the first stone tools in eastern Africa 3.4 million years ago up until recent decades. It is of most importance for learning about prehistoric societies, when there are no written records for historians to study, and which makes up over 99% of total human history, from the Paleolithic until the advent of literacy in any given society. Archaeology has various different goals, which range from studying human evolution to cultural evolution and understanding culture history.

asteroid belt is a region of the solar system between the orbits of Mars and Jupiter (2.2 - 3.3 A.U.) in which most asteroids are located. The Asteroid Belt or Main Belt, probably contains millions of asteroids ranging widely in size from Ceres, which at 940 km in diameter is about one-quarter the diameter of our Moon, to bodies that are less than 1 km across. There are more than 20,000 numbered asteroids in the asteroid belt.

astronomy is a natural science that deals with the study of celestial objects (such as stars, planets, comets, nebulae, star clusters and galaxies) and phenomena that originate outside the Earth's atmosphere (such as the cosmic background radiation). It is concerned with the evolution, physics, chemistry, meteorology, and motion of celestial objects, as well as the formation and development of the universe.

atmosphere An envelope of gases that surrounds the Earth, the Sun, and other planets and stars.

atom The smallest particle of an element that can exist on its own. It is therefore the basic unit of all mater. Atoms, have a nucleus, surrounded by orbiting electrons.

aurora australis An aurora that occurs in southern regions of the earth. Also called *southern lights*.

beach This is a geological land form along the shoreline of an ocean, sea or lake.

berry A usually fleshy or pulpy fruit, typically with two or more seeds developed from a single ovary.

California A state of the western United States on the Pacific Ocean. It was admitted as the 31st state in 1850. The area was colonized by the Spanish and formally ceded to the United States by the Treaty of Guadalupe Hidalgo (1848). California is often called the Golden State because of its sunny climate and the discovery of gold during its pioneering days. Sacramento is the capital and Los Angeles the largest city. Population: 36,600,000.

cardamom A rhizomatous Indian herb *(Elettaria cardamomum)* having capsular fruits with aromatic seeds used as a spice or condiment.

carnivorous plants are plants that derive some or most of their nutrients (but not energy) from trapping and consuming animals or protozoans, typically insects and other arthropods. Carnivorous plants appear adapted to grow in places where the soil is thin or poor in nutrients, especially nitrogen, such as acidic bogs and rock out cropping.

cauliflower An herb *(Brassica oleracea* var. *botrytis)* in the mustard family, related to the cabbage and broccoli and having a whitish undeveloped flower with a large edible head.

cave A hollow or natural passage under or into the earth, especially one with an opening to the surface.

cereal, grains, or cereal grains are grasses cultivated for the edible components of their fruit seeds (botanically, a type of fruit called a caryopsis): the endosperm, germ, and bran. Cereal grains are grown in greater quantities and provide more food energy worldwide than any other type of crop; they are therefore staple crops. Grain is both a fruit and a vegetable.

deciduous means "falling off at maturity" or "tending to fall off" and is typically used in reference to trees or shrubs that lose their leaves seasonally and to the shedding of other plant structures such as petals after flowering or fruit when ripe. In a more specific sense deciduous means the dropping of a part that is no longer needed, or falling away after its purpose is finished. In plants it is the result of natural processes; in other fields the word has a similar meaning, including deciduous antlers in deer or deciduous teeth, also known as baby teeth, in some mammals, including human children.

delta A usually triangular mass of sediment, especially silt and sand, deposited at the mouth of a river. Deltas form when a river flows into a body of standing water, such as a sea or lake, and deposits large quantities of sediment. They are usually crossed by numerous streams and channels and have exposed as well as submerged areas.

desert A very dry area of the world, which usually has less than 250 millimeters of rainfall a year. Most deserts are rocky or sandy.

emu is the largest bird native to Australia and the only extant member of the genus *Dromaius*. It is also the second-largest extant bird in the world by height, after its ratite relative, the ostrich. There are three extant subspecies of Emus in Australia. The Emu is common over most of mainland Australia, although it avoids heavily populated areas, dense forest, and arid areas.

entomology is the scientific study of insects, a branch of arthropodology. At some 1.3 million described species, insects account for more than two-thirds of all known organisms, and have many kinds of interactions with humans and other forms of life on earth. It is a specialty within the field of biology. Though technically incorrect, the definition is sometimes widened to include the study of terrestrial animals in other arthropod groups or other phyla, such as arachnids, myriapods, earthworms, land snails, and slugs. Entomology is rooted in nearly all human cultures from prehistoric times, primarily in the context of agriculture (especially biological control and beekeeping), but scientific study began only as recently as the 16th century.

eucalyptus is a diverse genus of flowering trees (and a few shrubs) in the myrtle family, Myrtaceae. Members of the genus dominate the tree flora of Australia. There are more than 700 species of Eucalyptus, mostly native to Australia, and a very small number are found in adjacent areas of New Guinea and Indonesia and one as far north as the Philippine archipelago and Taiwan. Only 15 species occur outside Australia, and only 9 do not occur in Australia. Species of Eucalyptus are cultivated throughout the tropics and subtropics including the Americas, Europe, Africa, the Mediterranean Basin, the Middle East, China and the Indian Subcontinent.

fruits are the fleshy or dry ripened ovary of a plant, enclosing one or many seeds. A fruit is a mature ovary and its associated parts. It usually contains seeds, which have developed from the enclosed ovule after fertilization.

genetics a discipline of biology, is the science of genes, heredity, and variation in living organisms. The fact that living things inherit traits from their parents has been used since prehistoric times to improve crop plants and animals through selective breeding. However, the modern science of genetics, which seeks to understand the process of inheritance, only began with the work of Gregor Mendel in the mid-19th century. Although he did not know the physical basis for heredity, Mendel observed that organisms inherit traits via discrete units of inheritance, which are now called genes.

gravitation or gravity, is a natural phenomenon in which objects with mass attract one another. In everyday life, gravitation is most familiar as the agent that gives weight to objects with mass and causes them to fall to the ground when dropped. Gravitation causes dispersed matter to coalesce, thus accounting for the existence of the Earth, the Sun, and most of the macroscopic objects in the universe.

hammurabi (Akkadian from Amorite *Ammurāpi*, "the kinsman is a healer," from *'Ammu*, "paternal kinsman," and *Rāpi*, "healer"; (died c. 1750 BC)) was the sixth king of Babylon from 1792 BC to 1750 BC middle chronology (1728 BC – 1686 BC short chronology). He became the first king of the Babylonian Empire following the abdication of his father, Sin-Muballit, extending Babylon's control over Mesopotamia by winning a series of wars against neighboring kingdoms. Although his empire controlled all of Mesopotamia at the time of his death, his successors were unable to maintain his empire.

headland A point of land, usually high and with a sheer drop, extending out into a body of water; a promontory.

herpetology is the branch of zoology concerned with the study of amphibians (including the frogs, toads, salamanders, newts, and gymnophionae) and of ectothermic (cold blooded) reptiles (including snakes, lizards, amphisbaenids, turtles, terrapins, tortoises, crocodilians, and the tuataras).

Ichthyology is the branch of zoology devoted to the study of fishes. This includes skeletal fish, cartilaginous fish, and jawless fish. While a majority of species have probably been discovered and described, approximately 250 new species are officially described by science each year. According to FishBase, 31,500 species of fish had been described by January 2010. There are more fish species than the combined total of all other vertebrates: mammals, amphibians, reptiles and birds.

insectivorous plant also called a carnivorous plant, captures prey items, such as insects, spiders, crustaceans, mites, and protozoans, as a nitrogen source. Many insectivorous species live in freshwater bogs, where nitrogen is not present in available form, because the pH of the water is extremely acid.

meteorology is the interdisciplinary scientific study of the atmosphere that focuses on weather processes and short term forecasting (in contrast with climatology). Studies in the field stretch back millennia, though significant progress in meteorology did not occur until the eighteenth century. The nineteenth century saw breakthroughs occur after observing networks developed across several countries. Breakthroughs in weather forecasting were achieved in the latter half of the twentieth century, after the development of the computer.

microbiology is the study of microorganisms, which are unicellular or cell-cluster microscopic organisms. This includes eukaryotes such as fungi and protists, and prokaryotes. Viruses and prions, though not strictly classed as living organisms, are also studied. In short; microbiology refers to the study of life and organisms that are too small to be seen with the naked eye. Microbiology typically includes the study of the immune system, or Immunology.

mineral is a naturally occurring solid chemical substance that is formed through geological processes and that has a characteristic chemical composition, a highly ordered atomic structure, and specific physical properties.

mountain is a large land form that stretches above the surrounding land in a limited area usually in the form of a peak.

mycology is the branch of biology concerned with the study of fungi, including their genetic and biochemical properties, their taxonomy and their use to humans as a source for tinder, medicinals, food (e.g., beer, wine, cheese, edible mushrooms) and entheogens, as well as their dangers, such as poisoning or infection.

nutrition is the provision, to cells and organisms, of the materials necessary (in the form of food) to support life. Many common health problems can be prevented or alleviated with a healthy diet.

optics is the branch of physics which involves the behavior and properties of light, including its interactions with matter and the construction of instruments that use or detect it. Optics usually describes the behavior of visible, ultraviolet, and infrared light. Because light is an electromagnetic wave, other forms of electromagnetic radiation such as X-rays, microwaves, and radio waves exhibit similar properties.

ornithology is a branch of zoology that concerns the study of birds. Several aspects of ornithology differ from related disciplines, due partly to the high visibility and the aesthetic appeal of birds. Most marked among these is the extent of studies undertaken by amateurs working within the parameters of strict scientific methodology.

ovule literally means "small egg." In seed plants, the ovule is the structure that gives rise to and contains the female reproductive cells. It consists of three parts: The integuments forming its outer layer, the nucellus in its center. The megagametophyte produces the egg cell for fertilization. After fertilization, the ovule develops into a seed.

oxygen An important gas which the human body's cells need for energy. when we breathe, our lungs take oxygen from the air and pass it into the bloodstream, which carries oxygen around the body.

ozone layer ozone is a kind of oxygen that occurs as a layer in the stratosphere. the ultraviolet rays coming from the Sun react with the oxygen in the atmosphere and form ozone. Had the ozone layer not been there, all life forms would have perished because of the heat and the harmful radiation emitted by the Sun.

penguin Any of various stout flightless marine birds of the family Spheniscidae, of cool regions of the Southern Hemisphere, having flipper like wings and webbed feet adapted for swimming and diving, and short scalelike feathers that are white in front and black on the back.

photosynthesis Animals inhale oxygen and exhale carbon dioxide. Green plants are the only plants that produce oxygen and make food, which is called photosynthesis. Photosynthesis means "putting together with light." This takes place in chloroplast, which have chlorophyll in them. Chlorophyll absorbs the sunlight. From sunlight, green plants combine carbon dioxide and water to make sugar and oxygen. Green plants use sugar to make starch, fats, and proteins. There are tiny pores called stomata. Carbon dioxide and oxygen enter and leave through the stomata respectively.

pickle An edible product, such as a cucumber, that has been preserved and flavored in a solution of brine or vinegar.

plants Any of various photosynthetic, eukaryotic, multi cellular organisms of the kingdom Planate characteristically producing embryos, containing chloroplasts, having cellulose cell walls, and lacking the power of locomotion.

polar regions Earth's **polar regions** are the areas of the globe surrounding the poles also known as frigid zones. The North Pole and South Pole being the centers, these regions are dominated by the polar ice caps, resting respectively on the Arctic Ocean and the continent of Antarctica. Polar sea ice is currently diminishing, possibly as a result of anthropogenic global warming.

preserved To save from decay by the use of some

preservative substance, as sugar, salt, etc.; to season and prepare for remaining in a good state, as fruits, meat, etc.; as, to preserve peaches or grapes.

roots The usually underground portion of a plant that lacks buds, leaves, or nodes and serves as support, draws minerals and water from the surrounding soil, and sometimes stores food.

sahara A vast desert of northern Africa extending east from the Atlantic coast to the Nile Valley and south from the Atlas Mountains to the region of the Sudan. During the Ice Age (about 50,000 to 100,000 years ago), the Sahara was a region of extensive shallow lakes watering large areas of vegetation, most of which had disappeared by Roman times. Introduction of the camel (probably in the first century A.D.) led to occupation by nomadic tribes who moved from oasis to oasis in search of water.

seed A Seed is a small embryonic plant enclosed in a covering called the seed coat, usually with some stored food.

shrubs are defined as woody, semiwoody or herbaceous perennial plants, branches arise from the base of the plants, and grow up to a height of about 0.5 to 4 metres. The plants are usually erect and bushy. Most of the shrubs are very hardy, require little attention and grow in all types of soil. Shrubs flower regularly every year and produce flower of almost all the important colours-white, light yellow, golden-yellow, pink, scarlet, salmon, crimson, rose, violet, light blue, deep blue and some are sweet scented.

solar system consists of the Sun, the nine planets, their moons, and other heavenly bodies, like asteroids, meteoroids, comets and clouds of dust floating in interplanetary orbits. all the heavenly bodies, including the planets, are governed by the gravitational pull of the Sun.

soybean A southeast Asian annual leguminous plant *(Glycine max),* widely cultivated for forage an Eucalyptus soil improvement and for its nutritious seeds.

stamen is the male reproductive organ of a flower. Each stamen generally has a stalk called the filament and, on top of the filament, an anther and pollen sacs, called micro sporangia. The development of the micro sporangia and the contained haploid gametophytes, is closely comparable with that of the micro sporangia in gymnosperms or heterosporous ferns. The pollen is set free by the opening of the anther, generally by means of longitudinal slits, but sometimes by pores, as in the heath family, or by valves, as in the barberry family. It is then dropped, or carried by some external agent — wind, water or some member of the animal kingdom — onto the receptive surface of the carpel of the same or another flower, which is thus pollinated. It is the part that contains the sperm cells.

thermodynamics In science, thermodynamics is the study of energy conversion between heat and mechanical work, and subsequently the macroscopic variables such as temperature, volume and pressure.

Vegetable usually means edible plant or part of a plant other than a sweet fruit or seed. This usually means the leaf, stem, or root of a plant.

volcano when pressure from the molten rock beneath the earth's surface becomes too great, the rock, usually accompanied by lava or gases, escapes through a fissure or vent in the crust of the earth. "Volcano" is the term given to both the vent and the conical mountain left by the overflow of the erupted lava, rock and ash.

weather The state of the air or atmosphere with respect to heat or cold, wetness or dryness, calm or storm, clearness or cloudiness, or any other meteorological phenomena; meteorological condition of the atmosphere; as, warm weather; cold weather; wet weather; dry weather, etc.

wind vane mechanical device attached to an elevated structure; rotates freely to show the direction of the wind

woodland Land covered with wood or trees; forest; land on which trees are suffered to grow, either for fuel or timber.

Index

The page numbers mentioned in **bold** type refer to main headings.

Junior Encyclopedia series

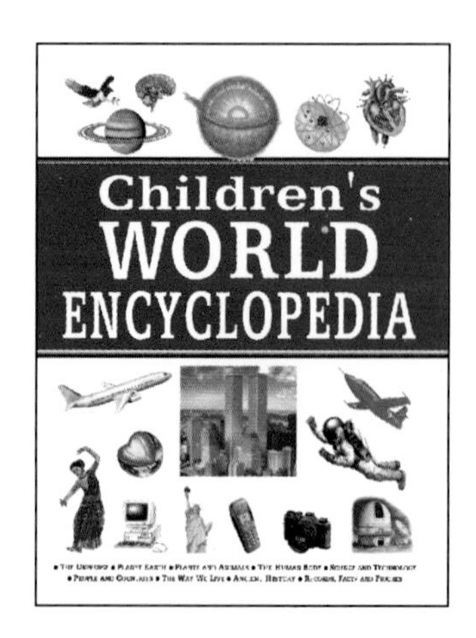

Children's World Encyclopedia
size 7.5"x10"in
320 pages

Rs. 325.00
ISBN 81-7582-048-9

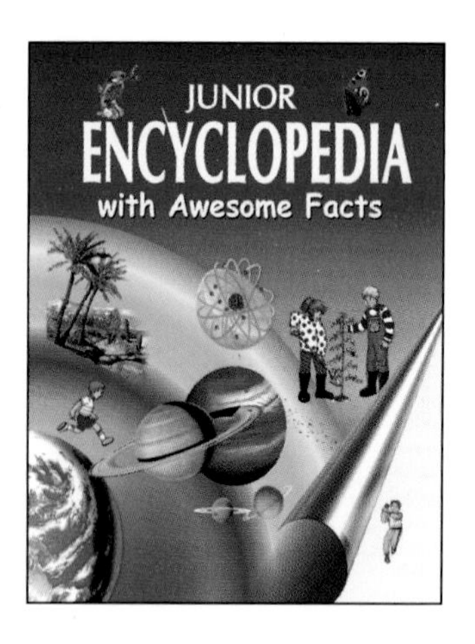

Junior Encyclopedia with Awesome Facts
size 7.5"x10"in
320 pages

Rs. 395.00
ISBN 81-7582-102-7
978-81-7582-102-6 (new)

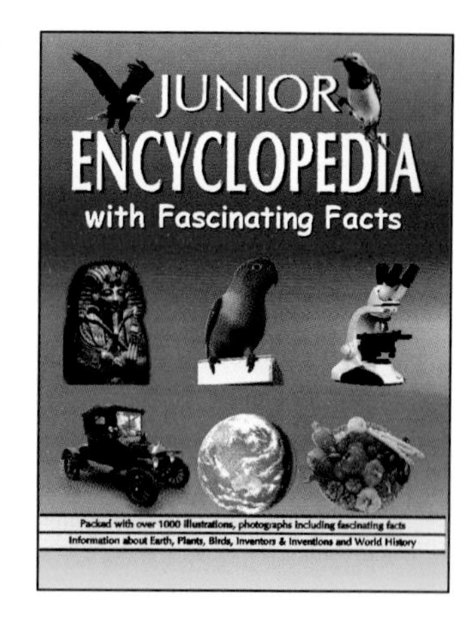

Junior Encyclopedia with Fascinating Facts
size 7.5"x10"in
320 pages

Rs. 425.00
ISBN 978-81-7582-133-0

Children's Junior Encyclopedia
size 7.5"x10"in
196 pages

Rs. 295.00
ISBN 978-81-87057-57-4

Encyclopedia of Space and our moving Earth
size 6.75"x9.75"in
104 pages

Rs. 125.00
ISBN 81-7187-218-2

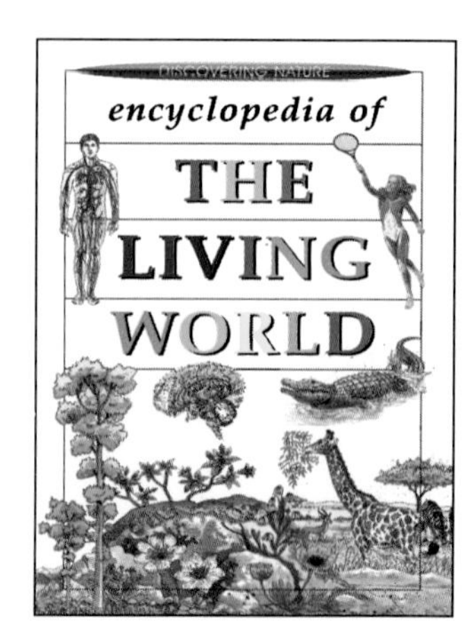

Encyclopedia of The Living World
size 6.75"x9.75"in
104 pages

Rs. 125.00
ISBN 81-7187-217-4